Women and the Politics of Schooling in Victorian and Edwardian England

Women, Power and Politics
Series Editors: June Hannam and Pauline Stafford

Books in this series explore women's excercise of power in Britain and Europe from the ancient world onwards. In the burgeoning area of women's history this is an increasingly important theme, and one which provides a place for women's history and its insights within the traditional concerns of mainstream history. In view of the wide date range, 'power' is broadly conceived, involving, for instance, the religious and familial as well as the political.

Queens, Concubines and Dowagers: The King's Wife in the Early Middle Ages
Pauline Stafford

Also to be published in the series:

Art and the Construction of Early Medieval Queenship: Dynastic Legitimacy and Family Piety
Erin Barrett

Edwardian Ladies and Imperial Power: Organizing for Empire
Julia Bush

From Helena to Eirene: The Byzantine Empress, 4th to 8th Centuries
Liz James

Women and the Poor Law, 1870–1948
Moira Martin

Women and the Politics of Schooling in Victorian and Edwardian England

JANE MARTIN

Leicester University Press
London and New York

Leicester University Press
A Cassell Imprint
Wellington House, 125 Strand, London WC2R 0BB
370 Lexington Avenue, New York, NY 10017–6550

First published 1999

British Library Cataloguing in Publication Data
A catalogue record for this book is available from the British Library.
ISBN 0 7185 0053 9

Library of Congress Cataloging-in-Publication Data
Martin, Jane, 1959–
    Women and the politics of schooling in Victorian and Edwardian England / Jane Martin.
        p.   cm. – (Women, power, and politics)
    Includes bibliographical references (p.) and index.
    ISBN 0–7185–0053–9 (hardcover)
    1. Women in education – England – History – Case studies. 2. School board members – England – History – Case studies. 3. London (England). School Board. 4. Politics and education – England – History – Case studies. 5. Women – Education – England – History – Case studies.
    I. Series.
    LC2057.M37   1998
    379. 1'531'08209421–dc21   97–45897
                                                            CIP

Typeset by York House Typographic Ltd, London.
Printed and bound in Great Britain by Bookcraft (Bath) Ltd, Midsomer Norton, Somerset.

Contents

Acknowledgements

This book builds on a project, funded by the Economic and Social Research Council and the Open University, exploring the role of women in the education of the working classes, 1870 to 1904. Their support during a period of four years is gratefully acknowledged. Furthermore, I am grateful to my colleagues in the Sociology and Politics Division at Nene University College, Northampton, for supporting my study leave in the autumn of 1996.

The process of research has resulted in many debts to librarians and archivists but I should mention in particular the staff at the British Library and the London Metropolitan Archives, as well as Sophie Badham, College Archivist at Royal Holloway, University of London, Kate Perry, Archivist of Girton College, and Ron Roffey at the South-East Co-op Archive in Powis Street, Woolwich. The staff of the library at the Open University were also of assistance in procuring materials, above all the inter-library loan staff.

But most of all I want to express my thanks to Rosemary Deem and Carol Dyhouse who supervised my Open University doctoral thesis and consistently offered warm support and encouragement at every stage of the research process. They both provided excellent comments on the work and excellent suggestions for revisions. Kevin Brehony, Judith Ford and Brian Simon have also given encouragement over the long term. Indeed Judith not only played a key role in keeping my spirits up, she also read and commented on a previous draft of the book and thereby saved me from many stylistic lapses. More recently, I have benefited from the help and advice of June Hannam, who made many useful editorial suggestions on an earlier draft, and Joyce Goodman who shares my enthusiasm for the history of education and who kindly agreed to read the whole manuscript. David Englander and Rosemary O'Day also read and commented on various parts of the work. Special thanks go to Emma Austin for her patience, speed and accuracy when putting the text on disc.

Over the years my family have provided essential support and encouragement and I want to thank my brother, Joe, for his help with the original book proposal and my mother for reading the end product. My warm thanks go also to Paul, Emma and Ben for living with me and 'my women' for what must seem an interminably long period of time.

Some portions of this book have appeared in print previously but all have been revised and include significant new material. However the author wishes to thank Taylor and Francis for permission to quote from the following articles:

'"Hard-headed and large-hearted": women and the industrial schools, 1870–1885', *History of Education*, 20 (3), 1991, 187–202; 'Entering the Public Arena: the female members of the London School Board, 1870–1904', *History of Education*, 22 (3), 1993, 225–40; 'Fighting down the idea that the only place for women was home? gender and policy in elementary education, 1870–1904', *History of Education*, 24 (4), 1995, 277–92.

For Mary

1 London and the Politics of Mass Schooling

Introduction

In August 1879 an elite gathering of London's activist women held a campaign meeting at the Kensington home of Mrs Thomas Taylor. Their objective was to establish a committee for promoting the candidature of women in the forthcoming elections for the directly elected, single purpose educational authority called the London School Board. Accordingly, one past member, two unsuccessful candidates and three serving members were among those present, as well as Mrs Augusta Webster, who had just come forward in Chelsea. Three months later their efforts were rewarded when nine women were elected to the Board, five of them topping the poll. It was a sign of the women's strength that they accounted for 18 per cent of the total membership, the pinnacle of female representation during the Board's 34 years of existence.

This book is about the women who ran for and served on the School Board for London. Altogether 326 Londoners sat on the Board, including 29 female representatives.[1] Excluded from national politics on the grounds of their sex, it is important to remind ourselves that opportunities for women in local government increased greatly in the last third of the nineteenth century. The Municipal Franchise Act of 1869 was the first of a number of measures which were to effect women's democratic participation, and the following year the passing of the Education Act gave all women the right to serve as representatives on the thousands of school boards set up in and after 1870. Moreover it was announced in Parliament that female involvement was both intended and wished.

As a result a slow trickle of women contested the various elections and six years later some 41 were elected school board members. Yet Mrs Webster was unhappy with this performance and her platform for the 1879 triennial elections was peppered with remarks drawing attention to the need to encourage women's election to public office. She supported her demands in a number of ways. First, by making the point that school governance had a long history in women's religious and charitable activities and yet, out of the 50 members of the London School Board, only four were women. Second, women as a group were presented as the saviours of the nation's children. Finally, she was particularly critical of the fact that the education of working-class girls was 'planned and ruled almost entirely by men' (*Englishwoman's Review*, 15 October 1879: 445–6). The focus here concerns the implications of this struggle to achieve a breakthrough for women in British politics. First, the geographical location is considered before briefly summarizing the existing debate in the literature on gender and policy-making in English education. Second, some of the concepts feminists have used to analyse differences of power and advantage between men and women are defined. These concepts are then used to illuminate the position of women in local government in late Victorian and Edwardian England. Needless to say, in what follows the emphasis is on the links between women representatives and educational decision-making during the period between the major Education Acts of 1870 and 1902.

London's women activists

Eager to secure greater equality with men, by the 1870s Augusta Webster was part of a much larger network of activist women. In London and elsewhere, members of the first women's movement in Britain pressed for educational, economic and social rights for women. Higher education was slowly opened up to them, professions such as medicine admitted their first female entrants, and the suffrage organizations used the traditions of female philanthropy to gain access to government, administration and the law.

This book concerns itself with the problems and progress of women as they actively sought political power. By the 1890s there were about 2500 school boards in England and Wales and although it is difficult to quantify the level of female involvement at any one time, it is possible to cite estimates (Rubinstein, 1986: 166). For example, Honnor Morten, who was a member of the London School Board from 1897 to 1902, suggested there were about 188 women so serving in 1898 (Morten, 1899a: 60). Following the elections held between January 1901 and September 1902, the Women's Local Government Society published figures showing that a total of 167 urban and rural education authorities had returned 132 female representatives. Thus while the last quarter of the nineteenth century saw significant breakthroughs for women in school board politics, at a national level they were still only a fraction of the male representation.

In contrast, 29 of the 326 members of the London School Board were women, which constituted nearly 10 per cent of the local membership. This was significant for several reasons. First, it provided a crucial testing ground of women's abilities both as political candidates and as elected representatives. Second, London's role as capital city meant that activities there were closely watched elsewhere and in this sense local aspects of urban educational policy were (and still are) of more than parochial interest. Third, it is evident that the school boards wielded enormous influence over the growth of the elementary school system in a specific locality, with the power to finance schools out of rates and make good any shortfall in school places. Elected every three years, board members were responsible for ensuring local educational needs were met, erecting buildings where these were lacking, providing teachers and, if they thought proper, enforcing the attendance of non-exempted children under 13 (see Simon, 1981). Clearly this was no small task in a city where, as Honnor

Morten herself pointed out at the turn of the century, the elementary school children 'outnumber the whole population of New Zealand by fifty thousand' (Morten, 1899a: 62).

Indeed by 1870 continued population growth meant the shortage of school accommodation was most acute in London, whose sheer size came to symbolize middle-class preoccupation with social relations at this time. Physical change was one thing, but it was more than this, the capitalist city seemed to have destroyed the very fabric of society. Virtually all British towns and cities were characterized by an immense gulf between the classes but nowhere was the geographic division of wealth as complete as in London, the largest city in the world. In general, differences among poor neighbourhoods were lost in a pervasive single image of 'outcast' London as the middle-class residents of the West End sought to convey the gulf of experience that separated them from the population of the East End and the area south of the Thames. Intrepid social explorers who ventured into the slums brought back many and varied accounts of life in this dark and mysterious social world, while the more imaginative scenarios reveal a complex of moral and physical revulsion. On the whole, the casual labour class was represented as 'the Other', to use the language of Michel Foucault, defined as everything the middle classes were not. Although essentially different, this Other was itself then split into two camps: the 'worthy' and the 'unworthy' poor. Consequently, the people on the wrong side of 'the abyss' stood for all that was shifty and feckless and were clearly in need of rescue and reclamation. In the words of the scientist and educator T.H. Huxley, one of the first members of the London School Board, the Polynesian savage 'in his most primitive condition' is 'not half so savage, so unclean, so irreclaimable as the tenant of a tenement in an East London slum' (quoted in Briggs, 1977: 315). Indeed it was widely assumed that the character of the new city population had been warped by deteriorating social conditions. As the novelist Arthur Morrison put it in the 1890s:

> The East-end is a vast city, as famous in its way as any city men have built. But who knows the East-end? It is down through Cornhill and out beyond Leadenhall Street and Aldgate pump, one will say, a shocking place, where he once went with a curate. An evil growth of slums which hide human creeping things; where foul men and women live on penn'orths of gin, where collars and clean shirts are not yet invented, where every citizen wears a black eye, and no man combs his hair.
>
> (*Macmillan's Magazine*, October 1891: 460)

Yet for thousands of women philanthropists this was not a separate, unknown world, but one in which they found fulfilment and freedom of movement. As Frank Prochaska (1980) has shown, women were increasingly prominent in the world of organized philanthropy and by the 1870s a wide variety of middle-class women had established themselves as an active presence in the lives of the poor. Indeed the first women members of the London School Board all had close links with the various philanthropic societies involved in this 'rescue' mission. It is these women who are the subjects of this study.

Women and education

It is of course well understood that the great majority of middle-class Victorians engaged in voluntary community work saw education as a means of securing the welfare of children. Thus, it is within this context that the parameters of this study have been set. Its main focus is an analysis of education as social policy, the neglect of which Janet Finch (1984) complains and Rosemary Deem *et al.* (1995) seek to redress. A view of education as social welfare has a long history which can be traced back to nineteenth-century debates about the enforcement of compulsory school attendance and the introduction of school meals. Not surprisingly, the need to enforce attendance provoked intense concern and ultimately it proved impossible to sustain a rigid distinction between education and broader social problems, including the means to relieve poverty and distress. In part, this was because the provisions of the 1870 Education Act repeated the concerns of middle-class social workers, researchers and reformers with the classification, segregation and surveillance of the poor. Within this remit, the legislation effectively demarcated public elementary schools from other educational institutions according to the scale of school fees charged, which could not exceed 9d a week. Unlike the state schools for which it was responsible, the London School Board was at all times dominated by members of the middle and upper classes and could count peers and MPs among its members. Only three candidates of working-class origin were elected: the former Chartist and cabinetmaker Benjamin Lucraft, the trade unionist George Potter, and Mary Bridges Adams, the daughter of an engine fitter who trained as a pupil teacher. Moreover it goes without saying that most of the electors were middle class and, as a consequence, they did not send their children to the board schools.

The Victorians made little attempt to hide the class nature of education. Cecil Reddie, giving evidence to the Bryce Commission in 1894, spoke for the great majority when he urged that there should be: 'the school for the Briton who will be one of the muscle workers . . . the school for the Briton whose work requires knowledge of the modern world . . . the school for the Briton who is to be a leader' (cited in Lawson and Silver, 1973: 344). Although this class nexus was crucial to struggles over schooling, it also had a distinct gender dynamic. For while the principle of compulsion underpinning the educational legislation of the 1870s made no distinction of sex, the outcome of state policies on education for girls and boys was not identical. In practice, a pattern was soon established that rendered the expansion of the girls' curriculum gender specific. However, this does not mean that sole responsibility for the shape of provision lay with the male officials of the Education Department. It is also important to look in detail at the power and influence afforded the new agents of local authority, some far from the corridors of Whitehall.

Again, neither the school board franchise nor the qualification for election excluded women by virtue of their sex. This book argues that London's activist women played a crucial role in the formation of a state education system both as teachers, as school managers and as members of the School Board. Yet while the work of London's women teachers has been charted by Dina Copelman (1996), the level of female involvement in school governance remains largely unexplored. Characteristically, what little research has been conducted on such women is contained within general histories of Victorian feminism, where a concentration on the suffrage issue has meant the contribution of a few leading names is largely measured in terms of the unique quality of the female contribution, forming an apprenticeship for and platform from which to secure full political enfranchisement. This skewed picture has been further distorted by a tendency for historians of women's education to concentrate their attention on the schooling of the middle classes where girls and women were placed in separate institutions. In this respect an enduring image has developed of a small but vocal group of female activists spearheading the campaigns for access to secondary and higher education for girls and women. However, a concentration on middle-class schooling has exacerbated the tendency to neglect the tradition of direct female involvement in the provision of universal education for the working classes. This is unfortunate, for it means the history of state education has fallen short of the ideal in terms of equality of representation and treatment of women, despite the feminization of the teaching profession in the nineteenth century.

The subject has not been ignored entirely. Patricia Hollis (1989) provides a valuable insight into the world of those who held office on school boards, in her pioneering study of women in English local government between 1865 and 1914, while Annmarie Turnbull (1983a) has focused attention on the female members of the London School Board. But in general, women's involvement in educational decision-making has been neglected in the literature focused on women, feminism, and education. Nonetheless, it is only by considering the nature and actions of local school boards that it becomes possible to see the vital post-1870 period in elementary education with clear eyes. In this context, the focus shifts from the level of government policy for education (in which women had no direct say), to the women involved in what Felicity Hunt (1991: 11) refers to as 'a middle level of decision making which intervenes between government policy and actual school practice'. Like Hunt, I choose to call this 'organizational policy', although the concerns are somewhat different in the period preceding the 1902 Education Act, which forms the starting point in her study. In this book organizational policy is concerned with the nature of the school curriculum, policies for enforcing attendance, the provision of facilities, responsibility for budgets and staff appointments, as well as the related issues of training, hiring, salaries, promotions and pensions for all the Board's employees.

This study is, in the main, an investigation of female experience on what was then the world's largest educational parliament. As such it reflects the concerns of some commentators that the narrow perception of events, epitomized by an extended tradition of class-based analysis within the history of education generally, needs altering (Hunt, 1991). Hence feminist work in recent years has drawn attention to the fact that this requires a new dimension to our historical thinking through the use of gender as a category of social analysis, that is, the psychological and cultural constructions of role and behaviour – male and female. For example, Hilda Kean (1990) has considered the interacting dynamics of class and gender relations in her analysis of the socialist and feminist response to state education policy in England and Wales between 1900 and 1930. Here the concept of gender is used to decipher the power relations in the School Board for London, including the decision-making process at the Board's regular weekly meetings. Indeed, although influence is difficult to isolate, as Annmarie Turnbull (1983b) has explained from the standpoint of the domestic subjects movement, certain women did manage to carve out a place for themselves within the new schools. In the late nineteenth century, what Turnbull found was that a growing focus on cooking and sewing owed as much to the ladies urging a syllabus grounded in the knowledge needs of women as to the narrow conceptions of women's capacities held by the male officials of the Education Department. From the start, women were among the prime movers and most consistent supporters of these courses and yet the women themselves and their field of endeavour have been made invisible by an account of education that excludes the traditional female role and of an educational system shaped and inspired by masculine ideals.

Even though using power in the historical context is not easy (because key data may be missing), it is important to identify the particular theories of power used in this analysis of female activism. Of course it is necessary to distinguish between having power and exercising power and the central theme will be the visible and less visible dimensions of power as evidenced in a specific 'gender regime'. In this instance, there is a concern to examine relations of power between males and females attracted to service on the Board, as well as the women members themselves. However, while it is possible to chart the ability of individuals and alliances to directly influence the decision-making process, it may be difficult to isolate ability to set the agenda of politics and it may only be possible to suspect the impact exerted by the structural constraints surrounding social action (Deem *et al.*, 1995).

Essentially the distribution of political power reflects certain biases in the way society is organized that make it easier for some individuals and groups to see their objectives come to fruition than others. Using the framework of power proposed by Stewart Clegg (1989), it becomes possible to identify the different 'circuits of power' instantiated within a specific organizational setting. Thus the impact of women's contribution will refract not only the circuit of 'facilitative power' embedded within the rules and regulations of the School Board itself, but also the circuit of 'dispositional power' framing relations between elected men and women, as well as diagonal gender–class relations underpinning the London school system. Here it is useful to draw on the concept of gender balance that is being developed by Joni Lovenduski, Helen Margetts and Patrick Dunleavy. To simplify, this typology draws out the sex and/or gender biases of contemporary politics by distinguishing between positional, policy and organizational balances. But it is the first and third dimensions that are crucial here. Thus positional balance 'refers to the numbers of men and women in organisations as a whole and, within those organisations, to their presence in decision-making positions' (see Lovenduski, 1996: 5–6). By contrast, organizational balance alerts us to the biases integral to the rules, values, norms, structures and policies of a specific organization – that is, Clegg's notion of 'facilitative power'.

By drawing on concepts such as these both women's history (as defined by its subject matter) and feminist history (as defined by its perspective), offer fresh insights into the dynamics of the relationship between women and politics in late Victorian and Edwardian England. However there has been relatively little research into women's efforts in local government in this period – partly perhaps because of the fact that historically politics tends to be dominated by masculine and middle-class definitions of political significance. Certainly it is arguable that a concentration on the rules of formal politics and specifically political arrangements – parliament, government departments – has exacerbated a tendency to marginalize the struggles of some excluded groups which, from this standpoint, do not count as politics at all. Seen from this perspective, Victorian feminism may be considered an extreme and minority movement, while the names and details of all but the most eminent women's lives have tended not to be preserved as were those of their main contemporaries who led lives of social action. As others have made clear, this exclusionary process has its own history and is clearly in marked contrast to the emphasis on the public activities of male bureaucrats and politicians found in mainstream accounts of the nineteenth-century political process. Yet a focus on gender as a category of analysis highlights the problems associated with a rigidly compartmentalized model of a social world divided into masculine public and feminine private spheres. In practice, it is impossible to sustain the artificial demarcation between private lives and public commitments implicit within the accepted parameters of formal politics. Like all social movements, the nineteenth-century women's movement is as much the history of friendships, emotional attachments, and social and intellectual networks as it is the history of organized campaigns and lobbying. As Philippa Levine (1990) points out, it is impossible to understand either the politics of women's oppression or that of their defiance, without seeking a much broader definition of the meaning of the word 'politics'. To what extent, for instance, did the leaders of the nineteenth-century women's movement live out their political values in private as well as in public life?

An analysis of the moral sensibilities and cultural assumptions at the heart of political debate is vital in understanding the growth of public education in nineteenth-century England. Then, as now, education policy reflected a series of political victories in which social groups that benefited from and supported institutional reform gradually won out over those who were disadvantaged by it. The winners clearly included elements of the middle and upper classes, as well as the educational professionals who would be running the new bureaucratic system. Certainly many of the important figures in the Victorian feminist movement, such as Emily Davies (1830–1921) and Elizabeth Garrett (1836–1917), played an active part in the construction of the new system. Moreover, this is hardly surprising in view of their concern with extending political and employment rights for middle-class women. Unlike some of the more radical activists involved in the second wave of feminism in the 1960s and 1970s, they did not seek a feminist revolution. Instead they campaigned for reform from within. Drawing specifically on liberal ideas about natural justice, Elizabeth and Emily argued that individual women should be as free as men to determine their social, political and educational roles. Consequently, although they dreaded breaking the boundaries of social convention, they were prepared to press the demand for an increased presence of women in local decision-making. As Elizabeth Garrett wrote to Emily Davies during the 1870 election campaign for the London School Board:

> It is no use asking for women to be taken into public work and yet wish them to avoid publicity. We must be ready to go into the thing as men do if we go at all, and in time there will be no more awkwardness on our side than there is on theirs.
>
> (Elizabeth Garrett to Emily Davies, 24 October 1870)

Significantly, neither were complete novices to the world of social reform politics and both publicly argued that women had interests that were best represented by women. Like many of their twentieth-century counterparts, they placed great emphasis on the need for a feminist consciousness-raising strategy and were part of a wider movement to force women's concerns on to the political agenda. Nevertheless, thirty years later the sight of these 'platform women' was still unusual enough to provoke interest in their activities and this alone would seem to justify an analysis of their contribution to elected office. As important, as Annabelle Sreberny-Mohammadi and Karen Ross (1996: 105) point out, is the need to look at the 'manner in which the mediated presentation of politics is gendered'. For instance, writing in 1887, the social investigator Beatrice Potter (later Beatrice Webb), not only acknowledged her interest in powerful women like the secularist and 'real orator', Annie Besant but also presented a critique of 'women orators' in general:

> But to *see* her speaking made me shudder. It is not womanly to thrust yourself before the world. A woman, in all the relations of life, should be sought. It is only on great occasions, when religious feeling and morality demand it, that a woman has a right to lift up her voice and call aloud to her fellow-mortals.
>
> (*Diary of Beatrice Webb, Volume One 1873–1892*, 1986: 223)

But what do these rather sparse details suggest? Is Beatrice a reliable witness to contemporary public opinion? Or were her contemporaries generally more receptive to female participants in the caring sphere of social politics? In the years that followed Forster's 1870 Education Act, a significant number of British women played an active public role in the administration of local educational services, although it can be argued that most of the benefits were felt by independent single women who were better placed than their married counterparts in the 1860s and 1870s to take advantage of the expanding work, educational and political opportunities.

However, as will become apparent during the course of this book, elite and middle-class women who sat on school boards did experience difficulties. Despite the fact that women members were unusually well represented on the London Board, they were still in a minority and operating within what Jill Matthews speaks of as the gender order: 'a historically constructed pattern of power relations between men and women and definitions of femininity and masculinity' (cited in Connell, 1987: 98–9). Following the approach taken by Bob Connell in his study of gender and power, this work uses the terms 'gender order' and 'gender regime' in order to break down the overall structure of gender relations in nineteenth- and early twentieth-century Britain. Therefore, it argues that in order to understand the close relationship between structure and agency in individual lives, it is necessary to make sense of the way in which the macro-politics of the gender order shape social practice within any given 'gender regime'.

Accordingly, while sexual stereotyping became more pervasive in a variety of ways both inside and outside the Victorian home, it is important to remember that male authority is neither distributed among all groups of men, nor is it evenly secreted across every department of social life. Relations of power are diffuse, uneven and contested and in some circumstances women have authority. For instance, as historians such as Patricia Hollis (1989), Seth Koven (1993, 1994), Pat Thane (1993) and Annmarie Turnbull (1983a) have recognized, possessing the right to vote and hold local office gave women ratepayers access to precisely the political venues that immediately complicated, and partly contradicted, the general connection of authority with masculinity. Consequently, the term 'gender regime' as it is used in the following chapters should be seen as a fluid category used to describe the state of play in sexual politics within just one of the locally elected, single purpose educational authorities called school boards.

Local government was the linchpin of the Victorian state. It was also the key arena for the design and provision of social welfare at a time when the only approved role outside the home for women from wealthy families was unpaid charitable work. In the late 1860s and early 1870s expanding political opportunities opened up new gender and class roles for women which, while they transgressed the doctrine of separate spheres for men and women, might be represented within the traditional framework of complementarity. Because school board work could be presented as a legitimate extension of the traditional female role of nurturing the young, the wider political climate was especially attractive for single women seeking independent and useful lives. For those fortunate enough to be able to make choices unfettered by financial insecurity and social isolation, the politics of education conformed to larger patterns of female philanthropy in the nineteenth century and offered both single women and childless married women alike the chance to project a womanly and motherly persona by devoting their lives to the rough and wayward children of the urban poor.

Conclusion

It is my personal view that these neglected institutions offer an extremely fertile area within which to explore the ways women negotiate a space for themselves in the public world, when given the opportunity to do so. Likewise, Carol Dyhouse (1987: 23) points out that 'education was (and is) one of the few areas of public life where women have achieved a measure of status and authority'. Despite the potential dissonance of gender roles and hierarchies, women members of the London School Board made a significant contribution to the area of organizational policy by defining issues, building institutions and expanding the capacity of local authorities to deal with social problems. At the same time, they were unable to participate in the education policy of government and the action of government departments. Although their public activities were both wide-ranging and influential, elected women were restricted to particular spheres in local government which were most receptive to female involvement. Hence the concept of the state is central to the principal themes of this book. In particular, it needs to be appreciated that the British state in the later nineteenth and early twentieth centuries was characterized by a small, but strong, heavily masculinized core, directing the key activities of a variety of local government bodies responsible for the delivery of particular social services in their communities. Not surprisingly, the functions delegated to local authorities were those judged less essential by the male politicians in central government.

Nonetheless, as members of an elite circle of civic-minded reformers, these women combined individual service with institution building in order to facilitate the education of the people. A belief in the meaning and value of individual striving was central to their achievements and provided a justification for their gender and class roles in a way that ultimately reaffirmed the worth and status of their class and its culture. The great majority never doubted for a moment that elites, men and women like themselves, were the rightful arbiters of a particular philosophy, morality and culture. To this extent at least, the sharing of a common culture among the 'urban gentry' represented on the Board was an important resource for middle-class women members (Stedman Jones, 1984). Sharing a particular relationship to culture, they inevitably acquired certain family linguistic and social competences, quite apart from such qualities as style and manners, that effectively set them apart from their working-class constituents and the children attending the state elementary schools.

This study supports the view presented in the work of Pierre Bourdieu (1976, 1977) that the relationship between family background and patterns of socialization is crucial to an understanding of the cultural inequalities that underlie the overt and hidden curricula of schooling. Thus Bourdieu's work is developed to explore the ways in which relationships among the sexual division of labour, the social division of labour, and particular forms of culture influence struggles over the meanings and practices selected and distributed in school. For the middle-class women who ran for and served on the Board, the possession of certain cultural capital and a certain ethos helped reconcile the tensions between personal aspiration and a sense of what was socially acceptable, not only at an individual level, but at the level of public image and public behaviour (Dyhouse, 1987). Antonio Gramsci's focus on the importance of intellectuals is also significant here. He argued that the intellectual contributions of every individual who 'contributes to sustain a particular conception of the world or to modify it, that is, to bring into being new modes of thought' (1971: 9), are vital for societal change. Thus, the School Board for London offered a crucial testing ground for significant groups holding different economic, political and cultural resources and struggling to attain power and influence in late Victorian society. As a consequence, this book goes beyond the separate spheres model of female social action detailed by Patricia Hollis (1989), in order to examine how class and gender structures were dynamically interrelated in the politics of education.

Furthermore, a historical perspective on the relationship between gender and policy-making in English education has more than an antiquarian interest since, as Anna Davin explains briefly: 'a grasp of how sexual divisions have operated and changed is necessary for analysis both of the past and of the present' (1996: 1). Indeed Davin's work on childhood in the London working classes at this time has performed a great service in pointing to some of the continuities and differences in social, economic and cultural practices. Moreover a number of historians of education have highlighted the importance of history for the understanding of contemporary events and many commentators today see similarities between past and present educational reforms. Similarly, because these female representatives were among the first women in Britain to be elected to positions of this kind of political responsibility, some understanding of their lives and experiences provides a valuable insight into particular historical trends in the relationship between women and the political process in Britain. In this way the study also raises questions about what women can do for politics and what politics can do for women. Women are still significantly under-represented in many forms of public life, such as Parliament, the institutions of law and order, and influential non-governmental bodies. The proportion of women in the House of Commons did not exceed 5 per cent until 1987, although a Labour landslide election victory in May 1997 saw the figure rise to 18 per cent. Today, when the 120 'Westminster women' are a topic for debate, it is important to consider how we might network, lobby and campaign for change.

In the chapters that follow the various issues explored in this introduction are taken up in a detailed study of the lives and experiences of the 29 female members of the School Board for London. At the same time, it tries not to forget the many thousands of women who campaigned assiduously on behalf of the victorious candidates: writing and distributing campaign leaflets, donating funds and on polling day bringing voters to the polls. Chapter 2 considers the broad social, economic and ideological frameworks shaping these women's lives, and Chapter 3 examines the role and status of the London School Board, paying particular attention to the position of women on this key public institution. Chapter 4 takes as its main concern the links between private lives and public practice by focusing on key patterns that emerge from the individual biographies of the School Board women. In examining the extensive overlap of personal and political networks it considers what it was about these women that enabled them to make inroads into this exclusive world. This latter theme is explored further in Chapters 5 and 6, which focus on the administration of two key policy areas as seen from the perspective of female policy-makers struggling to secure a permanent place for women in local politics. Chapter 5 looks at patterns of access and provision for working class girls, and Chapter 6 focuses on the care and confinement of truanting children at risk. Chapter 7 concludes the analysis of the way in which women used both class- and gender-based themes in advancing themselves and their visions of education policy with an examination of broader social welfare concerns. Finally, Chapter 8 considers the impact of the

1902 Education Act on the political containment of women and the feminist opposition to it.

Note

1. The 29 women were: Annie Besant (represented Tower Hamlets 1888–91), Mary Bridges Adams (represented Greenwich 1897–1904), Jane Chessar (represented Marylebone 1873–6), Alice Cowell (represented Marylebone 1873–6), Rosamond Davenport Hill (represented the City 1876–97), Emily Davies (represented Greenwich 1870–3), Eugenie Dibdin (represented Finsbury 1897–1900), Margaret Mary Dilke/Cooke (represented Lambeth 1888–91), Constance Elder (represented Westminster 1897–1900), Margaret Eve (represented Finsbury 1891–1904), Elizabeth Garrett (represented Marylebone 1870–3), Edith Glover (co-opted after resignation of Emma Maitland in January 1903), Frances Hastings (represented Tower Hamlets 1882–5), Ruth Homan (represented Tower Hamlets 1891–1904), Susan Lawrence (represented Marylebone 1900–4), Maude Lawrence (represented Westminster 1900–4), Emma Maitland (represented Marylebone 1888–91, 1894–1902), Ellen McKee (represented the City 1897–1904), Hilda Miall–Smith (represented Marylebone 1900–4), Florence Fenwick Miller (represented Finsbury 1876–85), Honnor Morten (represented Hackney 1897–1900, Southwark 1900–2), Henrietta Muller (represented Lambeth 1879–85), Mary Richardson (represented Southwark 1876–85), Edith Simcox (represented Westminster 1879–82), Elizabeth Surr (represented Finsbury 1876–85), Helen Taylor (represented Southwark 1876–85), Julia Augusta Webster (represented Chelsea 1876–82, 1885–8), Alice Westlake (represented Marylebone 1876–88) and F. L. Wright (elected to succeed Mr Spink, resigned July 1893).

2 A New Role for Women?

Introduction

Organized around the sharpening divisions between the worlds of women and of men, this chapter is concerned with the broad context shaping women's experience of politics in the last three decades of the nineteenth century. Clearly the shift from a largely rural-based agrarian economy to one which was urban, industrial and based on wage labour was a long, slow and uneven process. Yet the changes involved were so momentous that their shadow fell across the lives of even those who were not directly affected. Economic change was one thing, but the sheer extent of social change heightened class consciousness to a quite new level and intensity. It is arguable that the impact of industrialization on relations between men and women was less dramatic than the impact on class relations. However, it was just as far-reaching.

Clearly it is relevant to examine the connections between inequalities in the domestic sphere and barriers to women's participation in the public sphere – not least because the realities of women's subordination were more complex than the familiar images of the 'angel in the house', the 'leisured lady', might suggest. In the first place, there was no absolute separation between the female world of household and family and the masculine world of business, politics and public affairs. Second, 'leisure' required a substantial income and only women in richer households could retreat from the material reality of the Victorian household. Thus although middle-class females were not generally working for money, neither were they leading the rather vacuous lives idealized by the prescriptive literature. In practice, many middle-class wives struggled to keep up appearances on relatively modest incomes, while their upper-middle-class counterparts also found the supervision of domestic staff could be arduous. It therefore follows that prescription must be tested against women's actual experience.

Here the emphasis is on the fluid and contested world inhabited by a well-connected group of activist women. So while it may seem diversionary to include a chapter on middle-class gender roles, it is a necessary excursion in order to show the ways in which the experience of hierarchy in the home constrains women's public commitments. Focusing on the macro level, the chapter first examines the construction of bourgeois domestic ideology in nineteenth-century England. This, then, provides a framework within which to explore the emergence of what Elizabeth Sarah (1982) calls 'first-wave' feminism in order to differentiate it from the feminist challenge which surfaced during the 1960s. Moving on, the second part of the chapter considers the emergence of the metropolitan women's movement in the 1850s, in particular the ladies of Langham Place and their connections with the feminist network to which many School Board women belonged. Finally, the chapter explores women's demands for the full political rights of citizenship in order to examine broad arguments about equality and difference, considered in the context of the ambiguous relationship between women and the political arena in late Victorian and Edwardian England.

Gender and class identity in nineteenth-century England

Accentuating the links between the rise of industrial capitalism and the marked expansion of the highly skilled and increasingly influential middle class, Leonore Davidoff and Catherine Hall (1987) suggest that the language of class formation was gendered. Their argument should by now be quite familiar. Taken as an ideal, they argue that the focus on hearth and home became an increasingly important criterion by which these middle ranks ensured a status of respectability and exclusivity. Daughters were largely educated for the marriage market and the low status alternative was assimilation into the ranks of those redundant women featured in the writings of concerned social commentators like the failed industrialist William Greg. In response to 'the surplus woman problem', published in the *National Review* in April 1862, Greg proposed that women who could not find husbands should emigrate to the colonies where there were far fewer European women than men. Nine years later the feminist Emily Faithfull (1835–95) would describe Greg's husband-hunting proposal as 'enforced transportation in a benevolent disguise' (*Victoria Magazine*, June 1871: 321). Contemporary public opinion appeared to coincide with that of Greg. The possibility that what some of these women wanted was the chance to lead an independent life was ignored.

Paradoxically, although their class applauded self-assertion, a limited feminine ideal portrayed middle-class women as passive decorative creatures. Thus it was widely recognized that, whereas middle-class Victorian males were to be active in the world as citizens and entrepreneurs, females were to be insulated from danger and temptation in the private sphere of the home. Significantly, these ideals were founded on a general belief in the principle that men and women were naturally different – not just biologically, but in terms of inherent personality. Buttressed by social and religious beliefs, medical and scientific practice, women's 'special' traits were felt to include: benevolence, compassion, humility, modesty, morality, patience, sensitivity and tact. In particular, it was assumed that a combination of maternal capacity, physical frailty and sexual vulnerability placed women in need of care and protection and, to this extent, the feminine ideal became a metaphor for the social patterning of gender. Consequently, as Jane Lewis (1986: 9) makes clear: 'both prescription and material reality imposed real constraints on women's behaviour and expression'. Furthermore, while all women were politically disenfranchised, the institution of marriage enshrined a double standard of morality based on gender. Defined as a legal minor, a married woman not only had:

> no right to enter contracts or own any property (including her earnings), but she had no rights over her children, whose guardianship passed from her husband to his nearest male relative at his death [. . .] an adulterous wife lost all rights to maintenance and was liable to be abandoned on the basis of a judicial separation; an adulterous husband suffered no penalty, could pursue a wife who left him on account of his infidelity and sue her harbourers, and if he abandoned her, could be made to provide support only on the basis of a court order establishing her need.
>
> (Taylor, 1983: 35)

In this context, a variety of religious, medical and scientific arguments became highly effective in dismissing unmarried women as society's failures. There was also strong support for new notions of gentility that required middle-class women to assume responsibility for creating a civilized domestic milieu (Dyhouse, 1986). What needs more emphasis is the uncomfortable consequence of living in a society in which a woman was seen as the wife, mother or daughter of some man:

> A girl could go on being somebody's daughter only so long as her father was alive, and after that, if she had not succeeded in becoming somebody's wife, she was adrift. Without money or the possibility of earning for herself, she was reduced to being dependent on her male relatives [. . .] With the laws of inheritance as they were, the single woman nearly always had narrow means; and her life was passed in trying to be as little in the way as possible.
>
> (Strachey, 1988: 17)

Obviously the way gender featured in the process of class formation was crucial to the social relations of citizenship, since it positioned women primarily within the home. But in the 1850s and 1860s an imbalance in the sex ratio and a common core of values that positively discouraged serious education and paid employment for middle-class girls, made 'the woman question' an important issue of the day. Overall, daughters of more genteel families were not expected to earn, but it became increasingly evident that a growing number faced an impoverished future if they did not succeed in finding a husband. Certainly middle-class girls were disadvantaged in the labour market because they were given knowledge that would make them more attractive in the marriage market, rather than knowledge that would give them vocational skills. Indeed the situation was exacerbated by concerns about social status and the lack of 'respectable' employment opportunities for upper-class and middle-class women. By 1850, small numbers of women mounted a challenge to prevailing sexual and social orthodoxies. As the wealthy Florence Nightingale (1820–1910) put it: 'Why have women passion, intellect, moral activity – these three – and a place in society where no one of the three can be exercised?' (from the autobiographical fragment 'Cassandra', first published in Strachey, 1988: 396). Seeking to transform and redefine the larger culture, these exceptional individuals organized to expose and express the legal inequalities and cultural injustices which hindered their sex. From these beginnings there emerged an alternative set of equal rights ideas espoused by a small but vocal minority of Victorian women, expressing a distinct philosophy reflecting a strong, positive sense of female identity. The end result was an eighty-year-long period during which the ideological struggle for women's rights was to transform the social problem of the 1840s – 'woman' into a political category (Alexander, 1994).

The mid-nineteenth-century metropolitan women's movement

As the customary historiography of the nineteenth-century English women's movement makes clear, the social origins of the early feminists correspond with those of the families which dominated the intellectual aristocracy identified and analysed by Noel Annan (1955). Moreover, the connection to the movements for anti-slavery, the People's Charter of 1838, the reform of the Corn Laws, and peace and temperance, has long been recognized. But although the emergence of the first women's movement in Britain is associated with the 1857 Married Women's Property petition, more recent work by Kathryn Gleadle (1995) has shown how much the ideas and networks related to the 1830s and 1840s. Her excellent monograph has performed a great service in articulating the links between the campaigners of the 1850s and an interesting group of radical, free-thinking men and women centred around William Johnson Fox (the Unitarian editor of the *Monthly Repository* and minister at South Place Chapel in Finsbury), whom Gleadle refers to as the 'radical Unitarians'. Unitarians combined belief in the one God with a stress on Christian values, and their separation from the Church of England stemmed from the Reformation and the events of the sixteenth and seventeenth centuries. The combined effects of a world dominated by the alliance of Church and State meant the Unitarians experienced a variety of disabilities. Thus while the repeal of the Test and Corporations Act in 1828 allowed nonconformists to enter Parliament and hold other public offices, religious tests for Oxbridge fellowships were not abolished until 1871.

Turning from the early feminists to the middle-class educators in this study, two of the women were the offspring of radical Unitarian feminists, while a third married into a radical Unitarian family. Rosamond Davenport Hill was the daughter of the radical Unitarian lawyer, Matthew Davenport Hill (1792–1872). Similarly, Helen Taylor was the daughter of the feminist Harriet Hardy Taylor Mill (1807–58), one of the original South Place congregants; and the upwardly mobile Mary Daltry gained an entry into the Unitarian world through her marriage to Walter Bridges Adams, the son of the political writer William Bridges Adams (1797–1872), whose progressive feminist views so outraged mainstream Unitarians in the 1830s. William had first married the eldest daughter of the radical Francis Place; when she died he married Sarah Flower, the daughter of Benjamin Flower, a radical Unitarian publisher and member of the original South Place circle. After Sarah's death in 1848, William married Ellen Rendall, who became Walter's mother and lived on until 1898. A well known civil engineer and paternalistic employer, William led the way in promoting the idea of associated housing schemes where families might occupy self-contained homes with shared access to kitchens, provisions, fires and libraries. In his opinion, this would both improve living conditions and emancipate women from their domestic ties (see Gleadle, 1995: 34, 37, 47–50, 99).

However the immediate precursors of the young women who formed the nucleus of the metropolitan women's movement were the writers and reformers connected with the radical Unitarian MP for Norwich, Benjamin Leigh Smith. This friendship circle included the Unitarian lawyer Thomas Noon Talford (who guided the Infant Custody Bill of 1839 through Parliament) and Matthew Davenport Hill. Like Smith, Hill came from a prominent Unitarian family whose educational projects earned a widespread reputation among liberal circles, and he himself publicly endorsed female suffrage during his successful general election campaign in Hull in 1832 (see Gleadle, 1995: 71). Moreover Benjamin's sister, Julia Leigh Smith, came to know the wealthy Unitarian widow Elizabeth Jesser Reid (who founded Bedford College for Women in 1849), and the writer and art critic Anna Jameson (1794–1860). Inspired by her aunt's friend, Anna Jameson, Barbara Leigh Smith (1827–91) promoted the cause of marriage law reform, while the support of sympathetic males like her father's friend, Hill, proved crucial to her first attempts at feminist propaganda. Indeed the close links may be illustrated by the fact that Anna referred to Barbara and her friends Bessie Parkes (1829–1925), Adelaide Proctor (1825–64), Anna Howitt (1824–84) and Eliza Fox as her 'adopted nieces' (Herstein, 1985: 71). More specifically, it was from these beginnings that Barbara Smith created the first women's network in Britain and was instrumental in founding the *English Woman's Journal* (1858–64), edited by Matilda Hays and Bessie Parkes. By 1860 their offices at 19 Langham Place housed the Society for the Promotion of Women's Employment, an emigration society and a school for industrial training, while the establishment of a social club marked another important cultural development. This included a library and reading-room designed to provide women with a forum where they might enjoy both education and recreation. In this way the moving spirits of this venture created space for politicized discussion about particular forms of legal injustice, and economic and social restriction.

Excluded from the established power centres of party and government, these unusually well-connected women were determined to pursue public activities and lives. They organized around broad based alliances, seeking to draw in strategically placed individuals of both sexes. Indeed, the campaign to reform the laws pertaining to married women, involving the establishment of a press, a centre for publicity and lines of communication, as well as the winning of influential allies through meetings, petitions, articles and lobbying, typified this approach. In essence, it provided the catalyst for several decades of equal rights campaigning for access to secondary and higher education, as well as greater employment opportunities and participation by women in public life and government. The widening opportunities in local government became a crucial aspect of their campaign strategy and participation in educational governance was fundamental to their demand for more women in decision-making positions.

Inevitably the initial group was small. Diana Worzola (1982) has charted the family background of these female pioneers and identified 32 committed activists, including Emily Davies and Elizabeth Garrett, the first two women members of the London School Board. Not all these campaigners were middle class, but again Diana Worzola has shown how the social origins of the women involved fit somewhere between the aristocracy and the respectable working class. The size of family fortunes varied, but as the daughters of professional or business men the background of the majority lay between the extremes of Frances Power Cobbe's ancestral home near Dublin and the St Albans grocery shop owned by Sarah Lewin's father. Some came from more traditional backgrounds; indeed Jessie Boucherett was the youngest daughter of a Lincolnshire landowner, an earnest churchwoman and fervent admirer of Disraeli. Irrespective of familial wealth, however, all the women resented the fact that as females their own personal circumstances depended upon the liberality of male relatives, whether it be fathers, husbands or brothers. For instance, Frances Cobbe actually moved to England to escape her brother's attempts to control her life after their father's death. Once there she maintained her independence by supporting herself through her writing.

A decade later, the size of the group remained a cause for concern. For example, during the winter of 1865 Emily Davies organized the Kensington Society, a discussion group for women interested in educational, political, social and moral questions. Again the society was never large; a membership list in the Davies papers at Girton College contains 67 names, including four School Board women: Elizabeth Garrett, Helen Taylor, Julia Webster and Alice Hare Westlake. However, the number increased at the end of the 1860s when the educational and suffrage campaigns enrolled many more supporters for the cause.

Significantly, the decision to initiate a series of single-issue campaigns enabled women to work with others with whose general and political outlook they sympathized, while avoiding those with whom they clashed. It also allowed for the clear expression of the very different ideas which existed within the movement as to what the movement itself was. This became more important as the organization spread across the country and proceeded to incorporate provincial networks of sympathetic women and men. Such mergers were never easy but Philippa Levine (1987) has stressed the importance of shared family and friendship networks. To a very large extent, this draws attention to the fact that feminism cuts across and includes women of diverse political allegiances. The distinguishing feature of feminist thinking was the focus on sexual difference, but a selective sampling of private correspondence and the journals of the movement itself reveals the differences among those absorbed in feminist politics, as well as a strong sense of the connections underlying the different campaigns. This meant the major issue became one of campaign strategy – the means by which these particular goals were to be attained. In theory, most activists were in agreement over the need to work through persuasion and to present the movement in a way that was socially and morally acceptable. In practice, there was considerable divergence over what precisely this entailed, especially the relative importance of style. For the more conservative elements within feminism this was largely interpreted as an emphasis on the need to maintain respectability, mainly by presenting themselves as womanly women. On the whole this reflected a need to reconcile self-image and behaviour, which meant doing their best to follow social prescriptions in their private lives and political commitments, while distancing themselves from more radical approaches that would prejudice the wider women's movement. Hence the ways in which the women's movement organized the agitation for better jobs, higher pay and greater personal freedom, as well as the demand for suffrage, varied according to the specific campaigns, and often by individual personality.

Nonetheless, it says much for the pervasiveness of the Victorian domestic ideal that most members of the early women's movement accepted as natural a sexual division of labour and of familial responsibility.[1] In general, the feminist assault was not on marriage as an institution, but on marital inequalities. The women of Langham Place turned their attention to the laws concerning a husband's absolute right to his wife's property and earnings (whether she was living with him or not); the double standards regarding divorce and physical abuse; and the vow of obedience which they saw as requiring a woman to forfeit her conscience and sense of moral responsibility. In 1870 women secured the right to keep their own earnings (whatever their marital status), but Mary Lyndon Shanley (1989) suggests the passage of the Married Women's Property Act of 1882 was of greater significance. In the first place, it enabled married women to function as independent legal personages. Second, it gave them the legal capacity to act as autonomous economic agents. This was an important psychological triumph which not only 'struck a blow at the whole notion of coverture and the necessary subordination of a woman's will to that of her husband' (Shanley, 1989: 103), but gave added impetus to feminist thinking about such issues as male violence against women and the double moral standards of their society. Out of these demands a new companionate model of the conjugal relationship was constructed to replace what had been a partnership based on inequality. In particular, the marriage between the social critic John Stuart Mill (1806–73) and Harriet Taylor was frequently lauded as an ideal type of spousal equality – a relationship that perfectly illustrated Mill's own ideal of marriage as a marriage of true minds (see Mendus, 1989: 171–91). Unsurprisingly, the liberal politics of Millicent Garrett Fawcett (1847–1929) meant her strongest political affinities were with Mill who objected to:

> the whole character of the marriage relation as constituted by law [. . .] for this amongst other reasons, that it confers upon one of the parties to the contract, legal power and control over the person, property, and freedom of action of the other party, independent of her own wishes and will.
>
> (Hayek, 1959: 168)

Certainly, Kate Amberley (1842–74) considered Mill's *Subjection of Women* the central text for the movement. Yet for Emily Davies and Barbara Leigh Smith Bodichon, it was his political purchase that counted and not his ideas on the woman question. However while Emily Davies wanted feminists to work closely with sympathetic men, this principle was established at the cost of antagonizing Mill's step-daughter, Helen Taylor, who advocated a separatist solution for women seeking change. In the short term, both Mill and Taylor opposed the establishment of mixed suffrage committees on the grounds that women needed to foster their own style and strategy with reference to organizational forms.

In harmony with the Victorian view of work as inherently virtuous, one of the most distinctive features of the early campaigns in the 1850s and 1860s was the emphasis on the transformation of women's lives through useful employment. Counterbalancing the focus on a carefully defined set of family duties pointed up by conservative social commentators, equal rights activists envisaged a future where women would enjoy the same economic rights as men. In this respect the ideas and example of Anna Jameson were extremely influential. As she put it in two drawing-room lectures in 1855, the progress of women was closely connected with the idea of specific needs and qualities that were considered to be naturally female. Indeed it was these 'special' capacities which would enable them to articulate women's concerns. Nonetheless, though she shared the dominant belief that the sexes had different capabilities and natures, Anna Jameson denied that women were inherently less capable than men and envisioned a future in which the sexes would work together to transform the character of the nation. In what amounted to a three-pronged attack on the doctrine of separate spheres, she used the language of reciprocal rights and duties to appeal for the incorporation of women as citizens. In this way the language of citizenship combined with the language of sisterhood. Jameson argued that women needed access to education and training, to employment and the professions, as well as to the administration of all public institutions caring for dependent women and children. Well aware that social convention made the idea of higher education or paid work for middle-class women problematic, she transformed the doctrine of separate spheres to argue that just as the family and household required the active cooperation of feminine with masculine brains and hands, so the voices of women should be heard in the wider sphere beyond. To work was a sacred duty, and Anna Jameson converted the taken-for-granted point of moral reference of the leading classes in English society to articulate a powerful political philosophy in which the idea of men and women working together in a 'communion of labour' was a central theme.

Based on the belief that they should be able to take part as individuals, irrespective of their sex, in the life of society, *Journal* contributors did not exempt other women from the need to work, but attention was directed towards the shortage of suitable employment for impoverished gentlewomen left without a male protector. To this end Barbara Leigh Smith proposed the industrial training of tens of thousands of middle-class women to open up social and economic opportunities. For instance, in a pamphlet entitled *Women and Work* (1857), she pressed the case for job-related training in a variety of occupations such as accountancy, book-keeping, nursing, teaching and watch-making (*Women and Work*, 1857: 16–17). One significant response to this rather grandiose plan came from Lord Brougham, who invited her and the rest of the Langham Place group to join the new National Association for the Promotion of Social Science (NAPSS), of which he was President. Established in 1857, this powerful pressure group presented itself as focusing on 'the practical rather than the theoretical aspects of social science' (Yeo, 1992: 67). It did much to open the way for women like Emily Davies and Rosamond Davenport Hill, whose close connections with the men of NAPSS – including Emily's brother, Llewellyn, and Rosamond's father, Matthew – offered a largely sympathetic conduit through which to develop their vision of a new social order.[2]

Generally speaking the Langham Place circle sought to communicate their conviction that women's inferior position was culturally, not naturally, determined. Indeed Sheila Herstein (1985) develops this theme by examining the reform of the British Civil Service associated with the Northcote-Trevelyan Report of 1854. This advocated a change, from existing Civil Service practice of appointment based on nepotism and patronage, towards the recognition of merit and talent. Led by Barbara Leigh Smith Bodichon, the framework in which the feminists worked was that of the growing professional concern with formal credentials. They were only partially successful. Although they did secure a greater degree of equal rights and opportunities for women, it must be remembered that the introduction of women into the civil service workforce was associated with the development of a hierarchical distinction between 'intellectual' and 'mechanical' labour (Drewry and Butcher, 1988). Ultimately the development of modern bureaucratic forms can be directly linked to a strategy that increasingly rested upon gender segregation in organizational hierarchies (see Martindale, 1938; Sanderson, 1990; Zimmeck, 1988).

By the mid-nineteenth century the professional middle class had secured a distinct cultural and economic presence in British society. As Mike Savage and his co-authors (1992) point out, the significance of this is brought out by their close links to the state, as well as their spatial bases in the urban arenas of London, Edinburgh and Manchester. The crucial point for the argument presented here is that W. Rubinstein (1987) estimates that by 1911 '44 per cent of middle class income was based in London ... even though it only contained 14 per cent of the population' (cited in Savage *et al.* 1992: 45). London had the largest number of middle-class housing developments and by the 1870s increasing numbers were living in rented houses in such leafy suburbs as Islington, Camberwell and Kensington. This should come as little surprise for two reasons. First, London was the centre of the British state and parliamentary politics. Second, it was the centre of the legal system and the learned professions. Thus the founders of the *Englishwoman's Journal* all came from professional families based in London.[3]

Eric Hobsbawm (1989: 165–91) has also considered the way in which particular changes in the capitalist economy impacted on certain members of the middle classes. In particular, he argues that the expansion of capitalist accumulation in the last quarter of the century brought increasing opportunities for the diversification of investment. As a result, the years leading up to the outbreak of the First World War saw a greater proportion of the middle classes leading leisured lives subsidized by private incomes. Moreover Hobsbawm (1983: 119) maintains that almost all the 170,000 'persons of rank and property' without visible occupation in England in 1871 were women provided for by stocks and shares, including shares in family firms formed into 'private companies' for this purpose. In this way, the era of railway, iron and foreign investment not only provided the economic base for the Victorian aesthete but also for those independent single women welcomed to the comfortable avenues of Kensington, the home of the first women's suffrage society. For some fortunate middle-class suffragists a substantial private income (of at least £250 a year), meant increased freedom of movement and produced a striking change in the position and aspirations of women (see Collini, 1993: 35–7 for a discussion of the sums required to sustain the public identity of a gentleman in this period). By the early 1880s the 'woman question' had moved to the centre of the public stage and feminism had become established as a major political force.

The idea of women's citizenship

In Ray Strachey's (1988) view a close correlation existed between nineteenth-century feminism and the eighteenth-century Enlightenment. For her, a number of key assumptions – like the optimistic faith in toleration and freedom – had a profound influence on this new kind of thinking about the rights of women. Further, it is suggested that the concerns and interests of the first feminists are deeply rooted in the Enlightenment's appeal to reason and natural rights. For instance, the conception of the individual as the starting point for all knowledge and action is seen as crucial to the conception of women (and men) as rational individuals with a right to property and to liberties of action and movement. Feminists extended the Enlightenment's faith in reason, science and progress and put the case that, when these were applied to social life, they would herald an end to all the traditional limits on women (as well as men). Thus contemporary ideals of individual liberty sanctioned and protected by the rule of law formed one of the most powerful points of moral reference and helped to shape the form of emancipation to which they aspired.

Yet Jane Rendall (1985: 7–32) has rejected rather favourable discussions of the historical connections between the women's movement and the Enlightenment to argue that the heritage is an extraordinarily confusing one. Moving away from an emphasis on the essential 'individualism' of classical liberalism as the key to the articulation of feminist demands, Rendall (1994) has entered into a dialogue with the mainstream of political history to establish a new framework for exploring the meanings of citizenship for the first generation of British suffragists. Rather than attach great weight to the key concept of individualism, recent revisions by John Burrow (1988), Stefan Collini (1991) and Donald Winch (1993) highlight the importance of changing philosophical attitudes among leading liberal intellectuals in the 1850s. This work has singled out the identifications forged around the newly coined concept of 'altruism'. This, then, provides a useful starting point to an exploration of the links between female activism and the language of personal philanthropy.

In mid-nineteenth-century England, the fear of being crushed by conventions carried huge psychological and emotional costs for single women who rebelled against the ascribed areas and roles of each sex. But for those with the drive and ambition to pursue interesting careers in public life, the spreading of the evangelical message crystallized women's participation in a whole range of religious activities (both educational and philanthropic), which took them out into the world. In particular, the idea that the home and the neighbourhood (including the church), were the anchors of a woman's existence helped to consolidate the role of middle-class women as social activists. Some continued the customary practice of ministering to the poor, the outcast and the infirm, and many became increasingly prominent in the charitable world as volunteer helpers, contributors and fund-raisers (see Prochaska, 1980). At the same time, others took the opportunity to carry their convictions into local government work as they began serving on local district councils, school boards, and poor law boards. In this way these female representatives extended their cultivating mission into new public areas of concern like the administration of poor relief and the development of the state system of elementary education.

But while the conventions surrounding the accomplished lady of leisure set clear determinants on social behaviour, it is important to emphasize the ways in which this self-designation of moral superiority provided the basis for that sense of cultivation and refinement that was an important theme of nineteenth-century social comment. In 1894, for instance, the *Woman's Signal* (the most important feminist paper of the period), carried an interview with Miss Harris, the head teacher of the Ben Jonson Street School in Whitechapel, who also attended the educational activities provided by the pioneer social settlement, Toynbee Hall. In response to a question about women managers for London Board Schools, she spoke in favour of their appointment because they understood the general concerns of women teachers and female pupils. Providing an example of such cross-class interaction to support her recommendation, she recalled an incident observed during a lesson on calico in which the teacher extolled the advantages of wearing unbleached cloth:

> A lady School Board member was present and the girls eyed her very curiously, wondering, no doubt what she would think of unbleached calico. At the end of the lesson, after thanking the teacher, she turned to the girls and told them that she was wearing unbleached underclothing, and strongly recommended them to follow their teacher's example.
>
> (*Woman's Signal*, 5 April 1894: 222)

It was argued that female representatives would articulate women's concerns. But of course public careers were facilitated by access to such resources as time, money and social status. Middle-class women *were* endowed with cultural capital. Moreover the culture of altruism was deeply embedded within liberal ideas of citizen participation and it is hardly surprising that the emphasis on family principles and the need for home influences in public life became one of the strongest arguments in favour of women's suffrage. Public work was a reflection of virtue and suffrage activists infused their construction of domesticity with a strong dose of civic maternalism. In the words of the *Englishwoman's Review*:

As voters, therefore, in the forthcoming School Board elections in London and many other cities, women to whom the care and education of their own families is a sacred charge should take this point seriously to heart. As Board School managers, and as members of the Boards, they are increasingly needed, and as no property qualification is necessary for a School Board member, there is not the same difficulty in finding suitable candidates that besets a Guardian election. We trust that women may feel this claim upon their motherhood, and bring to the State schools the thoughtfulness and tenderness which overflows from their home nurseries and schools.

(15 October 1888: 434–6)

Unlike conservative proponents of the domestic ideal, the middle-class leadership of the women's movement rejected earlier arguments stressing the links between women's particular moral and emotional qualities and their seclusion in the home. By contrast, the reformers argued that: 'while they were important within the home, womanly qualities were not derived from domesticity and would continue to be exercised by women in whatever capacity they chose' (Caine, 1982: 546). Discussions in pamphlets and periodicals tended to elaborate on Anna Jameson's ideas as a way of stimulating women to useful work, and the feminist circle steadily maintained her argument that the good of humanity required the 'active co-operation of feminine with masculine brains and hands just as much as the joint life of the individual homes of the nation' (*Englishwoman's Review*, 15 October 1888: 433–4). Louisa Twining (1820–1911), for instance, wanted to encourage more women to volunteer as helpers in the administration of the poor laws. Writing in the prestigious cultural periodical the *Nineteenth Century*, Twining used her social position to promulgate a vision of middle-class women as men's allies. Highlighting the need for women's influence and disturbed that there were so few ready to serve, she commended the work of women as public servants on the grounds that 'whatever changes may be brought about, none will be successful unless the necessity for their still more extended work and action is insisted upon, and the "communion of labour" between men and women yet further developed' (December 1890: 958). As Millicent Fawcett increasingly urged her fellow suffragists:

we do not want women to be bad imitations of men; we neither deny nor minimise the differences between men and women. The claim of women to representation depends to a large extent on those differences. Women bring something to the service of the state different from that which can be brought by men.

(quoted in Pugh, 1992: 3)

Firm believers that the citizen rights of the new social order should be extended to able and educated women, London's women activists were keen to demonstrate all the middle-class virtues of independence, self-improvement, self-discipline and public spirit. From early on, a knowledge that the pleasures to be derived from being a future lady and housekeeper were empty, increased a tendency towards profound self-contempt. In the words of Elizabeth Garrett, before moving to a permanent London home she was:

a young woman living at home with nothing to do in what authors call 'comfortable circumstances'. But I was wicked enough not to be comfortable. I was full of energy and vigour and of the discontent which goes with unemployed activities. ... Everything seemed wrong to me.

(Manton, 1965: 44)

Her sister, Millicent, echoed these sentiments and her autobiography, *What I Remember*, shows the importance she attached to this rejection of herself as a useless parasite. Mixed in with contempt for the 'selfishness' and 'egoism' of other women of her social class, her feminism was fuelled by a conversation she overheard between two clergymen's wives. As an exasperated Millicent later recalled, when asked what items sold best at charity bazaars, one of the wives replied: 'Oh! Things that are really useful such as butterflies for the hair' (Fawcett, 1924: 117). Of course the picture is further complicated by the fact that the very leisure of which the women complained secured them the opportunity for self-appraisal and shrewd self-analysis. Obviously women from such genteel backgrounds could hardly reiterate the heartfelt words of Hannah Mitchell, working-class socialist and suffrage worker, and say: 'I feel my greatest enemy has been the cooking stove – a sort of tyrant who has kept me in subjection' (1977: 240). Indeed the discovery that they were not alone in feeling this way, in tandem with their self-conscious awareness of belonging to a shared social world, provided a sense of solidarity and self-worth.

It is not surprising that the importance of social participation was perhaps the most influential mainspring to political action. Victorian London was the hub of the English charity world and, for middle-class women with the leisure and inclination, the theme of a metropolis at risk directed attention to the need for social service to the poor. Yet the characteristic preoccupations and assumptions of the leading activists may be seen as emblematic of the need for purpose deeply embedded in this class dynamic. In particular, a concentration upon the duties of altruism pertained directly to the class-based view of the world promulgated by the urban reformers.

In the analysis that follows, the sentimentalization of family life is considered a crucial aspect of the civic ideologies and practices of the period. At a time when ethical values stemmed directly from the teachings of the church, the emergence of activist interpretations of the gospel (which included evangelicalism and the highly influential Christian Socialism of Frederick Denison Maurice), was to have a direct bearing on notions of middle-class gender roles underpinning the social relations of citizenship. A certain expediency and pragmatism seemed necessary elements to the success of women's role in social reform politics and as Seth Koven's (1993) work on the 'borderlands' of local government and voluntary initiative clearly shows, a gender-based view of service provided a group of mostly middle-class women with a well-trodden path to power.

Excluded from the masculine sphere of parliamentary politics, women looked to local models of social and political action in which they might play a pivotal role as elected and appointed officials, as well as becoming social reformers, workers and activists in private sector philanthropic organizations. School board work had the added benefit of replicating women's familial duties and each of the leading ideas noted earlier lent weight to feminist claims about women's special suitability for this newly created role in wider society. Hence the concept of social mothering offered a critical pathway into the public sphere. In general, the imagery of motherhood and sisterhood, as well as the rhetoric of democratic participation and citizenship, were particularly potent.

The implications of this can be shown by reference to the fact that the tempo of women's participation in public life increased sharply in the 1880s and 1890s. As a matter of political principle, the feminist press advanced the conviction that women were by nature more caring, more ready for self-sacrifice and service than men, and encouraged women to use their growing civil rights as electors, party activists and elected representatives. Accordingly, they were able to report a significant number of women playing an active role in local authorities and voluntary organizations. By the end of the 1870s, for example, the number of women serving on school boards in England and Wales had grown from 3 to 71. But despite further steady growth during the 1880s, the five years from 1895 saw the most dramatic increase in the level of female representation as the number of school board women rose from 128 to 270. The socialist Margaret McMillan (1860–1931) was perhaps the most prominent of these women, serving on Bradford School Board from 1894 until its abolition in 1902. A key figure in the early Labour movement, she is renowned for her part in the movement for school feeding and child welfare. In particular, she led the campaign against the half-time system, helped secure the appointment of a School Medical Officer (the first in the country) and the installation of baths in the poorer schools. McMillan also co-operated with Robert Blatchford, socialist editor of the *Clarion* newspaper and founder of the Cinderella Club movement, which systematically fed and clothed slum children (see Steedman, 1990 for further details).

Like school board work, guardians' duties were also presented as specially suited to 'the motherly and the sisterly influence' (Twining, 1890: 952). Until the 1894 Local Government Act abolished all property qualifications, women came into poor law work only slowly. Previous to this, poor law guardians had to possess a high property qualification. The fact that the vote was calculated in accordance with the amount of property you owned did not help either female candidates (who were thought to be more generous with public money), or women ratepayers who were less likely to have multiple votes. Moreover, as Louisa Twining herself acknowledged, the work was often unpleasant and the presence of women frequently aroused hostility from male guardians and poor law officials alike. As a result, poor law work did not enjoy the same social status as school board work, neither did it attract individuals of the same social and political standing. In rural unions, Boards of Guardians were dominated by small farmers. In the towns it was small shopkeepers and businessmen, as opposed to the clerics and educationalists, who formed a consistent presence on the school boards (see Hollis, 1987).

Despite the anomalies which marked women's experience of local government, in 1875 Martha Merrington became the first woman to be elected to a

Poor Law Guardianship in Kensington. However, she was disqualified four years later when a ratepayer took legal action against her candidacy on the grounds that she was moving house when the election took place. Nonetheless, a slow trickle of women were elected, including the Somerset-born widow and author, Amelia Charles (1830–1900). Joining the Paddington Board of Guardians in 1881, Mrs Charles was one of several candidates of the Society for Promoting the Return of Women as Poor Law Guardians formed earlier that year. A generous subscriber to local charities, she took a special interest in the conditions of children in the workhouses and favoured a policy of boarding them out in country homes, rather than bringing them up in large institutions. She went on to consecrate her life to her civic duties, including nearly twenty consecutive years as a poor law guardian, six years on the Metropolitan Asylums Board, and membership of Paddington Vestry. As the only woman on the vestry, she joined the struggle over female eligibility to serve as members of the new London borough councils and was said to have been 'greatly disappointed' when women were excluded from this particular sphere of local government. Sadly, her story does not have a happy ending. Rejected on the grounds of her sex, she died on the very day the old vestry was superseded after the London Government Act of 1899. At this time she was widely thought to have been the longest serving female poor law guardian in England and according to her obituary in the *Paddington Times*: 'accomplished much useful work, supporting every progressive measure for the good of the poor' (9 November 1900).

With the exception of a few outstanding individuals, however, it was not until the 1890s that both women and working men stood in larger numbers. Thus whereas in 1890 Twining quotes figures of 100 females out of the 20,687 elected guardians in England and Wales, by 1895 there were between 800 and 900 women guardians (latter figures quoted in Rubinstein, 1986: 167). Karen Hunt (1996: 213) calculates that in the '1890s women as a whole constituted about 0.004 per cent of the national School Board membership and [...] about 0.03 per cent of the Boards of Guardians'. To use the typology proposed by Lovenduski (1996) and her colleagues, women's political under-representation meant a positional bias in respect of men in these organizations (see Chapter 1). Undeterred, in London and probably in other towns with a local suffrage society, some wealthy women combined the two fields of service by taking part in educational as well as poor law work.

Many of London's early women guardians were also managers of board schools, including Martha Merrington, who served as a manager at several schools in Notting Hill during the 1870s and the redoubtable Amelia Charles, who gained experience of social conditions as a manager of two board schools in Wapping. In addition, other women guardians joined the struggle over school attendance by accepting a nomination to serve as school board representatives on the various local committees responsible for enforcing compulsion. Elizabeth Lidgett, a Vigilance worker, joined Sarah Ward Andrews (another school manager) on the St Pancras Board of Guardians in 1883 and was appointed to Marylebone divisional committee the following year. Similarly,

Mary Anne Donkin joined Martha Merrington on Chelsea divisional committee in 1872 and later inherited her seat on the Kensington Board of Guardians.
As a consequence, these and other examples provide further evidence of extensive networks bridging the numerous worlds of women's activism. When Mrs
Henniker (a clergyman's widow who had 25 years' experience of ministering to
the poor), was elected head of the poll in Fulham in 1886, her supporters
included Augusta Webster who had herself been returned to the School Board
as representative for Chelsea the previous year. That same year Ellen McKee
joined the Marylebone Guardians and eleven years later she took over
Rosamond Davenport Hill's City seat on the School Board. Another future
School Board woman was less fortunate. In St Pancras Margaret Anne Eve was
defeated for the second time, although she went on to represent Finsbury on the
School Board in 1891. Finally, Henrietta Muller's sister Eva was a Lambeth
Guardian for a brief spell but did not seek re-election in 1883 due to her
impending marriage and move to Bradford, where she joined another woman
on the Bradford Board.

In both offices there was a gender dynamic to the work which meant that
middle-class women were frequently put into positions of power over working-
and lower-middle-class women. Almost all women came with an ethic of service
which rested upon wider social attitudes embedded in the culture of altruism
and the idea of character, although others posited more explicit notions of gender solidarity. Speaking of the franchise, for instance, Honnor Morten explained
that:

> There is no salvation through bettering one class or another, there is no redemp-
> tion that does not include the rich woman, as well as the poor [. . .] let the 'occu-
> pied' and the 'unoccupied' women then stretch forth their hands to one another;
> and then, standing firmly in a phalanx, find that they are a power in the land, and
> that the old days of their subjection are gone by for ever.
>
> (Morten, 1899a: 69–70)

Significantly, this statement suggests that gender identity was a key unity and a
force to be mobilized. In practice, the extent to which this followed the principle
of empowering women of different social groups was complex and riddled with
contradictions (Yeo, 1995). Partly, perhaps, because of the gendered notions of
citizenship explored by Carol Pateman (1989), middle-class activists pointed up
the association between women and welfare in their private role, in order to
widen the opportunities for women to enter public life. As Pateman makes clear,
men and women are incorporated into civil society differently. Quite apart from
the emphasis on property rights and paid employment as the key to citizenship,
the domestic ideal of separate spheres, which positioned women primarily as
men's dependants, served to perpetuate a range of exclusions among the
unpropertied and differently sexed. Not surprisingly, feminists pressed their
claims to political participation by mobilizing the argument that women in politics had an essential role to play in representing other women and articulating
women's concerns. But of course the way gender featured in the construction of
a positive class identity reinforced the claim that women speak with a different

voice. As a result, for some of these women, the combined effect of an emphasis on family principles and home influences produced a critical examination of
public policy in the administration of the poor laws and an expanding educational bureaucracy.

In one respect the concentration on the progress of women overlooks the per-
sistence of anomalies which marked women's public participation in late
Victorian and Edwardian England. Previously a woman might serve as sexton,
church warden or overseer of the poor, but all these offices were generally held
in low esteem. Sheila Herstein (1985: 25) has documented the example of a
woman who was granted the right to serve as sexton in which the view was
clearly stated: 'This is a servile ministerial office which requires neither skill nor
understanding [. . .] but this cannot determine that women may vote for members of Parliament as that choice requires an improved understanding.' And
there stands the suffragists' dilemma. Feminists wanted the full rights of political citizenship and couched their arguments in the language with which they
were most familiar. Reforms in women's status were seen as a reward for merit
and it was essential that women demonstrate their right to a public role. Hence
the emphasis on liberal notions of equality alongside the morally redeeming
qualities of work. In general, activists used the idea of a separate female character to argue forcefully that women could help to reform the social institutions
and practices inherited from an older social system. At the same time they
frequently found themselves constrained by prevailing ideas about masculinity
and femininity, and gender biases within political institutions and processes,
including the decision-making hierarchy.

To take the example of state elementary schools, it was widely assumed that
school board work was particularly suited to women's domestic skills and interests. In practice, this meant able and intelligent middle-class women came in
with an ethic of educational service shared by the great majority of their male
colleagues of a similar social standing. However, while the local educational
authorities were superior in social status to the poor law boards, education did
not loom large in parliamentary politics in this period. As Kevin Brehony (1987)
points out, poor attendance at the debates on the codes which regulated the elementary school system suggests the content and administration of schooling
excited little parliamentary interest. Moreover the fact that only one Education
Minister, Arthur Acland, was ever made a member of the Cabinet serves to reinforce the view that, 'in Parliamentary terms, schooling was low on the list of
political priorities' (Brehony, 1987: 90). However, women who held office
acknowledged that they were working within a system controlled by the male
experts and administrators running the Education Department, as well as those
serving in parliamentary politics and appointed to Her Majesty's Inspectorate.
Addressing the Coventry branch of the Women's Liberal Association on the subject of women's suffrage in June 1890, Florence Balgarnie of Scarborough
School Board explained that:

> women might flatter themselves they could act as members of School Boards and
> thus have quite enough interest in the Educational system, but the Boards and the

Code were regulated by the House of Commons. Had women had something to do with the making of the Code there would be none of the absurd waste of time in the Elementary Schools on crotchet [*sic*], hem-stitch, and tack, which sent a child out of school without being able to patch a gown or darn a stocking properly.

(*Women's Penny Paper*, 14 June 1890: 405)

Although they had no intention to destroy the existing political system, 'platform women' were consistently presented as unnatural eccentricities on account of their strong opinions and interest in intellectual pursuits. These were unconventional qualities and habits and it was widely assumed that many people felt far from comfortable in their company, while others attacked the high profile of those who took up various kinds of public social service far more directly. According to Margaret Lonsdale, 'that dreadful woman' was the kindest epithet applied to them and 'the meaning of it all is that the women who take up a personally prominent position in the world are distasteful to the good sense and refined feeling of the majority, and therefore that female influence in the world is degenerating' (*Nineteenth Century*, March 1884: 415). Given the conventions of the time, it is hardly surprising that suffragists represented local government in general as an extension of women's 'natural' duties:

We may be asked to assume why the responsibility of trying to maintain a healthier municipal life is particularly a woman's duty? [...] First, because the material, domestic concerns of life, so largely controlled by municipal management, are particularly the woman's province as a housekeeper. [...] Secondly, because the temperance and uprightness of the young, the moral elevation and education of the community, the amenities and harmonies of life, are her peculiar responsibility, and if she neglects them, and shuts herself up in selfish indifference or thoughtless ignorance, our national character must steadily deteriorate [...] women are less under political influences than men [...] less affected by class interests.

(*Englishwoman's Review*, 15 October 1886: 339–40)

Escalating the feminist campaign for inclusion within the developing institution of citizenship, the cause of child welfare was seen as consonant with woman's proper sphere in private and domestic life. Drawing on the participatory vocabulary of social responsibility, successive generations of female reformers envisioned a polity in which men and women would work together as moral beings and active citizens. Just as the process of class formation rested upon gender segregation, so did the social relations of citizenship. But while the ideal of participatory democracy may have been universal, for women the promise was only partially realized. Inclusion required that they be fully conscious of the privileges and duties of their citizenship, but as gender and class distinctions were mutually reinforcing, their tasks both as mothers and in the wider community were portrayed as an essential part of civic duty (Riley, 1988). In this way sitting on a school board provided some women with a bridge between the state and the developing realm of civil society. At the same time, like the poor law boards and parish councils, school boards were clearly an appropriate area in which women might serve their political apprenticeship and thereby focus attention on feminist demands for political incorporation in the new capitalist social order.

As women gained new confidence, increasing numbers took up the challenge despite the public political context in which they were required to act. Inevitably their motives and interests were mixed. The great majority utilized class interests. They also stressed that women were different from men. Frequently depicted as a 'treatment' or 'cure' for pathologizing social practices, mass compulsory schooling was part and parcel of a class cultural attack on the urban poor. The 'special' qualities of the more compassionate, self-sacrificing sex were clearly suited to the rescue of the socially unfit. Such notions were further reinforced by the public belief in women's ability to neutralize class consciousness. Free from the cut and thrust of commercial life, the religious and domestic skills of women were just what was needed for strengthening the 'character' of these new social subjects in the closing decades of the nineteenth century.

There can be little doubt that school board women wanted a political voice. They took it as their task to breach exclusively masculine bastions of political power and to set forth an ideal for imitation in public life. In so doing they set out to challenge existing institutions of power. They emerged as key players in the recomposition of British politics at a time when the boundaries between the state and civil society began to be redefined.

Notes

1. Although Elizabeth Garrett Anderson was a notable exception.

2. Although it should be noted that *Punch* never referred to it by any other name than 'The Universal Palaver Society'.

3. For instance, Bessie Parkes's father held a legal position in the Court of Chancery and the family home was in Saville Row (see Rendall, 1989: 36–70).

The Sages of the Embankment

Introduction

Fully acknowledging its exceptional nature, the British press greeted the formation of the world's largest educational parliament with a combination of awe and respect. At a time when Paris was enduring a grim siege during the Franco-Prussian War of 1870, *The Times* declared the great event of 29 November was the election of the first School Board for London: 'No equally powerful body will exist in England outside Parliament, if power be measured by influence for good and evil over masses of human beings.' To be elected as one of its members, therefore, not only carried with it an element of civic responsibility but served to convey a sense of status and prestige among one's peers. Nonetheless, the decision to step forward and campaign for office was especially significant for female candidates because school boards were the first elected public bodies in Great Britain to admit women on the same terms as men.

This chapter sets the context for the analysis which follows by providing a brief history of the School Board for London. It is divided into three parts. The first looks at the changing framework of local administration in this period, focusing on London politics and the particular problems which beset the centre and symbol of imperial and national power at this time. The second part considers the issue of female involvement in the politics of education – as voters, as political candidates and as elected members of the School Board for London. Finally, the chapter explores the gradual development of the London school system and the impact of women activists on the state system of elementary schooling.

Politics and the government of London

For a large part of the Victorian period civic policies and administration were complicated by a tangle of authorities and agencies, each with different boundaries, qualifications for office, voting procedures and rating powers. In London, for instance, the inner square mile of the City was governed by the Lord Mayor and closed corporations, while a considerable part of the metropolis was administered for certain limited purposes by the Metropolitan Board of Works (consisting of delegates elected by the 39 vestry and district boards). This constitution was changed by the setting up of the London County Council (LCC) in 1888, although the Metropolitan Asylums Board (established in

1867), poor law administrative districts (unions) and local vestries (districts for the supervision of health, or sanitation) survived intact.

It is generally agreed that London's problems were unique. As the urban historian David Reeder has put it: 'Victorian London was not merely passing through a series of transitional phases in architectural style, in economic organization, in demographic adjustment, and in governmental structure; it was also developing a new awareness of itself' (1982: 351). In demographic terms, the rate of growth was remorseless. Throughout the last quarter of the nineteenth century, London's numbers rapidly increased from three million people in the early 1860s to four and a half million in 1901 (Briggs, 1977: 312). By 1911, the area governed by the LCC had a population of seven million, nearly a quarter of the whole population of Britain. But most importantly for London's educational politics, the world's largest city was also a city of children. In 1871, for instance, 43 per cent of London's population were aged fifteen and under, and the East End of London contained the greatest number of them. Here again, special topographical and social factors fuelled the search for new categories and images adequate to the task of understanding London's pathological condition. On the one hand, people from the West End of London saw confident wealth. On the other, new techniques for social investigation, mapping and administering the city and its population fostered a much greater awareness of the growing gap between the rich and the poor.

During the 1880s and 1890s, the publication of pamphlets and books like the Congregationalist minister Andrew Mearns' *The Bitter Cry of Outcast London* (1883) gave inspiration to Liberal and Socialist politicians. Certainly the statistics of poverty, mortality and deprivation compiled by Charles Booth and his team of social investigators in the late 1880s and 1890s, were unchallengeable. Thus Annie Besant pressed the School Board to take a lead on the free schools issue and the fact that about three-quarters of London's population was categorized as 'poor' made it impossible to deny the logic of her argument that fees stood in the way of attendance.

In such circumstances political attention was increasingly focused on social questions and in certain quarters the unemployed themselves were seen as a potentially significant political force. This was especially pertinent in London – as Asa Briggs has suggested – since two facts made London's role in national history more dramatic at this time:

> First, the changes that were taking place in it were more pertinent than in any other part of the country. Second, it was acting in politics not merely as a national capital but as a centre of home-produced specifically London discontents.
>
> (1977: 327)

Asa Briggs links the prominence of London politics in the mid-1880s to the high incidence of cyclical unemployment in many of the London trades. Historically, this made the city's workforce especially vulnerable during periods of prolonged depression. Harris (1972) asserts that the plight of the urban unemployed worsened because the Inspectorate of the Local Government Board sought to impose greater uniformity and stringency on the administration of poor relief. In particular, London poor law administrators moved away from policies that permitted families to continue to live together as independent units, to practices that treated each member individually. Hence as Sue Hollen Lees (1990: 74) points out: 'although the mandate of the poor laws was to relieve the destitute, officials treated people differently according to their gender, age, and family status'. Class relations in the city became more volatile as the unemployed and the most important of the London socialist organizations, the Social Democratic Federation, began to agitate for public works and protective tariffs as a solution to unemployment. The winters of 1885–86 and 1886–87 were particularly severe and social tensions were heightened when the socialists began to hold street marches and meetings in Trafalgar Square. Although the Conservative government clamped down on signs of unrest, middle-class fears culminated in the events of 'Bloody Sunday' (13 November 1887), when two squadrons of the Life Guards were summoned up from Whitehall to charge one such demonstration in Trafalgar Square. In the words of J.W. Mackail, the biographer of the socialist leader William Morris:

> No one who ever saw it will ever forget the strange and indeed terrible sight of that grey winter day, the vast sombre-coloured crowd, the brief but fiery struggle at the corner of the Strand, and the river of steel and scarlet that moved slowly through the dusky swaying masses.
>
> (cited in Briggs, 1977: 329)

Overall, the continuing existence of a large casual labour class vulnerable to poverty and pauperism was a problem that seemed to pose itself with increasing urgency. But it is also important to remember that the vast majority of metropolitan workers were far less well organized than their counterparts in the great industrial cities of the provinces. As a consequence, the new unionism of the period inevitably centred on London. Initiated by the women employed at the Bryant and May match factory in 1888 (organized by Annie Besant and Herbert Burrows), the trend to organize the unskilled workers continued when Will Thorne started the Gasworkers' and General Labourers' Union at Beckton Gasworks in the early summer of 1889, culminating in the great London dock strike for a minimum rate of sixpence an hour.

Despite the surrounding confusion, this period of discontent and agitation saw a simultaneous growth in state expenditure on public policy and social welfare. Indeed many social and political movements had now taken on some commitment to the idea of a broad doctrine of social responsibility. Thus in the 1890s and 1900s arguments about the scope of state intervention (on matters of health and housing, education and training, employment and culture) were mirrored in intellectual developments among groups like the Fabian Society and the New Liberal political philosophers, who saw a need for increased government activity. In particular, they presented a philosophy that included a strong element of local government provision for schools, housing, libraries and museums, as well as certain essential services like gas and water.

All these initiatives had implications both for the work of the School Board and the debate about cities in Victorian England. Concern with the social distress of the unemployed, for example, not only raised problems of definition and classification with regard to the problem of unemployment itself, but with regard to its perceived victims within the working classes. These problems of classification and surveillance not only had implications for the educational legislation of the 1870s but, as the following chapters will show, were also important in shaping the response of consecutive members of the School Board for London to issues of social welfare. Pressure on the conventional liberal philosophy of self-help and the market economy saw permissive powers left to the discretion of local ratepayers and executed by local authorities working in tandem with the central state. Paradoxically, the extension of local government provision was grudgingly accepted by the end of the nineteenth century, not because individualist conviction had changed, but because it was assumed that the growth of civic power could provide a permanent check on the unwelcome growth of the official central state. In direct contravention of these expectations, however,   the process effected significant extensions in the welfare activities of local municipalities, thereby expanding the capacity of states to deal with social problems.

Against this background it was appropriate that factors of size and formation placed the London Board in a unique position within the embryonic state education system. This was because the School Board for London differed from its counterparts in the rest of England and Wales in two important respects. First, unlike the others, it was created under the terms of the Education Act of 1870. Second, while other boards were restricted to between five and fifteen members, the first London Board had 49 members rising to 55 by the mid-1880s. Moreover, unlike other cities, London was divided into ten vast wards (except the inner square mile of the City itself), who each returned a number of candidates. For instance, the electors of Greenwich returned four representatives and the division included the parliamentary seats of Deptford, Greenwich, Lewisham and Woolwich. Finally, because London politics had a strategic importance in the national debate on public policy and social welfare provision, this important British institution played a vital role both as a representative of, and in setting the educational standards for, other school boards to follow.

The issue of female representation

What is apparent is that Forster's Education Act created the most responsible elective position so far available to women. Writing about the 1876 election campaign, the *Graphic* (9 December 1876), for example, asserted: 'A member of the London School Board is not a very much less important personage than a Member of the House of Commons; for if his range of responsibility is narrower, his individual responsibility is, in his own sphere, far greater.' Consequently there is a need to explain why this concession was made and why it took the form that it did.

The first part of the explanation relates to the fact that educational policy-making clearly subscribed to conventional ideas about women's domestic skills and interests. The second part of the explanation followed closely: that politicians took a calculated risk on the grounds that the inclusion of certain carefully chosen individuals would tend to strengthen rather than destabilize local democracy. Essentially what makes these two explanations ultimately credible is the fact that the school board franchise incorporated a clearly defined group of elite and middle-class women into a well-established political framework connecting property with political representation. Qualification for voting at a school board election was based on the criterion of independence, so that all male, as well as single and widowed female ratepayers could qualify. However, the novel electoral system for the school boards (which allowed voters in a multi-member division to plump for just one candidate), can be understood only in the light of the religious squabbles and the philosophy of John Stuart Mill – in particular, his more recent preoccupation with the advance of democracy (see Collini, 1993: 160).

As Liberal MP for Westminster, 1865–68, and parliamentary spokesman for the Municipal Reform Association (founded by James Beal in 1866), Mill took a prominent part in the work of the Select Committee on Metropolitan Local Government where he pressed the case for the reform of London politics. Highly critical of the Corporation of the City of London which he described as a 'union of modern jobbery and antiquated foppery' (cited in Briggs, 1977: 331), Mill was especially concerned to establish a satisfactory mechanism for inducing persons of 'superior attainments' to offer themselves for elected office. The idea that all citizens should have equal weight in the political system remained outside Mill's actual doctrine. Then, as now, proportional representation favoured minorities and the likelihood was that a cumulative vote would secure the election of a larger number of Mill's favoured representatives. In terms of the debate about the local government of London, Asa Briggs (1977) argues that the only result of Mill's efforts was the usual parliamentary impasse, although he may deserve credit for the breath of democracy introduced by the School Board. In any event, a system of voting designed to assuage the fears of religious minorities that the new local educational authorities would be dominated by the Anglican clergy, seems to have favoured the representation of social minorities, especially of working people and of women.

Although the absence of any property qualification represented an ideal of inclusion for those wishing to sit on the School Board, financing an electoral campaign was an immediate problem for candidates with limited means. In addition, the fact that the work was voluntary and proved to be immensely time-consuming inevitably provided a further barrier for those on a low income. Many of the School Board women were wealthy enough to be, in effect, full-time but unpaid officials, but several relied upon daily or weekly journalism to supplement their income. For example, Florence Fenwick Miller gained advantage from her feminist connections, but the man she married (Frederick Alfred Ford) was never to prove very successful in business and this may have been a factor in her own decision to withdraw from the 1885 election campaign. Now the mother of two young daughters aged five and four, Florence had little choice but to rely on daily or weekly journalism to sustain her social position and was writing steadily for a variety of publications including the *Modern Review,*

Lady's Pictorial, Fraser's and *The Governess*. Yet she was also the author of several teaching texts and was about to become a weekly columnist for the *Illustrated London News*, a post which she held for the next 33 years (Van Arsdel, 1986: 39). Journalism also made a crucial contribution to the incomes of a number of other women who served on the Board including Annie Besant, Jane Chessar, Emily Davies, Honnor Morten, Edith Simcox, and Augusta Webster (a regular contributor to *The Examiner* and *The Athenaeum*, and the author of the somewhat modestly entitled: *A Housewife's Opinions*). Moreover, Edith Simcox actually mentions the question of funds in a diary entry written less than two months after her election:

> I don't care about the articles as an author – it wouldn't break my heart to give up for good ambition that way, but I wanted to earn money for the Notice B cases and other necessary expenses that exist from being on the Board – and – hang it! Just for once I will let myself pay.
> *(Autobiography of a Shirtmaker*, 9 February 1880)

Public careers clearly required financial security, as well as stamina and dedication. But involvement in the politics of education also facilitated a sense of self-fulfilment for middle-class women carrying out useful, unpaid womanly work, with women and girls as their primary clientele. Yet these now obscured individuals were powerful figures in their local communities and in the metropolis. School Board politics combined just the right degree of adversity and of hope to encourage supporters of the women's suffrage movement to make it a part of their work.

However, in attempting to explain why the historiography of British education has largely ignored their role, it is important to acknowledge the invisibility of women within a male-defined history accentuated by the publication of Sheila Rowbotham's influential text, *Hidden from History,* in 1973. As June Purvis (1991) points out, most educational histories of the nineteenth century focus upon the activities of 'great men' like James Kay (a secretary to the Committee of Council on Education) and Robert Lowe (a Vice-President of the Education Department), with the result that important figures like the female members of the London School Board have not been released from historical obscurity. This emphasis upon the role of great men as makers of education policy is, in part, a reflection of the tendency to minimize the importance of local government, both to the official central state and in the provision of essential services in late Victorian and Edwardian England. In any case the focus of research has been upon the origins of central government rather than the development of social policy at a local level. Such a bias is further compounded by the assumption that the administration and provision of education were not associated with high political office. For example, Anne Digby and Peter Searby (1981: 6) make the point that, with some notable exceptions, the Education Department (one of the largest within the central state bureaucracy), is conspicuous in its absence from the exhaustive debate among British historians on the causes and nature of the so-called 'Victorian Revolution in Government'. Similarly, it is possible to argue that the popular politics of schooling documented by socialist and Marxist historians remains on the margins within social and political histories of the nineteenth century generally.

On the other hand, recent work by Patricia Hollis (1989), Seth Koven (1993) and Pat Thane (1993) has had the effect of placing the role of local government in a much more positive light. Pointing to a weakness in the existing historiography, Koven observes a tendency to overlook the specific contribution of women in the development of public policy and social welfare provision in Victorian and Edwardian Britain. Quite apart from the usual debates about female invisibility, Koven notes that this exclusion 'stems partly from the fact that these histories have been written from the records of the official central state run by male bureaucrats and politicians' (1993: 94-5). Consequently, these studies continue the conventional pattern of being much less attentive to the often lengthy careers in public service pursued by women (and men) in their localities.

The London school system

As might be expected, the task facing the 326 Londoners attracted to service on the School Board was enormous. In 1861 the Newcastle Commission on 'popular education' had revealed that schools in London varied greatly and that local provision was in pitifully short supply. Ten years later the survey undertaken by the Education Department showed a shortfall of between 250,000 and 300,000 school places (Rubinstein, 1977: 232). Undeterred by the scale of the problem, 135 candidates contested the first election for the new local education authority. Historically, the 1870 campaign was unique in having a secret ballot – a precursor of the 1872 Ballot Act that made the secret ballot compulsory in all parliamentary and borough council elections, though it was not applicable to other local government elections.

Predictably, battle raged around the narrow question of religious instruction and those elected included men who had been prominent in local affairs, Anglican ministers, nonconformists, philanthropists, educationists and, of course, two ladies. They were both prominent women, Emily Davies for her work on behalf of women's advanced education and Elizabeth Garrett MD as Britain's first home-trained woman doctor. Both swept to the head of the poll in their divisions (Greenwich and Marylebone), and a resounding margin of 34,354 votes separated Garrett from the next candidate, the eminent scientist and educator, Thomas Huxley. No impartial witness, observed the *Daily Telegraph*, could doubt that this success held implications for the claims of women to a wider public and political life:

> If that will satisfy the ambition of the army of Amazons now menacing us [...] we might grin and bear it. But if Miss Garrett and Miss Davies make excellent members of the Educational Parliament, we shall be rather at a loss for good arguments to level at them when they try to enter the House of Commons. [...] Of course, they may break down. Miss Garrett if a motion of hers is rejected, may burst into tears, though those who know the lady deny the probability. Miss Emily Davies if called to order, may faint in the arms of Mr Hepworth Dixon, though why she

should do so nobody could possibly say. But if these things do not occur – if the ladies are calm, businesslike and useful, and keep to the point in public debate – what is to become of us men? What chance would a masculine candidate for Marylebone in Parliament have against Miss Garrett and her friends [. . .] and if Miss Garrett once enters the House of Commons, taking the oaths and her seat with a little rustle of dress, the supremacy of men is at an end. [. . .] We do not desire that result. We prefer the present division of labour. We prefer that, while men take the outdoor and public tasks, women should take the indoor and family tasks, not less noble if well done, not less useful if thoroughly performed.

(2 December, 1870)

London went to the polls on 29 November and the new Board held its first meeting on 15 December at the Guildhall. Yet despite the encouraging results, when the Board assembled the two women friends were asked to sit apart from the male members. This they refused to do and quite deliberately sat around the table with the main body. It was to prevent mixed-sex proceedings that some had opposed the election of women to the Board and Elizabeth and Emily were keenly aware of the significance of what they were asked. As Elizabeth noted in a letter to the businessman James Skelton Anderson (chairman of her election committee and her future husband) written later that day: 'I felt the atmosphere to be decidedly hostile, but of course that is not surprising and it is not a bad discipline to find it so after the intoxication of one's 47,000.' Although there was some suggestion that Elizabeth should take the chair (as the member with the largest majority), the socially conservative Emily was not amused:

> It is not being a woman (though that probably enhances it) but your youth and inexperience that makes it strike me as almost indecorous to think of presiding over men like Lord Lawrence etc. [. . .] I should be sorry for you to do anything which might give colour to the charge of being 'cheeky', which has been brought against you lately. It is true that your jokes are many and reckless. They do more harm than you know.
>
> (quoted in Manton, 1965: 209)

Ironically, Elizabeth was 34 and had been practising medicine for five years, but Emily need not have worried. In the event, Elizabeth asserted that she did not mind 'a little North East wind' from her friend and colleague, while Lord Lawrence was nominated by pre-arrangement. When it came to voting on the question of whether to pay the Chairman a salary (as the Board was empowered to do), the motion was defeated despite the fact that the permanent chairman of the Metropolitan Board of Works received a salary of £1,500 (Owen, 1982: 41). Members subsequently elected Lord Lawrence as Chairman and the thin-skinned Charles Reed (later MP and Sir) as Vice-Chairman, although he succeeded as Chairman in 1873. In retrospect Elizabeth wrote:

> I was sorry afterwards that I said so little, but I was really a little awed by the whole thing being so extremely like parliament, and by having to spring up so quickly to get a hearing after someone else had finished. The whole difficulty of speaking is so concentrated in that moment of swift self-assertion.
>
> (Elizabeth Garrett to James Skelton Anderson, 16 December 1870)

From the start, three parties were involved in the management of London's board schools – the Board itself (working through a School Management Committee), individual members and local school managers. Hence the School Management Committee was responsible for the management and discipline of board schools, the instruction given, estimating the costs and nominating, appointing, removing and setting the salaries of teachers. Such determinants notwithstanding, the financial power of the Education Department was also crucial to the Board's work. This was certainly true of the school curriculum since, as Dina Copelman (1996: 85) points out, the main effect of the hated system of payment by results 'was to inhibit curricular development and pedagogical innovation'. The power of the purse becomes clear when one considers Stuart Maclure's (1990: 45–6) estimate that the educational codes initially covered about 40 per cent of the cost of educating a child at a London board school, not to mention the local vestries and ratepayers' associations who were concerned about the drain on their own pockets. Moreover, although the Board was empowered by the Elementary Education Acts of 1870 and 1872 to borrow money from the Metropolitan Board of Works for the erection of school buildings, much of Board education began in flimsy iron structures that were in use for much longer than intended. This system of administration and finance, then, had a massive impact on the forms and content of schooling, on the resources available to schools and on real educational opportunities.

Ordinarily, the Board held open meetings every Wednesday, beginning at 3 p.m. and usually continuing until 6:30 p.m., although it was often much later. According to Thomas Gautrey (first secretary of the London Teachers' Association who represented the teachers on the School Board in the 1890s), these were often lively and sometimes hilarious occasions, especially the period following the election of the eighth Board in 1891. In particular, he recalled the occasion when John Lobb (FRGS and for fifteen years one of the members for Hackney) quietly deposited a human skeleton on the central table below the chairman (the Reverend Joseph Diggle). At the same time, a shocked Reverend John James Coxhead (vicar of St John's, Fitzroy Square, who represented Marylebone for eighteen years), rose to ask whether a member could display what he somewhat euphemistically referred to as 'emblems of mortality' when:

> Mr Lobb proceeded to start a sort of inquest on the 'bones'. Not only was he opposed to their use in schools, but to their being imported from the battlefield of Metz. If they must have them, let them be 'homespun' specimens. The Board, he said, had made itself ridiculous, which brought forth convulsive laughter given ironically. Then he dramatically said a woman cleaner had come upon one of these in a cupboard and had nearly fainted, and screamed loudly. Impatience followed hilarity, and finally Mr Lobb was 'closured'.
>
> (Gautrey, n.d.: 41)

Whatever their overall tone, the weekly meetings provided a forum for debate and decision-making on motions of policy. Essentially their main purpose was to hear the recommendations set out in reports from the various committees that conducted the work of the Board; these were then accepted, amended or referred back. Individual members then had a right to propose alternative motions of policy and debate them, before a vote was taken. Florence Fenwick Miller sets the scene:

> the Board-room was a spacious, lofty chamber with a gallery for the public at one end, facing a long table for the Chairman and other officers on a dais at the other end with a cross table below the dais for the press. The brown-leather-covered seats for members between the Chairman's table and the public gallery were arranged horse-shoe fashion around the carpeted floor [...] the chairmen of the several committees of the Board had a prescriptive right to the seats at the points of the horse-shoe and therefore next up to the chairman's dais and the press tables. In this and in all other matters the precedent of the customs of the House of Commons was followed.
>
> (unpublished autobiography cited in Van Arsdel, 1979: 14-15)

Above all, it is the accent on parliamentary tradition that is significant here. What is apparent is that the structural inventories underpinning the relations of power in this particular institution were both controlled by men and shaped in their interests. Women had to struggle to enter such places and their historical exclusion from elective office left them with little choice but to build upon, or try to undermine, this inherited foundation. Again, this was a difficult task given the evidence of both positional bias and male organizational gender bias.

Unaccustomed to the system of meanings embodied in the organizational setting in which they were now required to act, the social patterning of gender undoubtedly meant women members felt uncomfortable and out of place at times. Although many had responded to appeals from the suffrage movement to step forward and campaign for office, they had mixed feelings about their novel political and administrative experience. Indeed Henrietta Muller's comment on completing her service encapsulates this dilemma: 'At first the feeling of relief and freedom was very great but now I can only think of the little girls and the women teachers who are without a friend at the Board' (Henrietta Muller to Karl Pearson, December 1885).

In the light of the scale of the remedial problem facing the new educational authority, it is hardly surprising to find that the committee structure of the first seven Boards was largely predetermined by six key issues which laid the foundations of subsequent policy. Throughout the 1870s and 1880s, there were six permanent standing committees: Finance; Statistical, Law and Parliamentary (whose main function was to ascertain the shortfall in terms of school provision); Works and General Purposes, with a sub-committee on sites; School Management; Industrial Schools and Bye-Laws, for enforcing compulsion. In addition to the standing committees, there was also a growing plethora of sub-committees and special committees appointed for specific purposes. Essentially the latter were established in a rather haphazard way, tackling abuses when they arose and working pragmatically on glaring or well publicized controversies. This pattern was clearly evident, for example, in the formation of a special committee to consider the issue of 'over pressure' in schools that was causing an outcry in the mid-1880s. Unlike the public forum of the weekly Board meetings, however, the proceedings of the standing and special committees remained closed. As one might expect, Helen Taylor's demands for greater public account-ability in the wake of a series of allegations of child abuse at two of the capital's industrial schools in the 1880s went unheard. Nevertheless, all Board members were free to attend any meeting (should they choose to do so), but only those nominated to serve on the respective committees were authorized to take part in the proceedings.

Immediately after the 1885 election, the victorious candidates took the deci-sion that standing committees should be composed of members representing each of the divisions. Significantly, the level of female representation had just been halved, partly because Florence Fenwick Miller and Helen Taylor stood down, while Frances Hastings, Amie Hicks and Henrietta Muller were all defeat-ed at the polls.[1] Only Rosamond Davenport Hill and Alice Westlake retained their seats in the City and Marylebone, while Augusta Webster managed to win back Chelsea, having served as the divisional member for a single term in 1879. Previously there had been six women members (Hastings, Hill, Miller, Muller, Taylor and Westlake) and in 1879 nine women were elected (Hill, Miller, Muller, Richardson, Simcox, Surr, Taylor, Webster and Westlake), at which time every division except Greenwich had a woman among its members. As intimated earlier, as women became more powerful this provoked a reaction from their male colleagues. In 1880, for example, the Liberal leader, Lyulph Stanley, opposed the inclusion of another woman on the powerful School Management Committee, which he thought:

> was somewhat overweighted by the Trades Union spirit of the lady members [...] They were too ready to support large salaries for female teachers. The ladies did very intelligent and useful work in the committees and their influence was most desirable, but it could not be denied that they were a phalanx who were bound together for certain objects.
>
> (quoted in Hollis, 1989: 95)

Just four years later, the new ruling on the composition of committees made it even harder for a nascent women's party to make an impact in the Board. This was crucial because Marylebone and Southwark had previously returned two female candidates. In addition, for those who were more rebellious, the decision probably served to exacerbate any feelings of isolation and marginalization they might be experiencing. As Edith Simcox conceded in her diary, 'Lyulph Stanley is as insolent as usual and one can hardly be very useful on a committee when one's very existence is openly resented' (*Autobiography of a Shirtmaker*, 9 February 1880: 67).

When considered against the background of these reservations it is hardly surprising that only one woman, Helen Taylor, attained high office. However, Taylor's career on the Board constitutes an exception of some significance. Educated, socially aware and a convinced feminist, she had a reputation for being overbearing and forceful in her dealings with men. Indeed a piece of hate mail discovered among her personal papers vividly illustrates the misgivings generated by her unconventional behaviour. Ultimately it was felt to be contam-inating – it unsexed her:

H.T.
Disgusting Creature
Man in Petticoats –
Satans Masterpiece –
Her end
Destruction.

Yet in June 1883 members of the fifth Board set a precedent by promoting Helen to the position of Chair of the Educational Endowments Committee. Because it was then a permanent committee, this represented one of the highest positions on the Board. The three most senior positions in the Board's hierarchy were, of course, Chairman and Vice-Chairman of the Board and Chairman of the powerful School Management Committee. Perhaps her predominantly male colleagues took a finely calculated risk, acting in the belief that promotion might prove the best means of containing this individualistic and energetic character. In any event, the experience of her feminist colleague Henrietta Muller a few months later contained a salutary lesson for other women. Keeping her friend, Elizabeth Surr (now living in San Diego), abreast of the School Board gossip, Helen Taylor graphically described how, when the time came to elect a chair for a Special Committee for Swedish Exercises, Henrietta was passed over, despite the fact that it was she who successfully proposed the formation of the special committee. Contrary to all precedent, Lyulph Stanley and Alice Westlake immediately nominated the Reverend Charles Edward Brooke (who, like Henrietta, represented Lambeth) and he was elected, 'a direct insult to Miss Muller; and I was told she felt it bitterly'. Finally, Helen went on to say that had Henrietta included herself on her special committee the outcome would have been different for:

> I should (and I am the only person on the Board who would) have appealed to the gentlemanly feeling of Brooke not to insult Miss Muller by accepting; and I think I should have succeeded. Brooke is not a gentleman but is very anxious to be, I think he means to be honest, but is wholly framed by vanity. Stanley, Westlake and Co. govern him by it, and of course played into it by putting him up for Chairman. If they could have been defeated it could only have been by appealing to a higher and more legitimate vanity as I should have done.
> (Helen Taylor to Elizabeth Surr, 1 October 1883)

There was strong support for improving the state of physical education for working-class girls and this lack of female solidarity is interesting in light of the fact that Alice Westlake herself was a firm advocate of Swedish gymnastics in schools. Indeed it was she who invited Dr Mathias Roth, the most successful publicist of the system practised by Per Henrik Ling at the Royal Central Gymnastics Institute in Sweden, to present the case for teaching Ling's exercises in the elementary schools (Minutes of sub-committee, 11 December 1878). But whatever the underlying reasons for the failure to appoint Henrietta, the incident does point up the need to study diagonal gender–class relations when considering struggles over power and advantage in public life. Clearly the presence of women immediately complicated, and partly contradicted, the existing gender order, although the class cultural context of the political environment was also critical.

Nonetheless, at a time when female candidates were still a novelty, these formidable women exercised their right to play a part in public affairs and some, like Alice Westlake, appear to have been able to use their influence with their male colleagues. Yet it is also possible to argue that other women, like Henrietta Muller and Helen Taylor, failed to achieve the recognition they deserved because they challenged the male political establishment. On the one hand they were too independently feminist, on the other they espoused more radical politics. It certainly seems that Henrietta found her ambitions thwarted by a combination of male obstructionism and an interesting lack of female solidarity. The following account of her contribution to the workings of the Board, included among the pen portraits of 'sixty-five notable members' by Thomas Gautrey (first elected member in 1894), is illuminating for its mockery of her devotion to the cause of women's emancipation:

> This lady was one of the early women on the Board. [...] She claimed to be an emancipated woman and 'freed from the old dogma which condemned every woman to be a wife and mother'. 'Old maids', she said, 'used to be nerveless, inactive creatures; but now', she added, 'the celibate woman is the object of envy not only to the poor deluded married women, but to the men whose past had been ever robbed of the bloom which is life's sweetest gift'. Her sacred function as a femme libre was 'to protect the helpless and guard the young'. It cannot be said that this pioneer 'feminist' added much to efficient administration. By the end of her six years she seemed to tire, and faded out.
>
> (Gautrey, n.d.: 73)

In fact Muller, along with many others, was a victim of the Progressive backlash in the elections of November 1885, rather than any individual failing or 'tiring' on her part. She was also remarkable for her recent recruitment to the pioneering Men and Women's Club founded by Karl Pearson (the socialist and future eugenicist), to talk about sex (see Walkowitz, 1986, for a fuller discussion). Moreover, while she herself doubted her suitability and 'could not promise to behave prettily, but only to do as adversaries do in law', other female recruits like Elizabeth Cobb and Olive Schreiner were uneasy about her reputation as a 'manhater' (Karl Pearson from Henrietta Muller, June 1886; Walkowitz, 1986: 40). Yet it was Henrietta Muller who voiced the 'women's response' to Pearson's essay on the woman question that so outraged the female members at the club's first meeting on 9 July 1885. In a paper entitled 'The other side of the question', Muller delivered a stinging indictment of male hypersexuality, in which she argued that since 'moral strength' had replaced physical strength as the new criterion of social power, so the unequal power relations between the sexes would no longer be balanced in favour of men. Further insight into her feelings on the issue of working with men may be intimated from the circumstances surrounding a debate on prostitution in 1887. This precipitated a crisis in women's participation in the newly founded discussion group. Indeed, Henrietta angrily resigned, asserting:

it has become worse than useless to me, I hope to start a rival club for discussing the same class of subjects, but no men will be admitted - you will say 'this is prejudice', I will not stop to deny it. I will merely say that in my club every woman shall field a voice, and shall learn how to use it; it matters not in the first instance what her opinion may be, it does matter very much that she should learn to express it freely and fearlessly.

(Henrietta Muller to Karl Pearson, 29 March 1888)

Turning to the gender biases on the London School Board, it is notable that women members lacked policy experience, as well as the technical and social skills intimated by Muller. Furthermore, attitudes to and accommodation of women varied. As Elizabeth Garrett noted in a letter to Emily Davies on the eve of their retirement, John MacGregor was disparaging of women, but other male colleagues on the Industrial Schools Committee, like Mr Watson, Mr Scrutton and Mr Currie, were not (Elizabeth Garrett to Emily Davies, 9 November 1873).

The other dimension to women's experience lies in their relationship with the characteristic forms of popular politics, which grew from the organization of education itself, especially from the coexistence of the public and voluntary systems. Party organizations steadily increased their grip on political struggles in London and by the 1880s School Board elections were contested by two loosely organized groupings of individuals running as the Progressive and Moderate parties. Two patterns emerge. On the one hand, the Moderates were clearly aligned with the Anglican clergy and the Conservative party. On the other, the Progressives included all shades of Liberal opinion, now fortified by the new Socialist groups. Significantly, while Helen Taylor grew increasingly independent and critical of Progressive policy, her colleague Alice Westlake was comfortably ensconced within the male dominated Liberal party machine.

In general, it may be possible to argue that the great majority of these confident middle-class women declined to be intimidated, but gender stereotypes and social convention make it worth noting the comments of Honnor Morten and Elizabeth Surr. While she herself was complimented for her reticence, in 1877 Mrs Surr moved that, for important reasons the boardroom clock should be so placed as to be visible to the majority of members:

To most of us time is precious; and I don't think it well always to speak, even if we can always speak well. I have observed gentlemen rising three or four times in an afternoon only to express with fluent verbosity what has well been said by previous speakers (laughter). Why, gentlemen, if we ladies whose silence has hitherto been golden, and who are supposed to have such a free use of the unruly member, were to follow such an example our debates would be protracted till late in the evening.

(*School Board Chronicle*, 13 January 1877: 33–4)

Alluding once again to feminine reticence in the 1890s, Honnor pointed out: 'The silent, hard, conscientious committee work done by women as opposed to the blatant mouthing of the men on board days is most noticeable on large bodies. It is only at election time that words tell more than works'

(Morten, 1899a: 62). However the response of one male visitor who went to hear one of the debates at the all female Pioneer Club in the same period suggests the traditional attitudes of many men was slow to change. As his exasperated woman friend reported to the feminist periodical *Shafts*:

> Being asked what he thought of it and of the club, he replied, that what was said was very good, but that he did not like to see ladies speaking and it sounded very silly to hear them saying 'Mrs Chairman'. It is in this strain men usually utter their grumbles. It is not women cannot speak or women are illogical, or women are unbusinesslike – that they cannot say. If they could, it would be more reasonable, surely, than the usual utterances, 'I do not like to hear women speak', 'I do not like to see women on the platform', followed no doubt, by the thought – therefore they must not speak or go upon the platform.
>
> (*Shafts*, January 1896: 68)

The special qualifications of social status and personality were exploited with particular effect by Rosamond Davenport Hill, Ruth Homan, Helen Taylor and Alice Westlake, though only the example of Susan Lawrence will be considered here. Very tall, with short cropped hair, severe dress and a monocle, she was elected as a Moderate and subsequently used her knowledge and expertise as a statistician to support her attempts to limit the expansion of state provision. Apparently setting aside her own reservations, Susan frequently arrived at the the Board building on the Victoria Embankment in an ostentatious carriage and pair, having been pressed into it by relatives who presumably thought it was a useful strategy to let people see how grand a lady she was.

Irrespective of the social and political pressures on women members, they also had to adapt to the demands of public office. Many members regarded the School Board work as the main business of their lives and an indication of the workload can be gauged by looking at the Board's weekly timetable. During the first Board, the Statistical Committee met alternate Thursdays at 3:30 p.m., the Works and General Purposes on Mondays at 3 p.m., and the Finance Committee alternate Tuesdays at 3 p.m. The School Management Committee met every Friday at 3 p.m., the sub-committee of the Industrial Schools on Tuesdays at 10 a.m. and the Bye-Laws Committee alternate Thursdays at 2 p.m. The Committee responsible for teaching staff met at 4:30 p.m. on Mondays, Books and Apparatus every Thursday at 4 p.m., and the Charitable Endowments alternate Tuesdays at 3 p.m. (*School Board Chronicle*, 8 June 1872: 71). Indeed Gautrey reckoned that the central meetings reached as many as 750 a year, exclusive of local meetings and visits to the schools. A flavour of the practical implications is captured by the following entry in Edith Simcox's diary:

> Reached Mortimer Street at 9, looked round, then to Hart Street to see about pupil and assistant teacher, then to Vere Street for drawing examination ... then saw the visitor and received reports of truant cases caught by the visitors, managers meeting ... set off for the Rota, Works Committee and Educational Endowments etc – home reading Blackwood en route.
>
> (Edith Simcox, *Autobiography of a Shirtmaker*, 9 March 1880: 69)

By the 1890s, as Emma Maitland's weekly timetable shows, the workload was awesome. Mondays, Thursdays and Fridays were taken up with central Board work, as were alternate Wednesdays. The rest of the week was committed to constituency work – including the supervision of nine local schools, to which she nominated teachers, ancillary staff and resources. As Emma explained to Frederick Dolman during an interview for *The Young Woman* in 1896, she also played a part in developing schools for children with special needs, taking advantage of a visit to the continent to conduct an investigation into German and Austrian methods of teaching deaf and dumb children.

Many found the committee work too exacting and only half the members served for more than one term of three years. But while professional women like Elizabeth Garrett Anderson struggled to meet the requirements of public office, Socialists raised other class-based themes. Both Helen Taylor and Annie Besant demanded evening meetings to facilitate working-class representation, albeit with the support of the only working-class member, Benjamin Lucraft.[2] Helen emphasized the links between the bizarre hours of business and another deterrent for working people – the question of salaries for elective office. She considered this one of the most important principles of public life:

> one, that in her opinion would lead to the most beneficial results in public work. It was impossible that those interested in the Board's work – the working classes – should be represented upon it unless they were paid. The only reason against it was the additional expense. The Board should be a popular Board, and should really represent the working classes, and the parents of the children should have the chance of coming upon it.
>
> (*School Board Chronicle*, 3 March 1885: 234–5)

Historically, she was far ahead of her time here since payment of MPs did not begin until 1912. Thus it is notable that, while Benjamin Lucraft supported her motion calling for Board meetings at 7 p.m., he argued the payment of a salary would 'deprive bonafide working men of all chance of coming upon the Board. They would stand no chance against adventurers and place seekers' (*School Board Chronicle*, 3 March 1885: 234–5). Not surprisingly, given the political rationale underlying the 1870 Act, both motions were rejected. This was because the intention of the legislation of the 1870s was to lay the foundations of a state elementary education system that was provided, not that the working classes should assume responsibility for themselves. Annie Besant, elected to the Board in 1888, was one of the more outspoken and powerful voices on behalf of working-class interests. Representing the populous working-class district of Tower Hamlets, less than two months after her election she unsuccessfully moved that the Board meet at 6 p.m. since 'it was impossible for members of the class who sent their children to board schools to attend the meetings, therefore they did not seek seats on the board' (*School Board Chronicle*, 19 January 1889: 55). Essentially both issues highlight the dilemma facing working people. In theory, any adult was eligible to stand for election. In practice, it was tremendously difficult for those without an independent income or flexible working conditions.

The eighth Board took the administrative machinery in hand, streamlining the nine standing committees into six.[3] Again, a low female presence in the most powerful positions illuminates the male gender biases characterizing this public body. Appropriately enough, women consistently made up over half the membership of the Cookery, Laundry and Needlework Sub-Committee, the only sub-committee never to have a male chair. But as female members themselves recognized, in many ways this was only to be expected since the women's public networks generally exploited the conventional wife and mother stance with particular effect. However, as women rarely served on the Finance Committee, it does appear that both they and their male counterparts largely subscribed to conventional ideas about women's skills and interests. Acutely aware of the need to convince others in their social world that this was appropriate work for women, in 1873 Emily Davies concluded her farewell address to the electors of Greenwich with a plea for more women to step forward and take up their social responsibilities. By the end of the century Honnor Morten, professional nurse, journalist and member for Hackney, concluded that there were three main difficulties that kept women away from the work. First, the expense of elections, which generally cost a member £200, although Henrietta Muller spent several thousands in the 1880s. Second, the lack of experience in public speaking conspicuously attested to by Muller's experience in the Men and Women's Club in the 1880s. Third, the general lack of appreciation of the importance of these posts. Accentuating the links between the women's rights movement and the emphasis on service and a greater social purpose, Morten continued:

Note, again, the London School Board is, with the possible exception of the Paris Council the largest municipal body in the world, with annual budget of nearly three millions. Really it ought to be dread of responsibility, rather than apathy, which keeps the candidates for such bodies so limited. Obviously, if women have not the energy and courage to enter the fields of public service which are open to them, they will put a terrible weapon in the hands of the opponents of female suffrage. [...] Therefore, let women crowd on to all bodies and committees that will receive them, and there learn the country's laws administering the public funds, experience the discipline of associated action, and so broaden their judgement and enlarge their minds.

(Morten, 1899a: 63)

Notes

1. Amelia (Amie) Hicks (1839[?]–1917) was brought up by her uncle, but returned to her parental home when she was 14 and helped her Chartist Father in his boot-making business. Three years later she co-founded an evening school, which she ran for about two years in a cellar underneath the Soho bazaar. At the age of 25, Amie emigrated to New Zealand with her husband (a cabinet-maker) and three children where she ran a Home for Destitute Children and was variously employed as a boot-maker and rope-maker. Amie joined the Social Democratic Federation on her return to England and was later arrested for public speaking in Dodd Street, Limehouse, where the party had established an open air pitch in 1885. In both 1885 and 1888 she stood unsuccessfully as a candidate of the Social Democratic Federation in the elections for the London School Board. Amie Hicks achieved prominence for her work in organizing women in trade unions; she herself was secretary of the Ropemakers' Association and gave evidence to the Royal Commission on Labour (1891). A suffragist and temperance worker, she served on the Executive of the Women's Industrial Committee from 1894 to 1908, as well as being a member of the London Reform Union. (See Bellamy and Saville, 1978: 89–92 for more information.)

2. Benjamin Lucraft (1808–97) began work as a Devon ploughboy, became a cabinet maker after his move to London. Joined the moral force wing of the Chartist movement in 1848, and was an active member of the Parliamentary and Financial Reform Association which sought to inform public opinion through the publication of tracts. Financially secure because his sons had built up the cabinet-making business, Lucraft represented Finsbury on the London School Board, 1870–90, achieving prominence as Chair of the Educational Endowments Committee. He joined the campaign against the Contagious Diseases Acts and was supported by repealers in his unsuccessful candidature for the parliamentary seat of Tower Hamlets in 1879.

3. The Committee structure of the London School Board, 1891–1904:

School Accommodation and Attendance Committee: responsible for school accommodation (including the selection of sites), school attendance.

Works Committee: responsible for purchase of school sites, erection/enlargement of school buildings, furniture, general care of all Board properties (including ancillary staff, tenancies, coal, gas, water supplies).

School Management Committee: responsible for school management and discipline, curriculum and staffing.

Finance Committee: responsible for annual estimates plus any additional expenditure.

General Purposes Committee: responsible for legal work (including salaries and office control), work in connection with minuting and educational endowments.

Industrial Schools Committee: responsible for the administration of the variety of reformatory institutions established by the Board, as well as others used by the Board.

4 Entering the Public Arena: Women's Participation in Educational Politics

Introduction

This chapter explores the links between private lives, social networks and careers in public life by focusing on the biographies of the 29 women members of the School Board for London, 1870–1904. In examining the extensive overlap of powerful personal and political networks, it considers the extent to which these relationships provided the women with much needed support at emotional, intellectual and political levels. I will argue that connecting the ways in which School Board women negotiated their private and public lives is integral to understanding their achievements.

As members of a separately elected board of education these women shared a novel political and administrative experience. All political movements are as much the history of social and intellectual networks as they are of organized campaigns and lobbying but this seems especially true of first-wave feminism (see Levine, 1987; 1990; Holton, 1996). Male-dominated political establishments were not the only obstacles women faced and it is important to challenge a narrow definition of politics by presenting a more rounded picture of these women's lives. As Chapter 2 made clear, women's activism was partly dependent on several broad social and economic trends in English society. This chapter turns away from the broader social, economic and political context to consider the links between individual backgrounds, attitudes and experiences. The data on which this chapter is based are, therefore, mainly biographical in nature and so provide the basis for a life history approach both to the activists themselves and to their public work on the London School Board.

Sandra Stanley Holton, Philippa Levine, Jane Rendall and others have explored the personal relationships underpinning a developing feminist culture in nineteenth-century Britain. Olive Banks not only highlights the need to acknowledge the importance of change over time, with respect to the campaigns of first-wave feminism, 'but also in terms of its ideology, and, most obviously of all, in the social and political background of its leading campaigners' (1986: 149). Here the emphasis is on the social networks formed by female activists. Focusing on agents as the main unit of analysis, the chapter uses social network analysis to concentrate attention on the lived connections between personal and political worlds. In particular, there is a concern to explore the social networks built out of social relations on the basis of the principle that, as John Scott and Catherine Griff (1984: 9) make clear: 'agents are significantly connected to others, each of whom has similar connections to further agents. As a result, there exists a definite network of relations between agents.' Subsequent chapters will examine the links between time, place and attitudinal change, in so far as the evidence allows.

Thus the chapter begins by analysing the social background of the female sample. For this purpose important generational differences among female reformers and the connection between participation in women's social movements will be considered through the use of Banks' (1986: 4–5) generational schema. This provides a framework for investigating the political success of these women considered in terms of socioeconomic status, educational qualifications, political affiliation and marital and familial commitments, in so far as these were known. Finally, the chapter ends by exploring the development of powerful political and personal networks among School Board women themselves.

Who were the School Board women?

Following Olive Banks' (1986) study of the social origins of 'first-wave' feminism the main unit of analysis has been the cohort or generation based on year of birth. Generational differences between female activists are clearly important. Joyce Goodman (1995) has shown that in the early decades of the nineteenth century women governors in schools for working-class girls were not unusual, though their authority was curtailed by structural barriers. The removal of legal disabilities under the Married Women's Property Acts of 1870 and 1882 meant that more women were in a position to make educational endowments and act as trustees of schools. This needs to be emphasized while bearing in mind the approximation that only 10 per cent of women (including married women with settlements and unmarried daughters), were provided with an independent income under the law of equity (Perkin, 1989: 10–18). Legal changes clearly removed a powerful disincentive to women's participation in local government, as did the new sources of commercial, industrial and professional wealth and income facilitating a middle-class lifestyle and culture. Moreover, using the chronology proposed by Banks (1986) it becomes possible to illustrate very clearly the range of birth dates covered by the sample (see Table 4.1).

Table 4.1
Generational differences among School Board women (sample = 19)

Cohort One (<1828)	Cohort Two (1828–48)	Cohort Three (1849–71)
Rosamond Davenport Hill b. 1825	Annie Besant b. 1847	Mary Bridges Adams b. 1855
Elizabeth Surr b. 1825/6	Jane Chessar b. 1835	Margaret Dilke b. 1857
	Emily Davies b. 1830	Ruth Homan b. 1850
	Alice Garrett b. 1842	Maude Lawrence b. 1864
	Elizabeth Garrett b. 1836	Susan Lawrence b. 1871
	Emma Maitland b. 1844	Hilda Miall-Smith b. 1861
	Edith Simcox b. 1841	Florence Fenwick Miller b. 1854
	Helen Taylor b. 1831	Honnor Morten b.1861
	Julia Augusta Webster b. 1837	

Cohort One consisted of all those born before 1828 and so represented the first generation of School Board women. Not surprisingly, this was the smallest group. Only Elizabeth Surr and Rosamond Davenport Hill fall into this category and both were at least fifty when first elected. This was unusual since few Victorian women in their fifties would have enjoyed the robust health so often cited as an essential qualification for such high office (Bateson, 1895: 49).

The second cohort was born between 1828 and 1848 and this covers some of the most active members of the Langham Place circle. It includes, for example, Emily Davies and Elizabeth Garrett, as well as Elizabeth's sister, Alice. Both they and four of the other women who fall into this cohort subsequently joined the Kensington Society, a discussion group for women that met regularly at the house of Charlotte Manning (later first Mistress of Girton) in the mid-1860s (see Chapter 2). The most prominent woman in this group was Helen Taylor, although it also includes Emma Knox Maitland and Julia Augusta Webster. It seems likely that Frances Hastings, Henrietta Muller (died 1906), Mary Richardson and Alice Westlake, the second daughter of Thomas Hare who married John Westlake (1828–1913), also belong in Cohort Two. In 1851 John won a fellowship at Trinity College, Cambridge, a post he held until 1860, when he may well have resigned to marry. Moreover it should be pointed out that these less familiar women also came from upper-middle-class, Liberal and professional backgrounds. Augusta Webster, for example, was the daughter of Vice-Admiral George Davies (1800–76) chief constable of Cambridgeshire and Huntingdonshire and Julia Hume (1803–97), while Emma Maitland was the only daughter of John Rees, JP. Other significant feminists in the second cohort include the Socialist feminists Annie Besant and Edith Simcox. Finally, another largely unknown woman caught up in the campaign to reform the education of girls and women also falls into this cohort. Her name was Jane Chessar and she was born in 1835.

Cohort Three, born between 1849 and 1871, represents the last generation of School Board women. Several nineteenth-century suffrage leaders fall into this cohort including Florence Fenwick Miller and Margaret Dilke. This generation also included the socialist Mary Bridges Adams, the writer and lecturer Honnor Morten, the Liberals Ruth Homan and Hilda Miall-Smith, and the Honourable Maude Lawrence. The last woman born in this cohort was the main beneficiary from the later success of the suffrage campaign, Susan Lawrence.

The only one of the 29 School Board women to make the progression from local to national government was Susan Lawrence. She was elected to the LCC in 1910 as a member of the Municipal Reform Party but resigned in 1912 over the issue of the low wages and poor working conditions of women school cleaners. She speedily joined the Labour party and it was during the early years of the First World War that she became the first woman Labour representative on the LCC, and in 1919 was elected to Poplar Borough Council. For the next two years she was assistant to Mary Macarthur in organizing the National Federation of Women Workers. In 1921 she went to prison with other Poplar councillors for refusing to collect the Poor Rate. She stood unsuccessfully for Camberwell in 1920, but was returned to Parliament as Labour MP for East

Ham North three years later. Held in affectionate regard as 'our Susan' by the electors of Poplar, according to her friend and fellow Fabian Clara Rackham, it was as an expert in finance that Susan Lawrence won her parliamentary triumphs in 1928 (see Rackham, 1948: 21–2). After this she was rewarded with office as Parliamentary Secretary to the Ministry of Health, although her unconven- tional habit of 'sending round to Barker's for half a dozen inexpensive dresses to be sent to the Ministry and indicating her preference by simply raising her head for a minute from her papers and pointing with a pencil' (Vallence, 1979: 39), suggests she made few concessions to femininity.

To return to the question of generational differences among the School Board women, it seems likely that three other women whose dates of birth remain unknown also belong in Cohort Three. The three women are: Eugenie Dibdin (married in 1882), Constance Elder who married the Reverend Charles Robert Patey in 1898 (died 1940), and Edith Glover (died 1943). While I have only been able to discover when 19 of the 29 women were born, when those for whom it is possible to make a reasonable guess are added to the third cohort, this emerges as the largest grouping.

Drawing together the multifarious strands of these women's lives using the five success factors identified by Stacey and Price (1981) in their study of women, power, and politics, I shall now examine the links between the feminism of women members of the London School Board and the socioeconomic conditions necessary for putting their ideas into practice. This reflects a deliberate decision to avoid falling into the trap of divorcing a consideration of their public from their private lives. From a reading of published commentary, in conjunction with personal texts, it is possible to piece together an impression of the extent to which social and political homogeneity provided the women with much needed support at an emotional, intellectual and political level.

Taking each in turn, the first common factor identified by Stacey and Price was that of having been brought up in politically active families. Of the 29 female Board members, 10 women shared such an upbringing. In the case of Alice and Elizabeth Garrett, and their friend Emily Davies, the influence of siblings may have been significant. Elizabeth and Alice were drawn into radical political circles during the 1850s following the marriage and move to London of their elder sister Louisa Garrett Smith. Elizabeth and Emily were introduced to one another by a mutual friend, Jane Crow, whom Elizabeth met at a school in Blackheath run by the two Miss Brownings in the 1840s. In 1848 the Crow family moved to Gateshead where Jane became friends with Emily, the fourth of the five children of the Reverend John Davies and his wife, Mary Hopkinson. Shortly afterwards Elizabeth visited the Crows in their new home and it was there that she met Emily Davies (see Caine, 1992: 54–102).

Emily cultivated an active interest in public affairs very early in life. In the 1830s the family home was in Southampton and despite ill health her father addressed meetings calling for the abolition of slavery. Emily always regarded him as a conservative and at the age of eleven she and her elder brother William, aged thirteen, began to articulate their conservative views in the pages of their own weekly newspaper. Her commitment to the feminist cause was nurtured by a strong sense of relative deprivation and resentment at the educational and employment opportunities available to her brothers. In particular, her eldest brother Llewellyn shared her intellectual interests and gave her access to the world she most wanted to know. He himself had a very distinguished academic record at Cambridge and settled in London in 1851, having given up a fellowship at Trinity College to become an unpaid curate in Limehouse. Once there he became a follower of the·Christian Socialist Frederick Denison Maurice, rejecting his father's strict evangelicalism to become a prominent broad churchman. He later earned a reputation as a fashionable London preacher and philanthropist, devoting his time to the Working Men's College in Great Ormond Street (of which Maurice was the first Principal) and taking a keen interest in women's education. This was extremely significant for Emily as Llewellyn offered a gateway to a highly influential male network associated with educational and religious reform. In the late 1850s she accompanied her tubercular youngest brother, Henry, to Algiers and it was while she was abroad that she met Barbara Leigh Smith. On their return to England, Barbara introduced the three friends Elizabeth, Emily and Jane to Langham Place.

Like Emily Davies, Rosamond Davenport Hill was introduced to the world of politics and reform through members of her family. Both her father and his four brothers were all active administrators and social reformers, sharing an interest in a group of overlapping social concerns (see Gorham, 1978). These included the development of mass schooling, penal reform and the temperance movement; her father was also a founding member of the Law Amendment Society.[1] Like Llewellyn Davies, the five brothers also participated in the development of NAPSS (see Chapter 2). Rosamond's father, Matthew, was a friend of the Leigh Smith's and it was he who advised Barbara on the law pertaining to married women when she published her pamphlet in 1854 (see Chapter 2). Rosamond's brother, Alfred, drafted the Matrimonial Causes Bill at the request of Frances Power Cobbe in 1878.

Ruth Homan also belonged to a closely constructed familial network, although the Waterlow family combined public service with the success of a family business. Her father was Sydney Waterlow, co-founder of the printing house of Waterlow and Sons and one time Liberal MP, Alderman, Sheriff and Lord Mayor of London. Waterlow's friends included four male Board members: Sir Edmund Hay. Currie, Thomas Huxley, Samuel Morley and the Reverend William Rogers; his biographer, Smalley, records his having taken a lively interest in his eldest daughter's educational activities. Furthermore, her brother David (1857–1924), also became a County Councillor and Liberal MP, as did a brother of Mary Richardson. Two of Hilda Miall-Smith's uncles were Members of Parliament, one preceding his parliamentary career with a period on the Board, while Margaret Mary Dilke was the widow of Ashton Dilke MP. Finally, Alice Westlake was the daughter of the Liberal intellectual Thomas Hare, friend of John Stuart Mill and President of the London National Society for Women's Suffrage (*Englishwoman's Review*, 15 September 1876: 414).

Of the four other women who shared such an upbringing, Maude Lawrence was the fifth and youngest daughter of John Lawrence (1811–79, created Baron Lawrence in 1869). Like Matthew Davenport Hill, Lawrence enjoyed a rise in social status through the new activities of professional administrator and reformer, albeit largely in the colonies. Known as the 'Saviour of the Punjab', over a 39-year-period punctuated by bouts of ill health he held civic posts in Delhi and the Punjab before returning to India as third Viceroy in 1863. According to Thomas Gautrey:

> No man in public life at the time had greater prestige or was more honoured. Everyone acclaimed his capacity and his integrity. He had 'saved India, and was giving his unequalled influence and powers for saving London from illiteracy and ignorance'.
>
> (n.d.:43)

By contrast, Emma Maitland attributed her childhood interest in politics to the influence of her mother, who was a strong Liberal (*Women's Penny Paper*, 23 August 1890: 1–2). Helen Taylor obviously inherited a feminist tradition from her mother, the radical Unitarian Harriet Taylor-Mill. Finally, Augusta Webster was the niece of Joseph Hume (1777–1855) the friend and associate of the Utilitarian philosophers Jeremy Bentham and James Mill (the father of John Stuart Mill) and the radicals Francis Place and Richard Cobden (leader of the Anti-Corn Law League).

While coming from a politically articulate family obviously facilitated the process of learning how to 'work' the existing political machinery, this should not be allowed to detract from the fact that all the women had independent links with voluntary organizations. Fundamental religious doubts lay behind Annie Besant's entry to public life via the lecture circuit of the National Secular Society, the Fabian Society and Social Democratic Federation, before her conversion to theosophy, emigration to India and work for Indian independence in her capacity as President of the National Theosophical Society. Others like Edith Simcox and Mary Bridges Adams, who did not reach such esoteric heights but shared the same socialist credentials, came up through the ranks of the trades union movement. Edith Simcox ran a co-operative shirtmaking business employing women and in 1875 became one of six women delegates to represent the Women's Society of Shirt, Collar and Underlinen Makers at the Trades Union Congress (*Englishwoman's Review*, 15 October 1878: 465–9). Mary Bridges Adams, former pupil-teacher and headmistress of a board school, belonged to the Gas Workers' and General Labourers' Union and worked closely with the union leader Will Thorne. Her close connection with the organized labour movement was reinforced by her association with the Royal Arsenal Co-operative Society, whose education committee and local branches of the Women's Guild supported her candidature for the Board.

Perhaps of greatest importance, however, was the second factor identified by Stacey and Price (1981), that of coming from a middle- or upper-class background. Not only did all the London School Board women except Mary Bridges Adams fall into this category, but just how important it was for wealth to coalesce with specific familial gender regimes will be shown by reference to the group biographies of the Garrett sisters. Although their mother, a strict Evangelical Sabbatarian, had conventional expectations of her daughters, their self-made father, Newson, facilitated their independent lifestyle. It was he who provided Elizabeth with the necessary financial support to become the first British woman to pass through a recognized course of medical training and secure qualification in her own country; he also insisted on giving Alice the return fare when she opposed his wishes and married Herbert Cowell, a young barrister at the Indian bar. One must question how far this was the common experience among School Board women. There is no way of knowing precisely. Even if the other women had rather less affluent backgrounds, most of them lived extremely comfortable lives within families with strong traditions of charitable and professional work and an active interest in politics and social reform.

However, there were clear differences between female members in terms of the financial resources they could command and while they may have grown up in comfortable surroundings, all would have been conscious of their economic vulnerability. Yet whereas Elizabeth Garrett incurred no financial hardship in donating £100 to meet her election expenses and Henrietta Muller spent thousands, Florence Fenwick Miller only ran for a second term because Helen Taylor arranged a meeting with the educationalist William Ellis, who offered £100 to help fund her campaign. It may be that the required sum grew to match available resources. In 1899 Honnor Morten calculated that £200 was the average amount, though Rosamond Davenport Hill spent between £1400 and £1500 on three elections in the 1880s (Morten, 1899a: 61–2; Metcalfe, 1904). That some women experienced serious financial difficulty is underlined by the fact that Mary Bridges Adams felt compelled to ask for the assistance and support of fellow Socialists through the pages of the *Labour Leader*.

Despite differences in their socioeconomic conditions, they all received some sort of education. Educational background, the third common factor identified by Stacey and Price, was of crucial importance to the women on the Board, although their educational experiences varied enormously.

Little is known of Elizabeth Surr's early life, but her colleague in Cohort One was an educated woman. First educated at a local day school, Rosamond Davenport Hill spent a number of years at boarding school before finishing her studies at home under a visiting governess. Of the nine women with known birth dates in Cohort Two, Emily Davies, Helen Taylor and the young Annie Wood were educated almost entirely within the domestic circle (although in Annie's case it was largely in the home of Ellen Marryat, the sister of the popular novelist Frederick Marryat). It seems that the freedom to read widely was Helen Taylor's most formative educational experience. According to Kamm, her feminist mother Harriet:

gave the girl few, if any, organized lessons; but Helen, conscientious and methodical, had the run of her mother's library and, beginning at one end of a bookshelf, ploughed straight through to the end, sometimes understanding what she read often not [...] but it was a major part of her mother's system that her pupil should be encouraged to think for herself, to tackle different concepts which she could not fully grasp.

(Kamm, 1977: 114)

Although Elizabeth and Alice Garrett began their education at home, in 1849 Elizabeth and her elder sister Louisa were sent away to complete their education at Blackheath Boarding School for Ladies. Here the formal curriculum may have left something to be desired for Elizabeth later shuddered at the stupidity of the English classes. More importantly for her nascent feminism, it was while at school in Blackheath that a fellow student and future member of the Langham Place circle, Jane Crow, introduced her to the woman who was to become her closest female friend: Emily Davies.

The young Julia Augusta Webster first attended school in Banff. In 1851 the family settled in Cambridge where Augusta read widely as well as attending classes at the Cambridge School of Art. She and Elizabeth Garrett shared a passion for self-education, but whereas Elizabeth studied Latin, political economy and arithmetic at home in Aldeburgh, Augusta studied the Classics and foreign languages. Initially learning Greek to help a younger brother, she obviously attained a high standard since she went on to earn a reputation as an accomplished translator, poet, dramatist and essayist, translating the *Prometheus Bound* of Aeschylus into English verse and the *Medea* of Euripedes. Edith Simcox, too, was intelligent and apparently well educated. The third child and only daughter of George Price Simcox, variously described as a merchant and gentleman, her education was vastly inferior to that of her two brothers, both of whom went to Oxford. Despite this inequality, McKenzie (1961: 4) attests to the fact that she had 'a good knowledge of French and German as well as of English literature'.

An extremely delicate child, Jane Chessar attended private schools and classes in her home town of Edinburgh in order to prepare for a career in teaching. In 1851 she moved to London where she entered the Home and Colonial Teacher Training College, a progressive institution founded in 1836 for the training of primary school teachers and governesses. In the 1850s the Society had two practice schools in the Gray's Inn Road, one for students who intended to work in inspected schools, another for governesses and private school teachers. It seems likely that Jane attended the latter, established largely as a result of the enterprise of Frances Mary Buss. From the standpoint of this study, it is important to understand that the Home and Colonial was heavily influenced by the pedagogical ideas of Johann Heinrich Pestalozzi. In particular, it was Pestalozzi's insight that mothers are educators of their children and that teachers can learn from their methods that is significant here. At a time of expanding work opportunities for single women, teaching offered a career which appeared to rectify the most glaring irregularity in these women's private lives – their apparent rejection of marriage and motherhood. Linked with contemporary expressions of sexual difference, Pestalozzi's ideas about the mother as the model of the good educator gave his female disciples a moral imperative for entering the teaching profession. Indeed Jane's mentor at the institution was another unmarried teacher, Elizabeth Mayo, one of the first women in England to be appointed to a post in teacher training and the author of several teaching texts.[2]

In 1852 Jane was appointed one of the organizing governesses in the training of teachers for National Schools, specializing in the curriculum areas of Human Physiology and Physical Geography. Fourteen years later, ill health forced her to resign her position on the staff of the college, but she continued to give lectures and tuition classes, successfully preparing girls for the senior Cambridge examinations and teaching special subjects at Frances Mary Buss's North London Collegiate School and Camden School for Girls. Described as rather stout and plain of face and costume by one of her pupils, the eldest daughter of John Marshall (sponsor of the Ladies' Sanitary Association) – Jeanette Marshall nicknamed her 'Chessics' and the two attended meetings of the Royal Geographical Society, of which Jane was a keen member (Shonfield, 1987: 15–16). Another pupil of Jane, the American Eliza Minturn who entered Girton in 1875, founded the J.A. Chessar Classical Scholarship (still extant) at Girton in 1876 (Girton College Register, 1875). Furthermore, it seems likely that professional concerns also brought Jane into contact with Mary Frances Sim, who came to London in the 1850s to train at the Home and Colonial College (Smart, 1994: 18). Like herself, Mary was of Scottish stock and subsequently became known as an outstanding exponent of the educational ideas of Friedrich Froebel.[3] Significantly, the philosophy of Froebelianism was taken up by the Home and Colonial Society in 1859, while Miss Sim set up two private schools in the 1860s and 1870s. Out of this initiative she was appointed Kindergarten Mistress at Southampton Girls' College in 1875. It seems likely that this appointment allowed her to work closely with Jane Chessar, because when the Froebel Society began to give certificates of proficiency in 1876, Jane was an examiner and Mary supplied three of the successful student teachers.

As a result, by the time of her election to the Board in 1873, Jane was a figure of some repute in the educational world but, despite receiving the help and sympathy of Mary Richardson (with whom she lived at 6, Frederick Place, Gray's Inn Road), the strain of School Board work proved too much and her doctors advised her against seeking re-election in 1876. Despite her enforced retirement, Jane did not sever all ties with public life. She accepted an invitation to serve on the governing body of the Women's Education Union and supported their scheme to establish an evening college for women workers. She also joined the Teachers' Training and Registration Society founded by another Froebelian, Maria Grey, and was elected to sit on the Council of Cheltenham Ladies' College as the teachers' representative. In addition, she started a swimming club for London's women teachers and founded a ladies' debating society (where some of the third generation of School Board women took their first lessons in public speaking). Meanwhile, she was a regular contributor to *Queen* and other newspapers, edited Mrs Somerville's *Physical Geography* and Hughes's *Physical Geography*, as well as writing a teaching text. Finally, she joined the Somerville Club for Women shortly before leaving for Brussels to help at an educational conference, where she died of 'cerebral apoplexy' on 3 September 1880.

Angered by the exclusion of fee-paying women students from medical classes at Edinburgh University in the early 1870s, Florence Fenwick Miller enrolled at the Ladies' Medical College, London. She qualified with honours and subsequently took up practical work at the British Lying-in Hospital. Although women could not become legal medical practitioners until 1876, Florence maintained an office for the practice of obstetrics at her parents' home in Victoria Park until she entered public life at the youthful age of 22 (Van Arsdel, 1986: 26-7). Honnor Morten, too, was medically trained. Widely known as a hospital nurse and public health lecturer, she was a contributor to several leading newspapers and periodicals, as well as being the author of nursing and health text books. By contrast, the only organized schooling Ruth Homan is known to have received occurred much later in life and was in preparation for public office. Apparently acting in the belief that 'too much care cannot be taken in the proper cleaning of pots and pans' (Dolman, 1896: 130), Ruth took lessons in artisan scullery and cooking at the South Kensington School of Cookery before entering St Bartholomew's Hospital, where she worked as a probationary nurse for four months as well as attending the medical lectures. It may be that her father opened doors for her through his position, since he was the hospital treasurer.

Few details are known of Mary Richardson's early life, but she must have received some sort of education because she later shared a practice at the Inns of Court with the first woman solicitor – Eliza Orme. She became honorary treasurer of the Association to Promote Women's Knowledge of Law in 1878. After retiring from public life in London, Mary pursued a business career, having purchased the co-operative store at Bedford Park in 1888. Six years later she moved to Cornwall where she busied herself with literacy work, as well as accepting a place on the directorate of the Housel Bay Hotel and becoming a parish councillor. Significantly, her friend and colleague Eliza Orme is also considered a second generation pioneer in women's work (see Stone, 1994: 122). Awarded the Hume Scholarship in Jurisprudence, Orme trained as a conveyancy lawyer before going on to become one of the Lady Assistant Labour Commissioners (along with Clara Collett, May Abraham and M. H. Irwin). In 1894, much to the delight of Emily Faithful, she was appointed to the Departmental Committee of Inquiry into the Administration of Prisons. Both women belonged to the feminist network emanating from the Langham Place circle, as did Emma Knox Maitland, who was educated by governesses until the age of twelve and then went to a boarding school.

Six members of Cohort Three are known to have benefited from the increased opportunities for middle-class women in the last third of the nineteenth century. First, Henrietta Muller and Constance Elder were former Girtonians, while Susan Lawrence took the mathematics tripos at Newnham. Constance was an active member of the college tennis club and later left £1,000 (the Patey Fund, still extant in 1969) for making grants to students for expenses connected with their work during the summer term (Girton College Register, 1882; *Girton Review* December 1883, July 1884). Second, Hilda Miall-Smith, a product of Miss Buss's school in the 1870s, in 1882 became one of the first women graduates to receive her BA from London University. Entering the

Maria Grey Training College she proceeded to teach at South Hampstead High School and afterwards at the North London Collegiate. Finally, Mary Bridges Adams, Maude Lawrence and Honnor Morten were students at the non-residential Bedford College (see Chapter 2). Starting in the Lent Term of 1882, Mary attended evening classes in maths, English literature, French, Latin and Greek and, although she dropped a maths class after Easter, she supplemented her other studies with English language and English history. Fees at Bedford were a comparatively modest £10 10s per term, and in June 1882 Mary passed the University of London's Intermediate Examination in Arts. This was a qualification in itself and actually represented the first stage towards getting a degree (Bedford College Register AR201, College Calendar AR243). Thirteen years later, Honnor Morten (the daughter of a solicitor and niece of the novelist William Black) was among the first cohort of students to take the newly established Hygiene Course at Bedford College. She then qualified as a certified nurse and midwife, became organizing secretary for the Charity Organisation Society and manager of four East End board schools (Bedford College Register AR201, *The Times*, 15 July 1913: 11).

One other informal aspect of their education should be mentioned here and that is the habit of foreign travel. Eugenie Dibdin was actually born in France and received her education abroad, but she was not the only woman to share this opportunity. Constance Elder travelled widely in Germany, the Colonies and America, as did Annie Besant (funded by Ellen Marryat), Rosamond Davenport Hill, Ruth Homan, Emma Maitland, Helen Taylor and Augusta Webster. The daughter of an émigré German businessman, Henrietta Muller spoke six languages and is known to have travelled much (and alone) in Europe, America and Asia (Girton College Register, 1873). Ruth Homan was also an exceptionally experienced traveller. Widowed in 1880, the following year she accompanied her father, sister Hilda and brother Paul on a tour of Canada and the United States of America; and by 1896 she had been round the world three times!

Regardless of generational cohort, therefore, it would appear that the majority of female Board members did not receive the trivial education given others of their sex and class. Their self-confidence thus appeared to derive, in part, from the sharing of a common culture.

The fourth and fifth success factors identified by Stacey and Price (1981) were the ability to rely on the resources and support of their families and to avoid or minimize family commitments. Because single women were better positioned than their married counterparts in the 1860s and 1870s to take advantage of expanding political opportunities, it is hardly surprising to find that thirteen of the 29 female Board members were spinsters and therefore did not share a common experience in women's lives, marriage and family. Of the remaining sixteen, nine female representatives (Mary Bridges Adams, Alice Cowell, Eugenie Dibdin, Edith Glover, Hilda Miall-Smith, Elizabeth Surr, Alice Westlake, Augusta Webster and F. L. Wright) were married; and another four were married while serving – the widow Margaret Mary Dilke, Elizabeth Garrett, Constance Elder and Florence Fenwick Miller. Older women like Ruth Homan and Emma Maitland were widows when elected, while the notorious

Annie Besant was legally separated. Finally, of the married women, Alice Westlake was childless, while Eugenie Dibdin, Ruth Homan, Emma Maitland and Elizabeth Surr all had grown-up children. The only exception to the rule was Florence Fenwick Miller, who twice gave birth during her second term.

It will be readily understood that the opinions of contemporaries differed regarding the significance of marital status to the candidature of women for the Board. Hence *The Times* greeted the announcement of Elizabeth Garrett's engagement to James Skelton Anderson in 1871 by querying whether she ought to resign her seat on marriage 'since a conflict might arise between the rights of the husband and the duties of a wife' (7 January 1871). By contrast, Ruth Homan was reported as feeling that 'all things being equal, she should be inclined to give preference to married women, because there are many matters which the mistresses and parents would more readily confide to a married rather than an unmarried lady' (Bateson, 1895: 48).

Despite the importance attached to an evaluation of the success factors identified by Stacey and Price, this should not be allowed to deflect attention from the constraints and problems faced by women in authority. It should be acknowledged that the development of a specific female consciousness could not protect the School Board women from the prevailing social pressures regarding the conflict between traditional duties and public work. Nevertheless, by drawing on the women's letters and biographical writings, it is possible to sketch a more rounded picture of the conflicts these women faced between conventionally feminine desires and the urge to work in the field of public educational administration.

Unsurprisingly, two of the four women who were married while serving, Elizabeth Garrett and Florence Fenwick Miller, chose husbands who supported their efforts to combine successful careers and election to public office with marriage and motherhood. Elizabeth herself, anxious to reassure fellow women activists of her continued commitment to 'the cause', was convinced 'the woman question will never be solved in any complete way so long as marriage is thought to be incompatible with freedom and with an independent career' (quoted in Manton, 1965: 213). Furthermore Maria Grey reports that her friend and co-worker, the educationalist Frances Mary Buss, considered the marriage:

> a most fortunate event for the cause of better education and serious occupation of girls as it would allay the fears of so many mothers that their daughters, if highly educated, and still more if engaged in professional pursuits, would never find husbands.
>
> (Grey, *On the Education of Women*, Appendix XII, quoted in Sayers, 1973: 75)

Yet despite contemporary strictures regarding the ingredients for conjugal bliss, Elizabeth did more public work in the year of her marriage than ever before (Manton, 1965: 221). Again, her social and professional identities were equally significant to Elizabeth's break with prevailing norms and values surrounding domesticity and the cult of the home. Both before and after marriage and motherhood, her many activities were facilitated by her ability to employ other women of a differing social class to fulfil her domestic responsibilities. For instance, by the time her first child was born, the domestic servants employed to sustain the Garrett Anderson household included a cook, a housemaid, three general maids, a wet nurse and a nanny. Fortunately for her, as her biographer points out:

> One decision which a professional woman now has to make was, of course, spared her. The unquestioned custom of her class and time was a nursery life for children in the care of a nanny. No one suggested that a lady, however leisured, should take sole charge of her own children.
>
> (Manton, 1965: 234)

Nonetheless, having announced her engagement, Elizabeth found herself tormented by doubts: 'Lying awake at night, she felt she would almost die of the sense of guilt if she found herself after two or three years of marriage, out of the medical field.' Torn between her duty to other women and that owed her fiancé, Elizabeth avoided having to compromise her feminist principles by insisting that both her earnings, in the form of patients' fees, and her capital be legally secured to her. Hence the Andersons shared their considerable joint income by means of a common purse, to which each contributed and from which each could draw for current expenses (Manton, 1965: 215). The mention of duty is significant here as it shows how nineteenth-century feminists both adopted, and allowed themselves to be motivated by the passionate middle-class belief in the morally redeeming power of work.

For the independent single woman, voluntary work provided an invaluable means of catering for their emotional needs once marriage and family had been excluded. According to the biographer of the longest serving woman member, Rosamond Davenport Hill, Rosamond herself early dismissed all chance of marriage on the basis of her appearance:

> when talking over plans for the future with her governess one day, she said with quiet determination; 'I shall never marry. No-one would care for such an ugly girl as I am, except for her money'. So, before she was twenty she resolutely put aside all expectations of inspiring a love that was worthy of her, and mapped out plans and aspirations for a life in which marriage took no part.
>
> (Metcalfe, 1904: 16)

Accounts such as these provide a valuable illustration of the ways in which both single women of this generation, and their friends and relatives (such as Metcalfe), effectively altered the negative connotations of 'redundancy'. Having taken the positive decision for herself that marriage was not to be, Rosamond Davenport Hill achieved personal fulfilment through a lifetime of public service. She drew on the valuable experience of having been her father's companion, during which time she 'shared his thoughts, joined in the conversation of his friends and profited by their society' (Metcalfe, 1904: 16).

The School Board women's network

Whatever their material circumstances, since such women were denied access to existing channels of political influence, it is hardly surprising to find evidence of their reliance on the networking activities of other women. Polling day for the first triennial elections of the School Board for London saw the triumphant return of two women, Emily Davies and Elizabeth Garrett, as members for the divisions of Greenwich and Marylebone. Indeed Elizabeth actually received more votes than any other candidate in London and between three and four times as many as Professor Huxley, the next returned successful candidate in her division (see Chapter 3). Needless to say, this impressive victory meant far more than just another achievement in the careers of two well known and remarkable women. It was also a tribute to countless lesser known female volunteers who laboured behind the scenes in order to secure the necessary support for their illustrious protégées.

Although they themselves did not have to perform manual household duties, both candidates were single women leading full and demanding lives that severely restricted the time available for electioneering. Deeply involved in her efforts to establish a college for women at Hitchin, Emily Davies only accepted the invitation to stand for Greenwich in the face of some persuasive arguments from Paul Tidman (the uncle of one of her students at Girton). He stressed his desire as an elector to return a woman and his willingness to assume full-time responsibility for organizing her campaign. Similarly, it was only a matter of months since Elizabeth had achieved her ambition of becoming a doctor, having graduated as the first woman MD of the Sorbonne. Her days were filled by the private practice based at her home in Upper Berkeley Street as well as the Dispensary for Women and Children she had opened in Marylebone four years earlier.

Consequently both Emily and Elizabeth were considerably reliant upon the organizational abilities of their respective electoral committees. It follows that contemporaries attributed Elizabeth Garrett's astonishing success to 'thorough organisation and indefatigable exertion, as well as the high personal qualifications of the lady candidate' (*Englishwoman's Review*, January 1871: 1). Emily Davies found the whole experience of public speaking an ordeal and was surprised to find that it got no easier as the campaign progressed. Keeping another male supporter, Henry Tomkinson, abreast of developments she noted:

> it was quite easy at Greenwich, but at Blackheath I found it hard and I had an uncomfortable sense of failure when it was over – I felt that I had been nervously hurrying to get it over, and I am afraid the audience must have felt the same.
>
> (Emily Davies to Henry Tomkinson, 21 November 1870)

On the other hand, Elizabeth Garrett handled the situation with considerable aplomb. Confidently addressing crowds of over a thousand and then moving on to shake hands with enthusiastic women supporters which, Emily Davies was quick to point out, was a chief part of a candidate's business. The unsuccessful third woman candidate, Maria Grey, did not benefit from the organizational skills of a Skelton Anderson, and she also risked exposing herself to the attacks of the Anglican clergy by declaring her support for non-sectarian education. It is significant that she faced strong opposition for the seat in the shape of Lord Lawrence, Canon J. G. Cromwell (later Dean of St Paul's and avowed enemy of the Board Schools), Dr John Hall Gladstone and Robert Freeman (non-conformist member of the Metropolitan Board of Works), all of whom were respected local men. At a pre-election meeting on 28 November she was heckled by one man who enquired whether the prospective lady members would find it trying to see 'forty six hats and only three bonnets, forty six umbrellas and only three parasols?' To this Mrs Grey somewhat testily retorted: 'It is only a small minority, no doubt, the effect will depend on the nature and strength of the drops' (*The School Board of London. Three Addresses of Mrs William Grey in the Borough of Chelsea with a speech by William Grove, Esq, QC FRS*, 1871: 17–18; cited in Sayer, 1973: 5).

From the start the feminist press exploited the School Board elections with particular effect and the *Englishwoman's Review* concluded its analysis of the results with three main recommendations for future women candidates. First, it was important to have sympathetic press coverage and John Stuart Mill's letter to *The Times* proved invaluable in this context. Second, previous experience, achievements and connections (especially in the world of organized philanthropy), were critical to success. Finally, it was judicious to follow the prevailing view and advocate Christian religious teaching and Bible reading in schools (*Englishwoman's Review*, January 1871: 4).

It must be emphasized that the women who contested these elections had been sought out and invited by men, they did not take the initiative themselves. For example, Elizabeth Garrett accepted an offer from a deputation of Marylebone working men (including the fathers and sons of patients at her dispensary), while Maria Grey was presented as a candidate by Thomas Hare (a barrister and charity commissioner who urged women to join school boards in January 1871: his daughter Alice did so in 1876), Alsager Hill and Sir Charles Trevelyan (*Victoria Magazine*, 1870: 181–2). The fact that their electoral committees had male chairs not only reflected prevailing social mores but also the non-sectarian approach of Emily Davies and Elizabeth Garrett, both of whom wanted feminists to work closely with men. A cursory glance through the list of names composing Elizabeth Garrett's committee is sufficient to show that men outnumbered women by about two to one. Apart from her father, other prominent male supporters included James Anderson, Llewellyn Davies, Henry Fawcett, Thomas Hare, Alsager Hill, Arthur Hobhouse, Henry Sidgwick and John Westlake, as well as numerous colleagues from the medical profession. It also shows that Elizabeth had reached the point of enjoying an established reputation in a social-cum-intellectual circle. Like Henrietta Rowland who canvassed on her behalf and pioneered living among the East End poor (Koven, 1994), Elizabeth moved in a reforming world concerned with social issues, and desired to enter into the national fray.

Focusing on the role played by female support networks within the political sphere, it is significant to note how many women have been largely written out of history. Members of the Langham Place circle like Barbara Leigh Smith Bodichon, Frances Mary Buss, Emily Davies, Millicent Fawcett, Maria Grey, Octavia Hill and Julia Wedgwood, emerge as part of a phalanx of women. This becomes clear in Vicinus's (1985) study of two generations of independent women (those largely born in the 1840s and 1850s and a second generation born in the 1870s and 1880s). During this period the tradition of women working together was transformed into a network of women's organizations and institutions offering support for one another in the achievement of their public goals. Thus Emily's success was largely attributed to the exertions of the two honorary secretaries of her committee – Miss Lewin (possibly the Jane or Sarah Lewin included among the 32 active members of the Langham Place circle) and Miss Berkeley. Moreover, far from disappearing from the scene when the election was over, many of these women became deeply involved with elementary education, both as school managers and as members of local divisional committees dealing with issues of non-attendance and the remission of fees (see Chapters 2, 5 and 6).

Alice Westlake, one of the members of Elizabeth Garrett's committee, was herself destined to represent the division of Marylebone as a member of the third Board. Married to the Board's solicitor (himself an unsuccessful candidate in 1873), like Jane Chessar and Alice Cowell before her, Alice Westlake reaped the benefits of the well organized and hard-working committee of supporters established by the Garrett feminist circle. For although she did not stand for re-election, Elizabeth Garrett remained active in the Marylebone division, offering other women organizational support as well as sharing their platforms. In fact, as a member of the London School Board Election Committee, she did not restrict her activities to the confines of her old division but came to the rescue of female candidates in other divisions whose campaigns were foundering.

Persuaded to stand for election by Alice Westlake and Helen Taylor, in 1879 Rosamond Davenport Hill chose the unlikely seat of the City, where there were no female voters. Recognizing the need to mobilize support, Elizabeth quickly assembled a committee of MPs and QCs. Rosamond, a suffragist and campaigner for educational and criminal law reform, went on to become the longest serving woman member and never missed a single Board meeting in thirteen years. Nonetheless, it would be wrong to convey the impression that Elizabeth Garrett was the only woman member to play such a role. It was, in fact, rather like membership of a select and exclusive club in which serving members interacted with former and potential colleagues. Irrespective of personal politics, recognition of the demanding and demoralizing nature of Board work was tempered by a belief in its necessity as a means by which to demonstrate women's untapped potential as public administrators. For instance, despite the fact that ill health prevented Jane Chessar from seeking re-election, she went on to persuade Mary Richardson to stand in 1879. Yet another member of the Garrett circle, Mary recalled the debt she owed the friend who not only coached her in preparation for the election, but 'was the only person who ever taught me anything of business' (Bateson, 1895: 104). Similarly Helen Taylor formed the alliance with Fulham working women that helped Julia Augusta Webster head the poll in Chelsea in the School Board election of 1879.

Returning to the subject of Elizabeth Garrett's original election committee, although the majority of other women did not go on to serve as members, the committee provided a pool from which Elizabeth was able to recruit both school managers and members of the Marylebone divisional committee.[4] Thus the Board not only authorized the appointment of Mrs Hughlings Jackson, the wife of one of the honorary male consultant physicians at Elizabeth Garrett's dispensary for women and children, but those of two other women married to men in the medical profession. One of the more prominent was Ghetal Burdon Sanderson (1832–1909), elder daughter of Reverend Ridley Haim Herschell. Her brother became Chancellor of the University of London and her husband, John, was an eminent physician at Middlesex Hospital between 1860 and 1870, when Elizabeth Garrett was gaining her practical experience there in the guise of a nurse. Ghetal served on the committee until 1883 when the family moved to Oxford. She also acted as treasurer for the Metropolitan Association for Befriending Young Servants, founded in 1876, providing help and support for young servant girls (known colloquially as Mind and Behave Yourself!) (*Women's Penny Paper*, 6 December 1890: 100).

Besides the clusters of female representation in Greenwich and Marylebone, Westminster provides further evidence of another cluster of female activity among these socially homogeneous women. One of the women appointed to the Westminster divisional committee in 1872 was Lady Augusta Stanley, member of Girton's first executive committee. Related by marriage to a future vice-chairman of the London School Board, Lyulph Stanley, it cannot have been mere coincidence that Lady Augusta was joined five years later by Lyulph's mother, the Liberal Unionist Dowager Lady Stanley of Alderley. A close friend and supporter of Emily Davies, the Dowager Lady Stanley helped to raise funds for Girton, and enlisted Lyulph's help in writing to other possible benefactors. She was also closely associated with the Shirreff sisters (Maria Grey and Emily), who established the Girls Public Day School Company in 1872, a limited company set up to create and administer private girls' schools for the middle classes. Similarly, her daughter Maude served on Elizabeth Garrett's committee and became a manager of several London board schools; she was also a Westminster Guardian, as well as being active in the girls' club movement (*Englishwomans' Review*, 15 May 1878: 221).

Three sets of organizational connections were crucial to women on the Board. First, the influence of the Langham Place circle permeated women members throughout the lifetime of the Board. This is revealed by the service of Jane Chessar, Alice Cowell, Rosamond Davenport Hill, Emily Davies, Margaret Ashton Dilke, Margaret Eve, Elizabeth Garrett, Emma Maitland, Mary Richardson, Helen Taylor, Julia Augusta Webster and Alice Westlake. In fact both Margaret Dilke and Henrietta Muller served on the executive committee of the National Society for Women's Suffrage in 1890, while Margaret Eve's sister-in-law was a fellow member.

Further examples of the salience of the feminist political machine resound through the names of potential and unsuccessful candidates to the capital's educational parliament. Emily Faithfull turned down a request from a deputation representing the electors of the City of London in 1870, but three years later Paul Tidman persuaded Charlotte Burbury (died 1895) to stand. The daughter of Reverend Kennedy (Regius Professor of Greek at Cambridge, Canon of Ely and formerly headmaster of Shrewsbury), Charlotte married a master at Shrewsbury and led the feminist campaign to expand the educational and job opportunities of women. For ten years she was Secretary to the Cambridge Local Examinations, besides serving on the general committee of the Women's Educational Union (WEU) and the sub-committee for working women's classes. She was also a member of SPEW and Secretary to the London National Society for Women's Suffrage for a six-year period dating from 1871. As a consequence, her supporters included Elizabeth Garrett Anderson, and Alice and John Westlake, but she also canvassed the support of Helen Taylor (*Englishwoman's Review*, 15 January 1896: 57; Mrs Burbury to Helen Taylor 13 November 1873). Another colleague from the WEU who followed in Charlotte's footsteps in 1891 was Louisa Temple Mallet. A member of the inner circle of the Women's Local Government Society,[5] Emma Maitland was a close friend, as was Eva McLaren, the sister of Henrietta Muller. Finally, Elizabeth Garrett Anderson, Charlotte Burbury, Edith Glover, Florence Fenwick Miller, Helen Taylor, Julia Augusta Webster and Alice Westlake were among a group of feminists in London who decided to set up a Central Committee in 1879 (see Chapter 1). Its function was to promote the candidature of women for the School Board by offering help to the local committees established in the constituencies (*Journal of the WEU*, 15 August, 1879: 118–19).

The second set of organizational connections recall the recommendations of the *Englishwoman's Review* in 1871 regarding the need for women candidates to have done something philanthropic. Links between charitable and educational work were far from unusual and many women were active in both fields. Indeed the influence of the Charity Organisation Society (COS) was vital for instilling business methods and an enlarged sense of social responsibility. COS members co-opted to serve on the Board's administrative apparatus included Mary Anne Donkin (school manager in Chelsea, Poor Law Guardian in Kensington), Lucy Fowler (school manager in Southwark), Sarah Ward Heberden (née Andrews; school manager in Marylebone, Poor Law Guardian in St Pancras), Octavia Hill and Elizabeth Scott Lidgett (school manager in Marylebone, Poor Law Guardian in St Pancras).

Finally, party politics was of increasing importance to female candidates. The 1880s saw the formation of women's groups within the main parties and party allegiance is an important aspect of women's political work in the period. The Women's Liberal Federation was inaugurated in 1886 and six of the nineteen female members elected after 1885 were active members of local women's Liberal associations. Thus Margaret Ashton Dilke, Ruth Homan, Emma Maitland and Hilda Miall-Smith all held posts in their local associations, while Margaret Eve was a candidate of the Islington Liberal Association. In 1897 Ruth Homan was elected President of the Cornish Union of Women's Liberal Associations and her colleague, Emma Maitland, was a one time Vice-President of the Women's Liberal Federation. The Irish Home Rule schism of 1886 resulted in the formation of the neo-conservative Women's Liberal Unionist Association in 1888 and Alice Westlake later served on its general committee.

Four women were active supporters of the Conservatives. One, Eugenie Dibdin, was Treasurer of the Holborn Habitation of the Primrose League, Frances Hastings belonged to the East London Conservative Association and Susan Lawrence led the Tory party in the Newnham College Political Society in the late 1890s (Rackham, 1948: 20). Finally, Emily Davies always referred to herself as a Conservative (see Caine, 1992: 54-102). Of the ten other women elected in the period only Annie Besant and Mary Bridges Adams were active socialists. Annie Besant was a member of the Fabian Society from 1885 and the Social Democratic Federation (SDF) from 1888, while Mary Bridges Adams became an uncompromising Socialist in the early 1880s. However the SDF adopted a number of women candidates in the 1880s and 1890s. These included Amie Hicks, who contested the 1885 and 1888 elections, as well as the following three women who entered the contest in 1894 – Rose Jarvis who stood for election in Hackney, Edith Lanchester who stood in West Lambeth and Annie Thompson who contested Tower Hamlets. Like Mary, Annie Thompson received pledges of support from Will Thorne and Pete Curran of the Gasworkers' Union, as well as George Lansbury and Herbert Burrows (a friend and colleague of Annie Besant). Henrietta Muller and Edith Simcox supported the quest to unionize women and were associates of Emma Paterson, who founded the Women's Protective and Provident League in 1874. Indeed it was Mrs Paterson who persuaded Edith to accept an offer to stand for Westminster as the working-men's candidate. Edith also included Emilia Dilke (who presided over an influential reformist London salon in the 1880s and 1890s while also acting as a leader in the Women's Trade Union League), and Eliza Orme (see Chapter 2) among her friends and supporters.

Adopting an instrumental and pragmatic approach to the representation of women on school boards, it says much for the pervasiveness of the social patterning of gender that many School Board women stressed the fact that board school girls, as well as boys, should have their interests represented by members of their own sex. Although this may well have been a tactic designed to minimize potential antagonism, it may also have unwittingly nurtured the underlying chauvinism of many male members overtly revealed in School Board debates. Whatever their political goals, it remains true that they all asked for a share in government, irrespective of whether they shared that sense of identity that was characteristic of Victorian feminism.

Conclusion

The preceding discussion suggests several generalizations. First, a historical methodology highlights that the relationship between family background and a shared social world provided this sample of London's women activists with a much needed source of commonality and social integration. Second, as the previous chapter demonstrated, women's efforts in School Board politics were often part of a broader quest to consolidate a niche for women as voters, as political candidates, as organizers and as elected representatives. Finally, it follows that service on the Board secured and even strengthened women's class status. In the ensuing encounters the culture of altruism embedded in wider social attitudes would serve not only to develop a stronger female character, but also demonstrate to women's ability to take on new public roles and responsibilities.

Instead of highlighting the private world of home and family, the next chapter sets the stage for a multifaceted analysis of the policies and practices that most directly affected women members of the London School Board. It establishes the links between the School Board as a political and cultural nexus, and the basic structure of London board education. Here again there were contesting social visions, but Alice Westlake and Edith Simcox were not the only women to see the new School Board as 'utopian' (Gertrude Tuckwell, quoted in Copelman, 1996: 11). As Ruth Homan declared in her election address to the electors of Poplar and Limehouse in 1897:

> It will be my constant endeavour to do all in my power to secure for the children a fuller development of mind and body, helping them to grow up intelligent, healthy, and temperate, fitting them to take their place as good citizens, and to understand, while they have rights of their own they still owe a loving unselfish duty towards others less fortunate.
>
> (Fawcett Library, School Boards, 1890s)

Notes

1. The Law Amendment Society, established in 1844 by Lord Henry Brougham, functioned as a rallying point for a circle of utilitarian-influenced politicians and lawyers. While the utilitarians were interested in the reform of a whole variety of legal issues, they also revealed themselves to be sympathetic to feminist causes and took a progressive line on the issue of divorce reform. The Society attracted the support not only of such prominent lawyers as M.D. Hill, but also of many MPs, including Joseph Hume (see Gleadle, 1995: 128–9).

2. Elizabeth Mayo (1793–1865), teacher and writer. Between 1822 and 1834 she worked with her brother, the Reverend Charles Mayo (just returned from three years of teaching at Pestalozzi's school in Yuerdon, Switzerland), at a boarding school for upper-class boys in Cheam. The author of *Lessons on Objects* (1829), Elizabeth argued the child would be stimulated to learn by arranging and classifying objects and discovering their qualities; this method was universally used in the board schools and often became exercises in rote learning. The Home and Colonial Society later published two further teaching texts *Model Lessons for Infant Schools* (1838) and *Religious Instruction for Young Children* (1845) (see Aldrich and Gordon, 1989).

3. Like Pestalozzi, Froebel saw it as the task of the mother in the home, as well as the teacher in the school, to provide the right environment in which children might develop and grow. In tandem with the emphasis on play and the use of specific educational apparatus to help give the child's creative work the necessary structure and method, the ideals and methods of Froebelianism made a strong appeal to those concerned about the improvement of educational facilities and career opportunities for middle-class girls (Brehony, 1987; Smart, 1994).

4. Committees formed for each of the electoral divisions of the metropolis, consisting of the members for that division and other inhabitants or ratepayers of that division, nominated by the former. Constituting part of the Board's administrative machinery for enforcing the bye-laws relating to school attendance, members dealt with claims for the remittance of school fees whilst defaulting parents could be summoned to attend the committee in order to account for their child's absence from school, either to be excused with a caution or warned that a summons to attend the magistrate's court would follow.

5. Established by the Unitarian Annie Leigh Browne (1851–1936) when she brought together Mrs Amelia Charles, Mrs Matilda Evans, Caroline Biggs of the *Englishwomen's Review* and Lucy Wilson of the Vigilance Association into a Local Electors Association. The immediate objective was to secure female access to vestry politics, but the focus changed with the passing of the Local Government Act 1888, which provided for the establishment of county councils. So, in November 1888, the Society for Promoting the Return of Women as County Councillors was formed, with the Countess of Aberdeen (President of the Executive of the Women's Liberal Federation) as President, Mrs Eva McLaren (the married sister of Henrietta Muller) as first Honorary Treasurer and Mrs Louisa Temple Mallett (unsuccessful candidate for the London School Board) and Miss Browne as joint Secretaries of the Committee. Renamed the Women's Local Government Society (WLGS) in 1893, this upper-middle-class, Liberal and London-based women's organization was established on a non-party basis for promoting the eligibility of women to elect to and to serve on all local governing bodies. Apart from Annie, Mary Kilgour and Louisa Mallet, its inner circle also included Emma Cons (who had been appointed an alderman of the London County Council), Emma Knox Maitland, Ellen McKee and Eva McLaren, who had helped form the Society for Promoting the Return of Women as Poor Law Guardians a few years earlier. In this way the WLGS embraced a number of extensive networks bridging numerous worlds of women's activism in feminism and social reform politics.

Administering the Domestic Curriculum

Introduction

This chapter looks at the principles of curriculum building from the perspective of female policy-makers struggling to secure a permanent place for women in local government. In examining curriculum policies that were introduced for the schooling of working-class girls, it considers the strategies and tactics these women proposed and used in relation to the constraints and problems they faced as administrators and policy-makers in the field of elementary education. A central issue here is the quality and quantity of existing educational provision before the passage of the 1870 Education Act since this system provided the blueprint for the newly established state schools. Yet the growing disparity between the educational experiences of boys and girls also serves to introduce debates about the role of gender and class distinctions that were constantly evident and complexly related in the development of an appropriate curriculum for children attending London's board schools. As a consequence, the following sections examine both the state of 'popular' education before 1870 and the widening opportunities for middle-class girls in the last third of the nineteenth century. Most importantly, in looking at the politics of curriculum reform, key women members are placed within an ideological typology that focuses on their different educational and social world views.

Although a common element within feminism is the belief that women suffer injustice because of their gender, there are differing feminist agendas for change. Not all women School Board members saw themselves as working for the emancipation of their gender, nor as advocates of women's rights. Such views reflect both tactical and political diversity. With these assumptions in mind, critical reflection on their work involves going beyond their 'pioneering' status to examine the nature of their contribution to the workings of the Board. Was Millicent Fawcett right? Do women bring something to the service of the state different from that which can be brought by men?

As one might expect, the domestic curriculum was an area where School Board women could claim specialist knowledge and interests. To begin with, the electorate continued to entertain rather traditional views of the role women were to play in their new position. Second, the problematic relationship between contemporary feminist thought and conventional views of womanhood also created difficulties for women members. It must be emphasized that a feminist critique did not sink naturally into the Board's consciousness and the politics of curriculum reform were shot through with standard expectations of female roles. Thus women members who supported the expansion of the domestic curriculum for girls in state elementary schools were rewarded with promotion to positions of power in the Board's administrative machinery and characterized as 'typical' lady members. More critical women were depicted as outsiders.

The legacy of voluntary provision

As Chapter 4 made clear, all of these female activists were unusually well educated. Furthermore the change over time in the educational background of the School Board women reflects very clearly improvements in the education available to middle-class girls during this period. The connections between the educational backgrounds of women Board members and the stance they adopted on the question of the curriculum for working-class girls may have been important. To indicate the extent of social class differentiation, I will look first at educational provision for working-class girls, and then at educational provision for middle-class girls.

Research into educational provision before the 1870 Education Act shows that the schooling of working-class girls differed from that of working-class boys in several respects. First, the school attendance of girls was far lower than that of boys (Martin, 1987). Second, within the day schools organized by the two main religious bodies (which controlled over 90 per cent of voluntary school places), fewer places were offered to working-class girls than to working-class boys (see Hurt, 1979: 4). Third, differential stress was placed on appearance. Neatness and cleanliness were crucial for girls. Fourth, both the 1851 Census and the Newcastle Report a decade later, showed that even though girls and boys might be educated in the same schools, this did not mean that they shared all activities equally. During a period when it was assumed that men would be the major breadwinners, girls and young women were prepared for motherhood and domesticity and generally lost out in all the academic subjects save reading.

This pattern was reinforced in the Revised Code of 1862 when, as Anna Davin points out, 'failing to teach girls plain needlework became one of the few offences for which a school could lose its government grant' (1996: 143). As pointed out in Chapter 3, this was the era of payment by results when the size of the annual government grant depended upon attendance records and how well pupils performed in the annual inspectors' examinations (Simon, 1980: 114–19). Introduced by Robert Lowe, the principle effectively fastened a mechanical system of rote teaching, mainly confined to the three R's plus needlework, on the schools. Successive codes expanded the list of optional or class subjects on which grant was payable, but schools were not allowed to present any child for examination in more than two or three class subjects. The emphasis, therefore, was on a particular form of education that was increasingly differentiated by gender and social class. With regard to the needlework requirements, for example, the teacher and writer Clara Grant explained in her autobiography: 'in those days needlework was often taken daily during the whole afternoon, probably because the children made and mended garments for the neighbouring gentlefolk' (1929: 47). Since girls frequently spent the afternoon sewing they were therefore permitted a lower standard in the annual arithmetic examinations (Digby and Searby, 1981: 46). However this may have been a source of resentment among boys like Joseph Ashby (1859–1919), who recalled of his village National School in the 1860s:

> A specially hard time was the two 'sewing afternoons'. While the girls were collected together for sewing, the boys merely did more sums or an extra dictation, just the sort of thing they had been doing all morning. As they craned their necks to see what sort of garments, what colours, were coming out of the vicarage basket of mending, they were unusually tiresome to the poor pupil-teacher, losing their places over and over again, or misspelling words they knew perfectly well – forgetting everything.
>
> (Ashby, 1961: 17–18)

Here again, the association between women and domesticity was used as a rationale for the kinds of education offered working-class girls and the informal schooling in domestic work linked with erratic school attendance. As Anna Davin (1996) makes clear, girls were frequently expected to fulfil the roles of 'good wives' and 'little mothers' on wash days, or if their mother worked, was ill or having a baby. In the representative words of a Reverend Earnshaw, 'a mother cannot spare her daughters as much as her sons, boys are in the way at home, but girls assist in domestic work' (Newcastle Report, Parliamentary Papers 1861, Part 5: 183). Hence it seems evident that what Gaby Weiner (1994: 33) describes best as the four features of curriculum thinking – selection, differentiation, functionality and social advancement – were clearly visible in statements about the schooling of working-class girls and women in the last decades of the nineteenth century.

The assumption that women were destined for the domestic sphere was similarly reflected in the education of middle-class girls during this period. Unlike their male counterparts, these girls were largely educated for the marriage market, with the emphasis on social accomplishments before any sort of intellectual activity. Although the great majority were taught by their mothers and governesses at home, some attended small private schools, while those with very wealthy parents might attend expensive, fashionable boarding schools. For her class and period, therefore, Rosamond Davenport Hill was unusually well educated. She attended a local day school, went on to boarding school and completed her education at home with paid lessons from visiting governesses until she was 21. Emily Davies was less fortunate. Whereas her three brothers all went to well-known public schools and then to Trinity College, Cambridge, the Davies family paid little attention to their daughter's education. As a result, Emily received only a limited education (Caine, 1992: 63–5, 87–93). This included a brief spell at a day school supplemented by occasional paid lessons in languages and music.

By the 1840s, however, the unsystematic nature of this education was attracting criticism from professionals and wealthy businessmen – in particular, those aspiring to a new standard of gentility that would differentiate them from the newly rich (see Burstyn, 1980). Presumably some also recognized that their financial circumstances might not stretch to meet the need to support unmarried daughters who were not gainfully employed. Panton, writing in 1889, estimates that a grown-up daughter of a professional man would cost him £100 a year living at home, clearly an important consideration at a time when the income of a middle-class gentleman averaged between £700 and £1,000 a year (quoted in Banks and Banks, 1965: 173 note 3). There was growing pressure to improve governesses' teaching skills and in 1848 this led to the foundation of Queen's College, Harley Street. Linked to the greater competence expected of boys starting preparatory school, Queen's was sponsored by a male committee headed by Frederick Denison Maurice, Professor of English at the Anglican King's College. The approach of Maurice was a formative influence on both Emily Davies and Millicent Fawcett (Fawcett, 1924: 45), while Emily's brother, John, became Principal of Queen's in 1873. As might be expected, lectures were given by visiting male professors, while female teachers were known as junior tutors. Other female members of staff included the lady visitors – older women who, like Lady Henrietta Stanley of Alderley (see Chapter 4), volunteered to chaperone girls to lectures. A wealthy and influential patron, according to her grandson Bertrand Russell, 'she was an eighteenth-century type, rationalistic and unimaginative, keen on enlightenment and contemptuous of Victorian goody-goody priggery' (1967: 33).

Within six months Bedford College had opened with the broader aim of educating women who desired higher education. A close friend of Barbara Smith, Harriet Martineau, Mary Mohl and Anna Jameson (see Chapter 2), the founder, Elizabeth Jesser Reid, had a strong interest in schemes for elevating the moral and intellectual character of women. She also wanted to found a college which was organized by, as well as for, women. Unlike Queen's, Bedford was without denominational bias, although Reid had to compromise over the issue of school governance. Hence:

> The terms of the trust fund which Mrs Reid bequeathed 'for the promotion and improvement of female education' in 1860 (to come into operation after her death) stipulated that there should be at least three trustees, all of whom must be unmarried women, to administer the bequest.
>
> (Dyhouse, 1981: 63)

Aside from these new institutions, the movement to establish academically oriented schools for middle-class girls grew. Two very different schools were founded in the 1850s, the North London Collegiate and Cheltenham Ladies' College, the earliest proprietary girls' school in England. The first, founded in 1850 by Frances Buss (1827–94) was relatively unusual in having no class distinctions. The second, under the direction of Dorothea Beale (1831–1906), was highly selective. Both educators were early graduates of Queen's and Beale was actually on the college staff for seven years. The newly qualified Frances remodelled the North London Collegiate School along the lines of Queen's, offering an academic education at a moderate cost of nine guineas per annum

(Levine, 1987: 33). The close connections may be intimated by the appointment of Reverend David Laing as school superintendent. Laing was the secretary of the Governesses' Benevolent Institution and closely linked with Queen's, which was founded to train teachers and grant them certificates of proficiency. The Governesses' Benevolent Institution was formed in 1841 to grant annuities to aged governesses with no means of support, helping those in temporary financial difficulty and encouraging thrift among those who could afford to save.

In time the North London Collegiate became the forerunner of those schools for girls financed by the Girls' Public Day School Company (GPDSC), later the Girls' Public Day School Trust. The GPDSC was established in the summer of 1872 and by 1880 the company had opened 17 schools, with a total enrolment of over 2,800 girls (Ellsworth, 1979: 191). The great majority of these schools were determined to contest the idea that girls were biologically incapable of serious academic study, offering 'a sound, liberal education' that could lead to entry into the professions. Indeed the arguments advanced by Maria Grey, founder of the GPDSC, reveal the interacting dynamics of class and gender in this context:

> The Elementary Education Act provides for the girls of the lower classes equal advantages with the boys. But the ratepayers so heavily taxed for this provision, get no aid whatever in educating their own daughters according to their class in life, and are obliged to send them to private schools, the greater number of which give an education greatly inferior to thoroughness and value as mental training to the elementary schools.
>
> (*Journal of the Women's Educational Union*, 15 May 1875: 9–10, 24)

This argument was one with which most middle-class feminists sympathized. Maria Grey represented the views of many in articulating what amounts to a classically conservative framing of educational issues, where the stress is on social differentiation and an education suited to a person's station in life. Running for election to the first School Board for London, Mrs Grey was effusive in her support for the idea that a working-class education should include training in practical skills. Putting her case to a meeting of working men and women at the Cadogan Rooms on 28 November 1870, she argued that girls in particular should learn 'as their proper business, all the arts by which the wife and home can compete with the public-house' (Grey, 1871: 20). To what extent her attitude was representative of the attitudes adopted by women members of the London School Board remains to be seen.

1870–1885: Girls' education: an apprenticeship for domesticity?

The debate over curricular arrangements for working-class girls made apparent the problematic relationship between feminist thought and far more conventional views of womanhood. But to understand the complex interrelationship between gender, class and feminism, it is pertinent and useful to place members within the categories of ideological groups derived from the work of Raymond Williams (1965). Williams identifies three groups and ideologies that emerged most clearly in this period. The first group, the 'Public Educators', was composed of radical reformers like Thomas Huxley[1] and Benjamin Lucraft (see Chapter 3 notes), both of whom argued for expansionist educational policies. In contrast, the second group were proponents of educational policies based on economic arguments and sought to define education in terms of future adult work. A third group, the 'Old Humanists', argued that 'man's spiritual health depended on a kind of education which was more than a training for some specialised work, a kind variously defined as "liberal", "humane", or "cultural"' (Williams, 1965: 161). Nonetheless, as Williams concedes and this study shows, the public educators 'inevitably drew on the arguments of the defenders of the old liberal education, as a way of preventing universal education being narrowed to a system of preindustrial instruction' (1965: 162–3). The particular emphasis given to each or all of these three elements varies according to party politics, but connecting the ways in which different educational ideologies combine within the feminism of School Board women is integral to understanding their achievements.

Once assembled, the Board adopted a preliminary syllabus including basic reading, writing and arithmetic, plus needlework for girls, as well as morality and religion, music and drill. Yet within three months, members approved the appointment of a special committee, under the direction of Thomas Huxley, to devise a future programme of study and report back to the Board. In addition to the chairman, ordinary members included Emily Davies, William Green, Benjamin Lucraft and John 'Rob Roy' MacGregor. Named after the canoe he used to traverse foreign rivers, this larger than life character was immortalized by Thomas Gautrey for his action in presenting a local teacher, James Runciman, with a copy of his book – *A Thousand Miles in the Rob Roy Canoe*. MacGregor had just heard how the teacher had responded in kind when struck by an aggrieved father of a pupil at a school in his division, Greenwich. Indeed, the melodramatic Runciman subsequently inscribed the book 'Prize for Boxing' (Gautrey, n.d.: 57).

Meanwhile, the sub-committee held sixteen sittings, half of which were devoted to taking the evidence of experienced teachers – including Jane Chessar of the Home and Colonial Training College (see Chapters 3 and 4). Significantly, the curriculum planners went beyond the minimum mandated by the Education Department's codes. Huxley conceded the plan was ambitious and set forth what is 'desirable, rather than what is at present attainable' (SBL *Minutes*, 28 June 1871: 48). Hence during these first years, the syllabus in most schools followed the initial programme outlined above. Each pupil earned the same amount for successful examination performance (Weiner, 1994), but early moves to insist that older girls study household economy show that the sexes did not have access to a common curriculum. They also show the patronizing attitude of many men towards the women members.

The atmosphere is reflected in a series of clashes between William Green (another member of the Curriculum Sub-Committee) and Elizabeth Garrett Anderson on the issue. Moving an amendment to Green's motion that household economy be taught in the senior girls' schools, Garrett Anderson complained about the financial implications and practical difficulties. Substituting 'domestic economy' for the cooking and washing proposed by Green, Elizabeth asserted that the subject should be discretionary but that both girls and boys should be taught it. In her opinion the expense entailed in obtaining suitable premises, equipment and staff; the unnecessary wastage of food; the unlikelihood of people sending in clothes to be washed in the schools; and the risk of infection for children washing clothes – all were reasons for not teaching cooking and washing to the under-thirteens (*School Board Chronicle*, 1 July 1871: 198). Speaking a language of restraint and habit, she appealed to the liberal tenets of practical self-help to justify the teaching of domestic economy in a larger sense (including lessons on the need for fresh air, cleanliness and hygiene) as one of the ordinary lessons of the school. The themes of gender and class combine in a convincing political rationale enabling her to minimize the impact of gender differentiation, despite the misgivings of William Green. To the laughter of his colleagues, William admitted to having been frequently convinced by ladies but denied having been so that day. While they may have shared his sense of humour they did not endorse his opinion and Mrs Anderson's amendment was carried by 35 votes to 4.

Elizabeth Garrett Anderson did not object to the principle of working-class girls being taught cooking and washing *per se*, but rather to the age at which such instruction should begin. It is arguable that her prime concern was to avoid the devaluation of domestic skills. However, whilst her limited opposition to notions of subject–gender appropriateness within the Board school curriculum may encapsulate a positive conception of her sex's traditional activities within the home, it was a conception constructed within the context of class and gender power relations. The contrast between the efforts to provide new opportunities for middle-class girls and the kind of curriculum regarded as suitable for another section of the community, is the key to our understanding here. Liberal notions of equality were central to the feminist arguments of Emily Davies and Elizabeth Garrett. They both espoused an educational ideal that sought to reconcile academic excellence with ideas about a higher standard of middle-class womanhood. The new day high schools for middle-class girls adopted the curriculum ideas inherited from the public school tradition, yet compromised by stressing the benefits of education for the perpetuation of women's domestic roles. Overall, the particular emphasis given these aims and objectives may differ, but political manoeuvres at Board meetings reveal the impulse to repeat class and gender divisions in educational form.

The issue of subject–gender appropriateness was a recurring theme in the decision-making process regarding the selection, organization and distribution of educational knowledge. For instance, although John MacGregor, the Reverend Dr Miller and the Reverend J. Allanson Picton successfully argued that older girls and boys be taught book-keeping; mensuration was limited to senior boys. Further, while William Green worried that the Board would be made a 'laughing stock', analyses of exchanges over the teaching of freehand drawing show the way in which Thomas Huxley could deploy wit and sarcasm in order to assume an authoritative voice. As the *School Board Chronicle* records:

> Professor Huxley held it as an axiom that everybody might be taught to draw [...]
> it had not occurred to the committee that there were any particular reasons for
> excluding female children, whilst those who reflected on the employment of
> women might see that a certain elementary knowledge of art might be of use to
> them. He had just passed the office of a fashion journal, and as he looked at the
> drawings in the window he could not help reflecting that if women in general had
> a little more knowledge of art their attire would be more in accordance with aes-
> thetical principles than at present: but he would defer the judgment of the ladies
> who were members of the Board. (Laughter)
>
> (*School Board Chronicle*, 1 July 1871: 197)

Male members often disparaged their female colleagues, who faced certain difficulties against the 'dominant tone' of the men, but the reference to attire is
important as both women tried to avoid arousing hostility by conformity on the
question of dress. Emily Davies in particular engaged in a considerable amount
of stage management in her work for women's education, though Elizabeth
Anderson shared her views as to the importance of public relations.
Corresponding with Emily on the subject Elizabeth noted: 'I do wish, as
you said, the D's dressed better. She looks awfully strong-minded in walking
dress ... It is abominable, and most damaging to the cause ... I feel confident
now that one is helped rather than hindered by being as much like a lady as
lies in one's power' (quoted in Stephens, 1927: 59). Huxley's remarks presumably reflected his belief that as women's anatomy confined them to an inferior
position: 'The duty of man is to see that not a grain is piled upon that load
beyond what nature imposes; that injustice is not added to inequality' (*Reader*,
May 1865: 561–2). A critical William Green sought to exclude girls with the following illuminating comment:

> He could not help thinking that the Board was forgetting the class of children it
> had to educate and their necessities in after-life [...] what use would drawing be to
> girls, whose future occupation would probably be that of domestic servants or the
> wives of working men? He ventured to think that the only drawing such girls would
> require to know would be the 'drawing' of geese and other things for the table.
> (Laughter) [...] to educate girls in this way [...] would be to make them unfit for
> what some people chose to call the ordinary drudgery of every-day life. [...] Then
> there was the ratepayers' side of the question.
>
> (*School Board Chronicle*, 1 July 1871: 197)

In his speech Green combines a classic conservative statement epitomized by
the belief that schools should contribute to the maintenance of the status quo,
with concern about the level of the rates. Seeking to exert a very different influence from that of Huxley, Green promoted education in terms of training and
disciplining the poor as workers and citizens. By contrast, Huxley was clearly a
'Public Educator'. He argued that 'men had a natural human right to be educated and that any good society depended on governments accepting this principle as their duty' (Williams, 1965: 162). Including the 'Old Humanists',
Williams' model provides a framework for considering the educational philo-
sophies espoused by key individuals struggling to influence the process of curriculum development and change.

Thus Emily Davies counters the biological determinism of the next speaker, the Reverend Prebendary Thorold, with an argument combining vision with conventionality. Giving her reasons for voting in favour of the resolution and in opposition to Mr Green she argued that:

> drawing would not ... interfere with the essential subjects, because they were protected in some way or other – needlework, for instance, being amongst the subjects in girls' schools for which the Government grant was given [...] in the best girls' schools drawing was successfully taught without neglecting essential subjects, and she thought a practical experiment of this kind was worth a good deal of theorising. They would all agree with the last speaker that it was undesirable to make the education of girls such that it would discourage them from taking an interest on the daily duties of life; but she could hardly think that the way to make them take an interest in such matters was to make them entirely ignorant of everything else [...] what was wanted was to make the girls intelligent and capable of making their homes and their husbands comfortable, and of improving the present state of things which so often led the husbands to the public house. She thought education for girls should be a little wider and a little more interesting than it was at present.
>
> (*School Board Chronicle*, 1 July 1871: 197)

On other occasions Emily Davies placed pretty and docile-looking women at the front of public meetings called to discuss women's education. Here she uses the domestic vocation of the working-class girl as a conservative rationale for improving her schooling. Taking 'practical experience' rather than 'abstract theorising' for her thesis, she ensures the argument is based on rational formulations and cannot be dismissed as mere 'feminine' emotion. Far from expressing an educational philosophy which threatens the existing class and gender orders, the reasons cited in support of the resolution demonstrate that while there may be differences between the education policy statements of herself and William Green, their social aims were actually similar. Indeed Emily Davies always considered herself a conservative in politics and it is evident that both political affiliation and a moral authority grounded in the construction of positive class identity are essential to her warnings here.

By contrast, the working-class Benjamin Lucraft's expression of support for the resolution opposes the industrial arguments advanced by William Green and the more pragmatic response of Emily Davies. Aware of the inequalities of society, Benjamin Lucraft incorporates a demand for fairness with an elementary grass roots egalitarianism to convey a sense that education matters. He:

> hoped the Board would give the girls the same opportunity of learning drawing as the boys would have. If the Board were composed only of ladies, he felt sure they would vote for teaching the girls drawing, but seeing the Board was composed entirely of gentlemen, they voted in favour of their own sex. [...] He wanted to see the children of working men have an opportunity of rising, and he hoped the Board would get rid of all narrow views and strive to give the poor an education which should be on equality with other classes, otherwise the poor would have no opportunity of rising, and things would remain as they are.
>
> (*School Board Chronicle*, 1 July 1871: 197)

Benjamin Lucraft clearly wanted to prevent universal education being narrowed to a system of preindustrial training. It is accepted that schooling can offer routes to change, but he opposes the introduction of education policies tied to processes of class formation. Acknowledging the presence of gender antagonisms stemming from the composition of the Board, he infers that women members would uphold the solidarity of their sex over and above the barriers of class. Irrespective of whether the differences between Benjamin Lucraft and Emily Davies should be interpreted in terms of cultural difference, Lucraft maintained the stand he had adopted against further attempts to stultify the curriculum for working-class girls.

The debate was resurrected in 1889 and on this occasion Lucraft allied himself with another female member, Margaret Ashton Dilke, to challenge Board policy on the question of mechanical drawing. Although taught in all boys' departments, it was only taken in a few of the girls' schools and not necessarily as a subject for examination. Moreover, since government grant was paid on the basis of examination results, this was a significant distinction. By proposing that girls spend two hours a week on drawing Lucraft wanted to ensure it would become a grant-earning subject He achieved his goal and both Mrs Ashton Dilke and Mrs Maitland took the opportunity to attack the time devoted to needlework. The latter declared she would rather the Board fight the inspectors on this point than the girls spend less time on arithmetic and spelling as was permitted under the new code (*School Board Chronicle*, 1 June 1889: 562).

Making the most of opportunities to challenge the needlework requirements was a well-worn tactic among women Board members seeking room for manoeuvre within the restrictions of the Education Department's codes. All four women on the third Board supported Alice Westlake's motion that a deputation be sent to question the department over the time devoted to needlework in the new code of 1877, while in 1884 Florence Fenwick Miller headed a deputation from the London School Board that succeeded in getting the needlework requirements reduced (*School Board Chronicle*, 16 February 1884). Helen Taylor, Florence Fenwick Miller and Henrietta Muller all used their School Board position to publicize the subject's shortcomings. For example, while Henrietta was critical of the emphasis on needlework in schools in an 1879 electoral address (*South London Press*, 25 October 1879: 2), an extract from one of Florence's books reveals the strength of her feelings on the subject of unnecessary domestic work:

> Our sex's mute, inglorious Miltons, Shakespeares, and Bacons were smothered under the load of domestic labour. They were spinning and weaving, and planning and cutting, and laboriously stitch, stitch, stitching – needle pushed in and needle pulled out ... to make from the sheep's back or the linen yarn the finished garment for wear, all the clothing of mankind.
>
> (Miller, 1892: 96)

Thus from the earliest years needlework was regarded as a subject in which women members should interest themselves. This did not mean the men deferred to the women's judgement even when it was based on professional expertise.

Consequently the opposition from the two women members to plans to introduce cookery lessons for older girls in 1874 was not heeded, even though Jane Chessar based her opinion on twenty years' experience of teaching girls and was ably supported by her lay colleague, Alice Cowell. Addressing a meeting of headmistresses in 1877, Jane made her feelings on the issue clear:

> if one only had to do what was abstractly the best thing in education one would probably oppose the introduction of any industrial work into elementary schools at all, but, as teachers, they must carry out what was the desire of the Government and what appeared also to be the desire of the public.
>
> (*School Board Chronicle*, 3 March 1877: 243)

Whilst Jane's position is clearly distinguishable from that of the 'Industrial Trainers', her pragmatic response contains a kind of realism in the face of what she sees as public opposition and the actual structure and organization of elementary education.

Henceforth female opponents were to be placed on the defensive since the Education Department code of 1878 made domestic economy a compulsory subject for girls in state elementary schools. Undeterred, and with the support of Benjamin Lucraft and the trade unionist, George Potter,[2] Elizabeth Surr and Alice Westlake voiced their opposition to the use of purpose-built cookery centres for teaching practical cookery. These centres would entail female pupils physically leaving the school premises for a set period of time to receive lessons in cooking and cleaning, elementary hygiene and physiology, home nursing, and laundry work. However their different cultural backgrounds were exposed when Alice expressed the opinion that: 'the majority of the working-classes did not know how to make the best of cheap articles and how to cook their food to the best advantage'. To this Benjamin retorted: 'there was very little waste of food among the poor ... Mrs Westlake was not at all acquainted with the working classes or she would not argue in the way she did' (*School Board Chronicle*, 1 June 1878: 515).

But the next year Alice dropped all opposition to the scheme, although her claim that 'the cookery lessons were very popular' contradicts the findings of the special report compiled for the Education Department in 1896–97. Referring to the 1880s, it records that mothers frequently complained that their daughters 'wasted their time' in going to the cookery lessons. The Board's superintendent of cookery recalled: 'prejudice against it was almost insuperable, and parents put every possible obstacle in the way of their children attending the classes' (cited in Dyhouse, 1981: 90). Even that arch-exponent of cookery teaching, Rosamond Davenport Hill, was forced to admit that parental attitudes were mixed. Referring to the 'frivolous excuses' given for low attendance, she continues: 'the girls, [the parents] may remark, go to school to learn reading and writing; as for cooking they can learn it at home' (*Macmillans Magazine*, June 1884: 104). Both statements support the logic of Dena Attar's (1990) argument that the compulsory domestic economy syllabus was at best an irrelevance, at worst a tragic waste of time. Despite the imagery of rescue work taken over by the domestic economy reformers, it is worth remembering that the amount of practical cooking girls could do was severely restricted by cost, while the schemes of work set out in laundrywork textbooks were completely unrealistic in the context of the great majority of working-class homes (Attar, 1990: 45). The anomalies of power relations among girls and women are clearly expressed in the following extract from Julia Augusta Webster's discussion of the 1878 Domestic Economy Congress:

> As to teaching household processes in the elementary schools, for elementary education it certainly is an evil that girls whose only opportunities of intellectual training are those given them at these schools, and whose school career is necessarily timed to terminate while they are still children, should have a large portion of their school hours appropriated to household arts which could better be learned with opportunities of household practice. But, on the other hand, the evil of the common ignorance, slovenliness, and indifference as to these important home technicalities of working women is so great to themselves and to the nation that something must be sacrificed to impress them with a respect for housewifery.
>
> (Webster, 1879: 284)

Again, the contradiction reveals stronger social overtones, stressing the usefulness of this practical curriculum for working-class girls. But this statement represented only one point of view and the evidence suggests that the teaching of domestic subjects offered a clear expression of diagonal gender–class relations, with male working-class members supporting feminists of the middle class. Thus in 1878 George Potter allied himself with Florence Fenwick Miller, in a last ditch attempt at reducing the length of these classes. The two respectively moved and seconded an unsuccessful motion that cookery teaching start at 10.30 a.m. rather than 9.00 a.m. (*School Board Chronicle*, 11 November 1879).

Indeed far from encouraging the teaching of domestic subjects, most London School Board women struggled to minimize their impact on the education of working-class girls. The radical Helen Taylor, for one, deplored the fact that 'the girls were behind the boys in matters of learning ... because it was far more important for a woman to know how to count than to be able to use her needle' (*South London Chronicle and Lambeth Ensign*, 20 November 1880: 3). Even after cookery had been elevated to the status of a grant-paying subject (in 1882), she and Frances Hastings tried to modify the policy recommendations of the School Management Committee dealing with cookery. They proposed a cut in the number of lessons. But although five of the seven women members of the seventh Board supported these proposals, Alice Westlake and Rosamond Davenport Hill did not. Significantly both women belonged to what Florence Fenwick Miller referred to as the 'official ring', a 'party of members who voted for each other rather than for principles' (*School Board Chronicle*, 7 April 1883: 3). Largely composed of the chairs of the standing committees and those in their confidence, Fenwick Miller and her supporters argued that these members 'exercised an arbitrary authority, and gave no heed of suggestions or representations coming from outside the ring' (*School Board Chronicle*, 28 October 1882: 438). These comments also show the way in which some women members of the Board resented party discipline and a rigid allegiance to party. Among the Progressives, Mrs Miller developed into a major critic of her party leaders, adopting a very independent and feminist line. In this connection it is relevant to note that she and Elizabeth Garrett Anderson were said to have made 'admirable speeches, attacking and defending the so-called official ring during the 1882 elections' (*The Schoolmaster*, 28 October 1882: 475).

Nonetheless independent women teachers like Miss Thompson, the head teacher of Plumstead Road Board School, remained convinced that the 'evil' of 'over pressure' was intensified in girls' schools and that staff and pupils alike 'suffer in body and mind', (quoted in *The Schoolmaster*, 23 December 1882: 709). Operating outside the 'official ring', between 1883 and 1885 Hastings, Fenwick Miller, Muller and Taylor continued to challenge the extra demands imposed on girls. Despite their political differences, these women presented an undisguised gender solidarity and a sympathetic female commonality. Thus in November 1883 Florence Fenwick Miller proposed a reduction in the needle-work requirements in order to ease the pressure on girls and women teachers. These sentiments were warmly supported by the Moderate, Frances Hastings, who reasoned that the time wasted on needlework deprived girls of more nec-essary general knowledge. Male supporters included Benjamin Lucraft and T.H. Heller, one of the teachers' representatives. According to Heller, 'the lives of the female teachers were made at present simple slavery by the excessive demands upon them for preparing needlework out of schools hours and teaching it in school' (*The Governess*, 17 November 1883: 138). Four months later, Henrietta Muller responded to an external request that 'the attendance of girls at the cook-ery classes be not enforced' with a motion of her own. Once again Frances Hastings seconded the motion that the school management committee find out how many girls of what ages took cookery, and for how many hours, and also to 'consider whether Cookery properly speaking is an educational subject, and, further, whether it is suitable for young children of fourteen and under' (SBL *Minutes* 24 March 1884: 897). This move was blocked by other members and the women's effort to limit the growth of domestic instruction failed. But unlike Emily Davies and Elizabeth Garrett in the early years, Florence Miller clearly deprecated the class differentiation that shaped debates over the development of a distinctive working-class curriculum. As she pleaded with the readers of *The Governess* in one of the many articles she wrote on the subject: 'While the women of the upper classes are claiming equal intellectual opportunities with their brothers for themselves, are the women of the artisan classes to be perma-nently relegated to a position of female inferiority of educational advantages? And if so, why?' (5 May 1884: 228).

Essentially her opposition was futile so long as the majority of Board mem-bers shared the attitude of the Victorian male establishment towards school gen-der training and sexual divisions in the labour force. It does show the struggle to define what counts as school knowledge. Certainly there was an element of resistance to the dominant definitions of a sex specific education. Clearly it is important to acknowledge and seek to understand the involvement of women in accounting for the rise of the domestic subjects, but the evidence suggests it would be partial to see women and girls as its passive victims. As the debate detailed here suggests, minority groups can always produce a counter hegemony which is truly oppositional and cannot be incorporated into the dominant culture. It was this possibility that made the expansion of girls-only classes in domestic subjects a site of tension between proponents of the alternative views.

The question of an alternative form of education for girls brought conflicts and problems for female members. If rejection of the idea of sexual difference was crucial to the concept of a feminist tradition, Rosamond Davenport Hill would probably not be given that label. Women spoke with different voices and this presents a challenge to any notion of a single kind of feminism. So, whilst these political activists were self-conscious of their efforts to build new opportunities for women, it should be remembered that they also shaped their own response to specific education policies against a social thought preoccupied with the need to train or discipline the poor into an independent and self-maintaining existence.

The case of Rosamond Davenport Hill

Having settled in Hampstead with her sister, Florence, Rosamond Davenport Hill was elected as a Progressive member of the School Board on 5 December 1879. Previously based in Bristol, Rosamond and her two sisters (Joanna and Florence), took part in the struggles for the creation of the industrial and reform schools in the mid-nineteenth century, working alongside their father and Mary Carpenter in the movement for educational and criminal law reform. At the time of her election to the Board Rosamond was a well-known figure in social reform circles and an acknowledged expert in the treatment of wayward girls and women. Both father and daughters were early supporters of female suffrage (see Chapters 3 and 4) and Rosamond and Florence were among the prominent mid-Victorian feminists who opposed close connections between party politics and the suffrage campaigns in the 1880s. They also shared the class preoccupations prominent in reform circles, as evidenced by Rosamond's restrictive perspective on adult suffrage, as well as her views on education reform. She clearly accepted the conventional mid-Victorian view of woman's role and argued from within the paradigm of separate spheres to fulfil her role as social leader.

As a representative of the City, with its small resident population and single Board School, Rosamond had a light load of local work, which left more time to build a formidable reputation as an educational administrator which, Frederick Dolman explained, 'was second to that of none of her male colleagues' (1896: 129). In 1882 she was put in charge of the newly formed sub-committee responsible for cookery, laundry and needlework instruction (renamed the Domestic Subjects Committee in 1896). She is generally credited with administering the huge expansion in the teaching of domestic subjects during the 1880s and 1890s. Under her control and influence, for example, the Board established 140 cookery centres and 50 centres for laundry work. As a result, Henrietta Muller considered her 'a strong partisan and supporter of the School

Board policy' but 'not a friend of woman' (*Women's Penny Paper*, 24 November 1888: 1). By contrast, the journalist Charles Morley singled out the restorative potential of this teaching which he considered the 'birthright' of the daughters of the poor. Describing his visit to the four-roomed house in Bethnal Green where girls were taught how to cook and clean, as well as the values of thrift and self-sacrifice, Morley was fulsome in his praise for what he liked to call the 'school for the raising of the standard of the workers' homes' (*Studies in Board Schools*, 1897: 138).

Embracing the charitable with the policing impulse, Rosamond's educational philosophy reflected a firm belief in the value of really 'useful' knowledge, combined with conventional class and gender stereotypes. Within this framework of ideas, state funding for teaching girls domestic economy is presented as:

> a beneficent concession as regards the miserable dwellers in the slums of our metropolis ... knowledge which will enable these poor children to command somewhat higher wages than otherwise, as mere drudges, they could hope to obtain is of greater value to them than even a competent knowledge of the 3R's.
>
> (*Macmillans Magazine*, June 1884 : 99)

Here we see a clear enunciation of her belief in the reformative capacity of education. Such instruction would enable the girls to command higher wages, to maintain their independence from the state and to effectively combat the thriftless ignorance she considered to be the main source of poverty and of crime. As an 'Industrial Trainer', Rosamond promoted education in terms of preparing pupils for their future vocation as workers and citizens. For working-class girls this amounted to lessons in the rudiments of housework to inculcate a sense of individual responsibility and service to home and family. Fear of foreign competition – couched in the language of national efficiency – underpinned her support for the provision of a generalized technical education through the teaching of specific handicraft skills thought suitable for one sex only.

On the Board, she earned the nickname of the 'silent member', for Rosamond seldom spoke and was renowned for her habit of knitting during the debates. In the 1890s, Thomas Gautrey (n.d.: 56) recalls that this activity was ruled 'out of order', although the chairman relented after other members appealed on her behalf! When her continued silence also provoked a reprimand Rosamond was said to have retorted that it was the first time she had heard a woman blamed for holding her tongue. Nonetheless, the great majority of her male colleagues clearly felt more comfortable working with a woman in whom one can discern a tendency towards conformity with conventional femininity than the distinctly unconventional trio of Florence Fenwick Miller, Henrietta Muller and Helen Taylor. Significantly, Rosamond was one of a quintet of women whom contemporaries frequently depicted as the ideal type of a 'lady member'. All five were consistent supporters of the Progressive party. But while Rosamond Davenport Hill, Margaret Eve, Ruth Homan and Alice Westlake all gave special interest to girls' subjects, Emma Maitland consciously spread her work over a larger sphere, so that she might offer a woman's point of view on all aspects of the

Board's work. Interestingly, Ruth Homan consistently presented herself as a professional woman and it was she who succeeded Rosamond as chair of the Domestic Subjects Committee in 1897. Interviewed by Margaret Bateson in the 1890s for the book she was editing on the world of female professionalism, Ruth presents school board work as a new profession for women. Consequently, the final section explores the extent of women's support for domestic subjects and the consequences and effects of these social practices on the cultural categories, languages, images and ideas used to describe the value of woman's work on such a body as the School Board.

1886–1904: The wholesome art of housewifery

Having played a role as intermittent volunteer at a club for women teachers in the East End of London, Ruth Homan took the first step towards electoral office by becoming a school manager in Chelsea in 1887. The second step was to extend her knowledge of cookery, health and hygiene in order to equip herself for supervising an increasingly complex and differentiated curriculum for girls. Finally, her work for the Children's Country Holiday Fund gave her a personal acquaintance with the lives of the poor. Standing as a Progressive in Annie Besant's division of Tower Hamlets, Ruth took the unusual decision to leave her comfortable home in Kensington and take up lodgings in her constituency for the duration of the 1891 campaign. She not only headed the poll at a time when no other Progressive candidate occupied that position, but succeeded in polling more votes than any other woman candidate had previously done (Dolman, 1896: 130). According to one contemporary editorial, Ruth Homan represented the essence of the public spirited women offering themselves for service on behalf of poor and neglected children. In this stereotype she is projected as a 'type of her sister members', able to speak with an authoritative voice on the theme of service and domesticity because:

> few homes are so well organised as that over which she presides at Kensington. Every morning at half-past eight she arranges the duties for the day of her servant, breakfast having been served half-an-hour earlier. At half-past nine she is free to take her share of the work of the Board, whether she happens to be visiting any of the fifteen schools in Tower Hamlets under her supervision, answering letters sent by teachers, attending committee meetings, or visiting some industrial or house-wifery centre.
>
> (Morrison, 1897: 36)

Social class is crucial here. Ruth's status as scientific household manager is very different from the ideal of practical housekeeper upheld for working-class girls in the educational policies she was instrumental in framing. There was no expectation on Ruth to perform such domestic tasks as cooking and washing. She occupied the privileged position of being able to organize the manual labour of others. Indeed, it was this ability to employ substitute female labour that left her free to earn a reputation as an 'able and conscientious London School Board member' (Bateson, 1895: 48). Obviously this also raises the possibility of self-interest, for in some quarters the teaching of domestic subjects was intended to meet the concerns of employers worried about the apparent shortage of trained and contented servants (Attar, 1990). But whatever her own point of view, Ruth was an elected public servant and, unlike the domestic servants in her employ, she was depicted as a professional woman. Her cultural capital derived from social class position underpinning this combination of voluntary effort and professional label. In command of the cultural resources of education and time, the imagery of virtuous domesticity was particularly helpful to middle-class feminists like Ruth Homan who used their existing skills and interests as a way of moving into the public sphere.

Having completed a course in artisan scullery and cooking lessons at the South Kensington School of Cookery, Ruth consistently promoted domestic subjects, particularly encouraging the specialist teaching of practical housewifery. According to Millicent Morrison, who interviewed Ruth Homan before the School Board elections in 1897, the prevailing sentiment among working-class parents was one of gratitude. Yet, even if many parents welcomed more instruction of this kind, it seems that some thought the teaching derogatory and this generated a spirit of unrest which added to the problem of maintaining discipline and keeping the girls on task. At such times, the women members (Eve, Hill, Homan and Maitland) would, 'either singly or together, sail forth to cast oil upon the troubled waters. However, a chat with the children, especially if it is explained that they are being taught domestic *science*, usually has the desired effect' (Fawcett Library, Newscuttings, 'School Boards': 36). But despite the energetic and enthusiastic support for the development of gendered subjects on the part of Ruth Homan, Honnor Morten later expressed reservations. She argued that girls were made to specialize too early with the result that other subjects got neglected. She continued:

> There are a very large number of women on the School Boards now, and they ought to make their motto, 'Thorough grounding for the girls'. Unfortunately, it is the women members who so often press domestic economy lessons on babies, it being the thing of which they themselves have a little knowledge.
>
> (Morten, 1899a: 18)

As Honnor implies, support for the domestic curriculum enabled women Board members to extend their sphere of influence on the basis of their alleged 'expertise'. However, it is also important to remember the social and political contexts in which these women were working. As earlier studies on the content of working-class education have shown,[3] the number of recruits declared unfit for call-up in the Boer War (1899–1902) aroused fears about the health of the nation and the issue of 'national efficiency' took on a new importance in public discussion. Concern about the quality of maternal care enabled women members to develop a power base for themselves within what Thomas Gautrey referred to as the 'aggressive' domestic subjects sub-committee. This had been brought to the fore in 1883, when Gautrey objected to proposals for a long new syllabus of instruction in Home Economy on the grounds that the 'essential subjects' were being 'driven out of girls' schools' (*The Board Teacher*, 1 July 1889: 168).

But although Honnor Morten complained that the education of the girls stopped short compared with that of the boys, it appears that the teaching of domestic subjects for working-class girls was largely unchallenged by women members during the final years of the Board's existence. The elementary school curriculum which evolved during the nineteenth and early twentieth centuries is therefore seen as one which sought both classed and gendered cultural control. The fact that it was mainly girls who were taught to cook and clean reflects an uneasy compromise between the different educational ideologies espoused by the three groups identified by Raymond Williams and the social patterning of gender. While 'Industrial Trainers' stressed the need for training and discipline, within the populist ideology of the 'Public Educators' the way was clear for presenting the case in terms of the girls' dual location as working wives and mothers. Reminiscent of the 'Old Humanists' emphasis on character, others justified notions of subject–gender appropriateness by reference to women's 'special' role as 'moral' guardians of family life.

Advocates like Rosamond Davenport Hill stressed the need to develop all aspects of the child's personality by a combination of mental and manual training. She pressed for the introduction of practical studies relevant to the child's future occupation as conceptualized within the existing status quo. Furthermore, schooling working-class girls to be domestic servants and practical housewives conformed to the philanthropic conception of middle-class women's duties they brought to local educational politics. Thus, in 1897, Ellen McKee made the move from Poor Law Guardian in Holborn to representing the City as Rosamond Davenport Hill's successor both in temperament and politics. Following in Rosamond's footsteps, Ellen avidly supported the domestic curriculum her predecessor had helped to expand.

Whether supporters or detractors of the domestic curriculum, assertive and principled women representatives sought to minimize the element of gender differentiation involved. For instance, at the turn of the century Emma Maitland moved that boys be taught cookery on an experimental basis. She put the case that this would be useful to boys likely to become sailors or soldiers. Despite the derision with which it was greeted by some, the proposal was defeated by only a single vote. This interest in cookery as a vocational subject drew attention to national policy. For unlike the School Board, the Board of Education subsequently gave boys living in seaport towns a special dispensation to attend cookery classes (Yoxall, 1914: 49). Predictably, exhortations about the domestic ideal had no place in the new masculine courses, where the emphasis was on paid employment in a specific context.

Conclusion

In this chapter I have used Raymond Williams' typology to show the process by which particular forms of knowledge came to be included in the elementary school curriculum. The expansion of the domestic curriculum for working-class girls reflected an uneasy compromise between groups holding different economic, political and cultural resources and struggling to attain influence in the education system. As the element of resistance both inside and outside the Board makes clear, this development did not go unchallenged.

Women members were keen to press a distinctive women's line in School Board politics. In accordance with this view, the education of girls occupied a large part of the women members' contributions to debate. As one might expect, the domestic curriculum was an area where London School Board women could claim special knowledge and interests. Although the most frequent speakers were those who had become very active as opponents, at the other extreme there were few interventions by Margaret Anne Eve, Rosamond Davenport Hill and Ellen McKee. Not surprisingly, loyalty to the Progressive party line was instrumental in the promotion of Eve, Davenport Hill, Homan, McKee and Westlake to positions of power in the Board's administrative machinery. Nevertheless, both they and the outspoken critics of Board policy on the issue (Chessar, Cowell, Davies, Dilke, Garrett Anderson, Hastings, Maitland, Fenwick Miller, Morten, Muller, Taylor and Surr), deployed conventional ideas about women's domestic skills to articulate their differing demands. But their different voices are indicative of contradictions underpinning power relations among women. For whereas the quintet of female supporters used the disciplining and protective language of motherhood (Yeo, 1992; 1995), the critics offered images of sisterhood to constrain the overweening emphasis on domesticity.

However outnumbered, certain of the 'ladies at the Board' did produce a counter-hegemony that manifested itself in a resistance to a narrowing of working-class girls' educational opportunities. Essentially the presence of women Board members ensured that what was deemed 'a woman's question' remained on the agenda, irrespective of the ultimate fate of these strategies for educational change. As *The Governess* reported, after the Board spent nearly two hours debating the issue of 'over pressure' in relation to school needlework:

> The gentlemen did it with very bad grace, showing plainly that they would never have bothered about Needlework if they had not been compelled by the ladies at the Board. The subject was brought before them by Mrs Fenwick Miller, who was seconded by Miss Hastings, and supported by Miss Muller. The motion was that the School Management Committee should be instructed to consider what steps could be taken to diminish the over-pressure in Girls' Schools, caused by the time spent on Needlework. Mrs Fenwick Miller said that she had a return made to her by the teachers, from which she found that four hours and twenty minutes weekly, on average, was spent in the girls' schools on this subject. ... The result of this was that the girls were practically expected to learn as much as the boys in every four hours and forty minutes, as the boys are in every five hours and thirty minutes spent in school.
>
> (*The Governess*, 17 November 1883: 138)

Sensitive to the social and political context in which the debate took place, Florence qualifies her remarks with the comment that while she 'would be sorry to exclude either cookery, needlework or drawing from the schools, some limitation was wanted'. Clara Grant, one of London's women head teachers, would undoubtedly have agreed with her about the last point. In a sarcastic outburst against the declamations of Mrs Floyer, Examiner of Needlework, Clara publicized the ways in which this woman's enthusiasm for the subject knew no bounds.

According to Floyer, needlework could form the basis of lessons in drawing, spelling and writing and, if all else failed, on school days hampered by either poor light or hot weather, there was '"NEEDLE DRILL WITHOUT THE COTTON! KNITTING DRILL WITHOUT THE WOOL!" How good for the ratepayers!' (Grant, 1929: 48–9). However the obsession with drill also permeated the teaching of cookery. As Charles Morley observed during one of his forays into London's cookery centres, the practical component of the lesson concluded with pinafore drill, at which point 'little cooks stood in Indian file. At the word of command each one unlaced her neighbour's; each one folded her own up; each one took it to the locker' (1897: 133).

But although they may not have shared Mrs Floyer's proselytizing zeal, the issue of domestic subjects assumed a high profile for the majority of London School Board women. Obviously the elementary curriculum they helped shape points to the links between the distribution of educational knowledge and the gendered patterns of segregated labour markets. At the same time, the fact that many felt constrained to accommodate their behaviour to expectations about gender may explain why they generally adopted a more conciliatory tone than the daughter of the American feminist Elizabeth Cady Stanton, Mrs Harriot Stanton Blatch, who told an audience at the all-female Pioneer Club that she 'gave her life to the work of fighting down the idea that the only place for women was home' (*Shafts*, June 1895: 35–6).

Notes

1. Thomas Henry Huxley (1825–95), born Ealing, Middlesex. Studied medicine at Charing Cross Hospital. Fellow of the Royal Society and foremost exponent of Darwin's theory of evolution, Huxley was variously employed as assistant surgeon on *HMS Rattlesnake* (1846–50), Professor of Natural History at the Royal School of Mines (1854) and principal of the South London Working Men's College (1868). The author of a number of essays on theology and philosophy written from an 'agnostic' viewpoint, Huxley sat on several Royal Commissions and was perhaps the most influential exponent of the view that both scientific and literary studies were essential to an all-round education.

2. George Potter (1832–93), born at Kenilworth in Warwickshire, self-educated, apprenticed to a carpenter at Coventry. Came to London in 1854, member of the Progressive Society of Carpenters, prominent in the London Builders' strike of 1859. Ran an influential labour paper in London, *The Bee-Hive*, to encourage strikes in provinces. Organized the Conference of Trades in the summer of 1864, as president of the London Working Men's Association he opened the Trades Union Congress in 1868. Represented Westminster on the London School Board, 1873–82. Succeeded in getting a committee appointed, with Benjamin Lucraft as chairman, to enquire into endowments in the London School Board area which might (or should) be applied to education. From

the evidence produced in this and subsequent reports it became clear that substantial funds were being diverted from their proper purpose, a fact that Helen Taylor put to good use when calling for the abolition of school fees. Unsuccessfully contested the parliamentary seats of Peterborough in 1874 and Preston in 1886.

3. See, for example, Davin, 1978, 'Imperialism and motherhood', *History Workshop*, 5(1): 9–67; Dyhouse, 1976, 'Social Darwinistic ideas and the development of women's education in England, 1880–1920', *History of Education*, 5(1), 41–59, 'Good wives and little mothers: social anxieties and the schoolgirls' curriculum, 1977, *Oxford Review of Education*, 3(1) 1977: 21-35 and 'Working-class mothers and infant mortality in England, 1895–1914', 1979, *Journal of Social History*, 252–7. The subject is also examined in Dyhouse, 1981.

6 'The True Elements and Conditions of Warfare in Public Life': The Experience of Elizabeth Surr

Introduction

The previous chapter explained the process by which participation in the expansion of the domestic curriculum enabled some female Board members to develop an area of expertise upon which to build a power base. This chapter considers the extent to which the issue of industrial school management may also be seen as an emergent policy area for women. Clearly female representatives adapted to the mixed public arena of School Board politics in a variety of ways, ranging from strong partisan support for specific 'party' policies to the enunciation of a firm belief in the need to uphold the solidarity of their gender. During the late 1870s and early 1880s the London School Board was the focus of a series of allegations concerning the administration of industrial schools. Because female Board members played a key role, the controversy forms an obvious context within which to explore the conflicts faced by women in positions of authority in the late nineteenth century.

Focusing upon their contradictory experience at Board and committee meetings, this chapter considers how, and to what extent, women were able to exert power, authority and control through an analysis of two very different sets of power relations. First, there were the changes to relations between the home and the school considered in terms of the theme of compulsion. Second, there were the relations between School Board women, both as individuals and as colleagues working in a male-dominated political environment. The fact that education was a field in which women began to engage in public activity in the latter years of the nineteenth century, suggests a transfer of the authority and influence exercised by women in the private world of the home to the public arena of the Board.

The issue of industrial schools is especially pertinent here. State recognition of reformatory and industrial schools not only marked a radical change in penal policy, but involved the assertion of new powers of state intervention in parent–child relationships. As Margaret May (1981) has shown, the segregation of the neglected and ill-behaved child was one result of the growth of a system of public education which provided only for the more tractable and fee-paying working class. It also reflected a system of public assistance that made no direct provision for child neglect.

The notion of compulsion

Since the 1870 Act permitted school boards to make their own bye-laws relating to school attendance and to appoint attendance officers to pursue those evading the regulations, one of the first tasks facing the newly elected London Board was to decide how to make use of its powers to make attendance compulsory. Despite a public opinion in large part hostile to compulsion, lack of schools, and a small and inexperienced administration, London's own education scheme was already in place by 1871, a decade before that in many other parts of the country. Section 74 of the Act made mandatory a system of half- and full-time exemption for children aged ten to thirteen and the new London bye-laws kept children at school at least half-time until the age of thirteen, although London's legal school-leaving age had reached fourteen by the turn of the century. To qualify as a half-time scholar a child had to show that (s)he was 'beneficially and necessarily at work' which would reduce attendance to 10 out of 25 hours. This requirement was increased in 1879, when it literally became half-time, with children required to make five out of the ten weekly attendances.

Because many of the London trades had a high incidence of cyclical unemployment, fluctuating though always constrained economic circumstances ensured that the employment of children remained an essential part of the lives of the very poor. The 1833 Factory Act only prohibited the employment of children under nine in factories and textile mills, but despite provisions for government inspection, evasion was widespread. For a factory inspector attempting to cover East London it was like looking for a needle in a haystack amongst the multitude of small workshops and sweating dens making ample use of such cheap labour. The situation was exacerbated since the Poor Law Amendment Act (1834) was designed to make certain that nobody in receipt of relief was at any possible advantage over those who were in some kind of work. According to John Hurt, the principle of less eligibility meant that:

> The independent poor had been caught by the nineteenth-century version of the poverty trap. They were not so poor that they had to look to the poor law guardians for succour. On the other hand they were poor enough to have to send their children to work to avoid the poorhouse.
>
> (Hurt, 1979: 36)

Material hardship was compounded by the fact that board schools were legally obliged to charge fees (up to a maximum of 9d a week) and could only remit fees for a period of up to six months if parents pleaded poverty. In London, school fees averaged 2d a week, although families with more than one child attending the same school only paid half, unless it was a penny school. But despite the size of the fines imposed in the event of a successful prosecution for non-attendance, parents could often gain more money from their children's employment than they lost through fines.[1] Admittedly the chance of a successful prosecution was rare since the opposition of Police Court magistrates meant that it was common practice to simply issue attendance orders or to adjourn cases for a period to see if attendance improved (Philpott, 1904: 93–7). Journalists also exploited the popular anti-compulsion prejudice by publishing sensational and biased reports of school board cases (see Rubinstein, 1969).

School absenteeism was especially marked amongst girls. Not only was their average attendance consistently lower than that of boys, it was also more irregular, due to the fact that they were often expected to help at home with other younger children on wash days and if their mother worked, was ill or having a baby. Lessons on home economy and mothering led some mothers to question the value of the education their daughters were receiving and the obvious response was to keep them at home. Social and cultural values were reflected in a tendency for girl absentees to be treated sympathetically, while boys' non-attendance was defined as truancy and severely dealt with (see Davin, 1996). As a consequence, George Bartley informed readers of the journal published by the Women's Educational Union that many authorities were applying double standards when dealing with truancy in this period. See, for example:

> the authorities of the School Boards are severer in the case of boys absenting themselves from school than they are with girls. A sort of innate feeling, indeed, exists that school after all is more important to the boy than to the girl, so that if one must stay at home, of course it must be the girl, consequently we feel that the ill-effects of this evil, of a want of regularity of attendance will fall unevenly on the two sexes of the community.

> (Bartley, 15 May 1875: 98)

In simple terms what was new about the legislation of the 1870s was the extent of its operation. State-provided schooling required of the working classes something new and different, that is that their children should compulsorily attend an institution quite separate from a place of work or their home. As such it effectively accentuates the double edged element of power underpinning relations between those in authority and those over whom they wielded that authority – the working-class parental consumer and the child client.

For many of those living in poverty, the issue of compulsion was more than a bone of contention shaping their relations with the Board. It was one that highlighted the inability of these predominantly upper-middle-class agents to comprehend the social realities structuring working-class daily life. Yet as Phil Gardner (1984) has argued, the depth and resilience of independent educational activity shows that the working classes were not hostile to, or apathetic about, elementary education *per se*. What many resented was the imposition of publicly sponsored elementary schooling which, unlike the popular working-class educational system that predated and existed outside any state apparatus, was not attuned in personnel, in atmosphere and in organization, to the demands of working-class culture. As the depth and resilience of independent educational activity reveals, the main attraction of popular schooling was that it 'offered an open-ended flexibility in patterns of pupil attendance' (Gardner, 1991: 72). School hours were nominal and though fees were considerably higher than in either the denominational systems or the board schools, working-class private schools were far more flexible on the issue of non-payment.

By contrast, for educational reformers, the introduction of universal, state-funded elementary education was to provide the means of establishing the proper socialization of the working-class child. Just like the nineteenth-century reformers whom Anthony Platt (1969) collectively labelled 'the child-savers', the great majority were impressed by the need to repress, reform and rehabilitate specific social categories of children. Certainly such attitudes were further reinforced by subsequent contact with the social practices of working-class childhoods (see also Clarke, 1975; Gorham, 1978). Hence Board members were generally agreed that the absence of proper parental care was most to blame for absenteeism.

Challenging such moralistic explanations, Stephen Humphries offers an alternative, class-based interpretation. This is clearly seen in his analysis of mass schooling as part of a complex process of class conflict. Humphries sees this as involving the resistance of working-class youth to powerful attempts to inculcate conformist modes of behaviour through various bourgeois agencies of control, manipulation and exploitation. Citing truancy as an example of resistance behaviour or 'the persistent rule-breaking and opposition to authority characteristic of working-class youth culture that has traditionally been viewed as indiscipline or delinquency', Humphries (1981: 63) identifies three principal forms of irregular attendance in the early twentieth century: opportunist, retreatist and subsistence. Whereas opportunists only took the occasional day off, retreatist and subsistence truancy tended to be incessant and deeply ingrained. Essentially provoked by a sense of alienation to the form and content of board school education and the poverty and social deprivation which created the necessity for subsistence truancy in the first place, it is the latter two forms which are of relevance here.

It is arguable that such a framework provides a somewhat romanticized account wherein all oppositional behaviour is defined as resistance behaviour. Nonetheless Humphries' use of oral interviews does have the merit of giving a voice to a handful of those working-class children burdened by the implications of Forster's Bill:

> In the words of Bristolian Tom Radway, who occasionally truanted from school in the 1900s: 'We'd always be on the look-out for coppers on the beat or attendance officers on their bikes. They really put the fear of God in you 'cos they did the dirty work that had you sent to industrial school.'
>
> (Humphries, 1981: 69)

However, as this chapter will seek to demonstrate, it is too simplistic to interpret the phenomenon of irregular attendance in terms of straightforward cultural resistance to class-based repression. As John Hurt (1979: 212) so succinctly points out: 'Parental attitudes were determined largely on practical, knife and fork criteria,' making a rejection thesis based on political ideology hard to sustain.

Routine home visiting was essential to the process of securing compliance between family and school, and local attendance officers (or 'visitors') were to play a key role. A distinguishing feature of Victorian philanthropic efforts was the largely female practice of visiting the poor and the Board took the view that these officers should be women with experience in similar work (LSB Minutes, 28 June 1871: 172–5). There were three reasons for this. First, members thought women would be more likely to influence the mothers. Thus Emily Davies and Elizabeth Garrett wanted more women to be employed as visitors and put the case that the bulk of their work would entail dealing with mothers and considering excuses like lack of clothes and domestic difficulties. Second, it was thought that women were less likely to excite parental resistance. Finally, they were cheaper. The men were paid £80 per annum. In contrast, the women visitors were paid about a pound a week. Nonetheless, by 1873, there were only 17 women visitors out of a total staff of 116 paid officers (Report of the Bye-Laws Committee, 28 March 1873). In general, visitors were working-class men with a military background who may have been thicker-skinned than their female counterparts. They certainly needed to be. The former teacher Thomas Gautrey recalled his school's visitor of the 1870s having had a dead cat dropped on him from an upper window as he walked to work. In the opinion of John Reeves, a school visitor in London during the same period, it was the visitors who faced the most difficult task of 'enlightening the parents' (Reeves, c. 1915: 13). It would seem that W.E. Forster MP, agreed with him. Commending their work at the public opening of a London Board School he told his audience that attendance officers "'are entitled to have MP, after their names" as he regarded them as moral Policemen' (Reeves, c. 1915: 12–13).

Visitors were appointed to ensure that elementary children attended school with regularity. They kept a record of the relevant names and addresses and the schools they were expected to attend, as well as the names of children who were receiving instruction elsewhere and those who were absent, together with the reason for their non-attendance.[2] In addition, the street raid was another weapon at the disposal of the school authorities. Hugh Philpott, a contemporary chronicler of London education, recalls that these were occasions 'when all the visitors of the division, fifty or sixty in number, will spend a day in the streets interrogating the children whom they find there during school hours' (1904: 90). Moreover the appointment of 15 'street visitors' to look after children of the 'street Arab type' indicates the tension between care and coercion. Visitors were instructed to report any infringement of the bye-laws to a local committee, composed partly of members of the Board and partly of other inhabitants or ratepayers of that division. As a result, a formal written warning called an 'A' notice was served on the parent of the absentee requiring him [*sic*] to make the child attend school either full- or half-time. Alternatively, if there was a reasonable excuse, he [*sic*] could attend a meeting when the excuse would be considered (see Spalding, 1900: 124–32). In the words of Henrietta Muller:

> The Committee is composed of a few Board School managers (ladies and gentlemen, with sometimes a working man or two interested in education or philanthropy), nominated by the divisional representative, who, although himself an ex-officio member of the meeting, rarely finds time to attend it. Before this tribunal the parents of the children appear, and it is not uncommon for as many as seventy or eighty to be seen in one evening.
>
> (*Westminster Review*, January 1888: 703)

Predictably, despite Spalding's persistent use of the male gender, the parent was invariably female. Philpott (1904: 91) saw these as rather sorry occasions that were attended by a 'stream of tired looking mothers with an occasional father'. According to Muller, disease and weather were probably the most common explanations for low attendance, but mothers offered a variety of common obstacles: 'no boots', 'sickness in the family' and, in the case of girls, their use as 'baby-minders' (Muller, 1888: 703–4). More importantly, she herself was highly critical of the lack of uniformity in the administration of the compulsory clauses and used Board data to support her case. Drawing attention to the figures collated for the nine months ending March 1887, she concludes her analysis by noting that 'the great difference in numbers can only arise from the different views of the proper workings of the Act taken in these centres' (*Westminster Review*, January 1888: 704). The respective figures for each division were five children excused out of an elementary school population of 69,965 in Chelsea, six out of 94,320 elementary school children in Finsbury, 163 out of 49,182 children in Southwark, and 261 out of a school population of 99,366 in Tower Hamlets.

Ultimately, if all methods of persuasion failed, the Board had little choice but to issue a police court summons, a procedure which might eventually lead to the child's committal to one of two types of corrective institutions. The first category consisted of residential schools. Of these, truant schools were meant for persistent absentees whose attendance was unlikely to improve without a spell under strict supervision. In contrast, industrial schools contained children whose truancy was combined with homelessness, frequenting the company of criminals or beggars, being out of parental control, or otherwise in need of care and protection. As a result, some were the victims of 'unfit' parents reported by the Society for the Prevention of Cruelty to Children. Summoned to give evidence before the Departmental Committee on Reformatory and Industrial Schools in 1896, Rosamond Davenport Hill gave details of one small boy under seven years old then held in Brentwood Industrial School. The child had a huge scar on his shoulder sustained when his mother threw him on to the fire and, although the mother was sent to prison, she would have been able to reclaim him if the education authorities had not taken him into official custody. Consequently Rosamond had a very low opinion of the parents themselves. Parent–child communications were restricted to one institutional visit in three months. When pressed as to whether, if she were a mother, she would like her access restricted, these interchanges show that she had no qualms over the efficacy of her methods:

> If I were a mother, very much attached to my child, and had taken great care of it, I should not like at all to be separated from it; but many of these parents do not seem to care much about their children; they will take no notice of them in the school until the latter are about to leave, when they can earn money. Then the parents appear, and if they can, drag them back into their wretched homes.
>
> (*Report*, 1896: 528–9)

Obviously Rosamond represented the views of many in her bitter reaction to children working which, in tandem with the notions of childish innocence and dependence, were important elements in the moral regulation of the young (see May, 1973). On the whole, middle-class ideologies of a responsible Christian family life were juxtaposed with visions of families sunk in ignorance and vice, and the school authorities were unlikely to question their right to intervene. In the words of a School Board visitor who worked in the Boundary Street area of Bethnal Green during the 1870s:

> The whole moral tone was inconceivably low. ... There was scarcely a family but appeared to have some reason for fearing the police, and a large proportion of the men were on 'ticket to leave' ... Pickpockets, burglars, dog-stealers, and pugilists here abounded. They might frequently be observed examining their tools on the window sills, and practising robbery from upper windows. ... The children's lives were a constant round of sunless drudgery – they never played as children play, they never seemed even to think; they were prematurely old, and the victims of an awful cruelty. They worked at matchbox making many hours, and at other times assisted their parents in disposing of their wares in the streets. The mortality among the young children was appalling.
>
> (*Final Report of the School for London*, 1904: 227)

The Board leaned towards a policy of distributing the truants as widely as possible in order to effect a complete break with the past. In these cases residential schools would socialize the children by returning them to a state of dependency within a surrogate family, removed from the memory and associations of the past.

The second type of corrective school was the co-educational day industrial school. Although the 1876 Education Act provided for their establishment, the first Boards to establish such institutions were those at Liverpool, Oxford and Great Yarmouth. School hours were from 8 a.m. to 6 p.m. and the children attended for a maximum term of three years or until they were fourteen. Not until September 1895 did the London School Board open a day industrial school at Drury Lane, although the authority established a second school at Poplar in September 1901 and a third at Nine Elms in April 1902 (Philpott, 1904; Rubinstein, 1969). Thirty years on it seems that the regime of full-time schooling was accepted by most working-class parents. The Board's figures show that average attendance gradually improved from 65.8 per cent of the pupils on roll in the Board schools in 1872 to a figure of 88.1 per cent in 1904 (*Final Report*, 1904: 220). However, these statistics are notoriously unreliable, not least because government grants and, until 1883, teachers' salaries depended directly on average attendance levels.

Although length of stay was largely determined by behaviour, truant school children were allowed home 'on licence' after one to three months. By contrast, industrial school children were usually released for licensed residential employment at fourteen or fifteen, but could be recalled (if necessary) until they were sixteen. In each case the Board assumed parental as well as educational responsibilities; it was hardly likely that a parental contribution would be easy to obtain. Hence officials were warned of the need:

to be careful not to play into the hands of dissolute parents who are only too pleased to get their children clothed and fed at the public expense, the parents' contributions being generally but a fraction of the cost of keeping a child at an Industrial School, even if it is possible to enforce the payment at all.

(Philpott, 1904: 96)

At first, the Board exercised its power to contribute to the maintenance of existing industrial schools and sent its own juvenile offenders to such schools. But the number of cases soon exceeded the number of places and three residential schools were established in the 1870s, two more in the 1890s, and a sixth in 1903. More importantly, all but the Gordon House Girls' Home (1897) were for boys only. They were all semi-penal institutions, organized on the assumption that the inculcation of appropriate character traits, habits and knowledge might redeem those most in danger of contamination from the 'moral diseases' of the city streets.

In April 1876 the proposal to establish a truant school was greeted with favour by all save the two working-class members, Benjamin Lucraft and George Potter. Even so, they expressed widely differing opinions on the proposed policy. Thus whereas Benjamin Lucraft voiced total opposition on the grounds that such schools interfered with the classical liberal theory of individual liberty, George Potter did not object in principle, but considered the establishment of such schools to be a duty that belonged to other agencies (*School Board Chronicle*, 9 April 1876: 425). Despite failing to defeat the motion, the two men successfully moved that the proposal be referred to a special committee to lay down the details of their establishment. Ironically, neither one of them was elected to serve on it.[3]

The case of Upton House

The Board's first truant school opened in November 1878. Despite local opposition the chosen site was Upton House, Hackney, and the school was duly certified as fit to receive 60 boys.[4] The exclusion of girls may have reflected ideas concerning the relative importance of education for girls, but Benjamin Lucraft had other ideas. He thought that it was because the school was to be run on the silent system, a regulation which prohibited conversation in order to eliminate the potential for corruption from others – an essential feature of Victorian prisons. In the opinion of the Truant School Committee, corporal punishment was not a sufficient deterrent for these boys. What was required was 'a moral impression of a power beyond the parent' (*School Board Chronicle*, 29 April 1876), in other words a treatment to stimulate conscience and discourage recidivism. Hence the fundamental purpose of schools like Upton House was to inculcate obedience, discipline, honesty, cleanliness and sobriety. Opposition to the scheme centred on a diagonal gender-class alliance between Benjamin Lucraft, George Potter and Elizabeth Surr (first elected in November 1876), who adopted a variety of delaying tactics. So incensed was Lucraft that he declared:

institutions like this were a disgrace to the country, a device of trying to keep down the lower strata of the people where they were now. This notion ... was all a notion of snobs – well, it might or might not apply to members of this Board. Better schools had superseded the ragged schools and these truant schools were a step backwards.

(School Board Chronicle, 28 July 1877: 81)

However, Elizabeth's objections to the school are an expression of her concern over the boys' welfare, and do not necessarily stem from such a class-based analysis. She was the first member to question the use of corporal punishment and the nature of the boys' diet and, with the support of Helen Taylor and Florence Fenwick Miller, was largely responsible for uncovering the appalling mistreatment of boys in both Upton House and St Paul's Industrial School. Unlike Benjamin and Elizabeth, however, neither Helen nor Florence opposed the establishment of such a school. Helen did not agree with Benjamin's point about the liberty of the subject, while Florence retained her belief in this approach to the moral regulation of the young, despite also supporting the campaign to uncover the truth about what was going on in both schools. Nevertheless, the stance taken by all three women on this issue provides an indication of the lengths to which they were prepared to go in defence of a moral principle they believed in.

Doggedly determined, for the next six months Elizabeth continued to raise issues of concern, both in public at weekly Board meetings and in private in her capacity as a member of the Industrial Schools Committee. Fellow members included J. Allanson Picton and Thomas Scrutton, though the only other woman on the committee was Alice Westlake who did not offer any support for the line she was taking. Hence Elizabeth was very much a lone voice on a committee with a clear male positional bias (see Chapter 1). Finally, as all her motions drawing the Board's attention to conditions in the school were defeated, Elizabeth took the initiative. She turned first to her Finsbury constituents and second, when she was still unable to move the Board to action, to the Home Secretary – the man with overall responsibility. In the face of the list of charges that her letter contained, including allegations of cruelty and mismanagement, the Home Secretary insisted on an inquiry. This shows the way in which, lacking the authority within the Board, Elizabeth was forced to apply external pressure in order to get the Board to take action. Speaking in Elizabeth's defence to a largely unrepentant Board, Helen suggests that women bring a more compassionate and caring approach to the policy agenda:

She would not readily forget the scene [...] when Mrs Surr entreated the Board to take into consideration the hardships undergone by the poor children at Upton House. Her protests were laughed to scorn, and it was upon such occasions that the value of a few simple feminine qualities were made patent. Taken at the very lowest, the report of the Special Committee was a tribute to the tact of Mrs Surr, and to her own good sense and judgment. The result was that the Board were obliged to own that there were serious grounds for complaint as to the management of this school.

(School Board Chronicle, 2 July 1879: 31–2)

Though careful to temper her rhetoric, Helen uses the occasion to make a tactical appeal to the balancing powers offered by the presence of women on the Board. Challenging conventional notions of female qualities, she manifests the feminist claim that women representatives make a distinctive contribution to the nature and direction of public policy (Norris, 1996).

In fact, the special committee to which Helen refers held its first meeting on 21 May 1879. Unsurprisingly, J. Allanson Picton and his colleagues Thomas Scrutton, Elizabeth Surr and Alice Westlake were all members; Helen Taylor attended every meeting. On the basis of the evidence presented – by fourteen boys aged between nine and twelve years, three parents, the school staff, an independent medical expert, the Board's architect, E.R. Robson, and Elizabeth Churcher (a mother of nine who lived next door) and her maid – the committee concluded there were serious grounds for complaint. Irregular punishments had been inflicted, without being recorded in the punishment book. These included the use of canes by subordinate officers as well as other violations which the majority report fails to specify beyond claiming that they did not involve systematic cruelty.

However, Elizabeth records her dissent, claiming there was systematic cruelty and lists a number of examples. These included lifting boys from the ground by their heads and ears. Those who were said to be of uncleanly habits were forced to lie naked on the stone sink of the lavatory on early winter mornings with the cold water tap turned on them; others were punished by making them sleep on the iron bars of a bedstead for nine weeks. One boy was shut in a cupboard within a cupboard, closed in by doors without light or any provision for ventilation for at least one night. Certainly the evidence suggests that apart from a persistent absconder, Golding, who was caned and chained by the neck to a block of wood, the most serious offence was that of bed-wetting. Indeed nine-year-old Richard Brownlie was made to carry his bedding on an eight foot pole from 9 a.m. till 7 p.m., with rests when tired and for meals (Minutes of Evidence). Elizabeth also disagreed with the committee's conclusion that the school was not operated on the silent system. This meant that boys were prohibited from other than essential conversation except for half an hour per day, during recreation. Her view was upheld by the Conservative Home Secretary in a letter to the Board dated 28 August 1879. The Board was asked to stop the practice as it broke the understanding on which the school was established and certified as an ordinary industrial school. With Alice Westlake accusing the other women members of coaching parents to complain, Benjamin Lucraft was stung to retort that:

> such treatment was only borne by the children because they were the children of the poor. Members denied cruelty because they belonged to another class. He knew this was so. The Board had no right to establish such schools. There ought to be an institution for kindness instead of having an institution for cruelty.
>
> (*School Board Chronicle*, 26 July 1879: 79)

While the lack of parental complaints may have been due to ignorance of the rules of the school, in reality there was little a concerned parent could do other than approach the institution directly or go back to the magistrate who had imposed the sentence. Neither option was particularly attractive, nor were they likely to be especially effective. As one mother who subsequently complained about her son's mistreatment at St Paul's Industrial School bitterly recalled, all that happened was that her son suffered further punishment in that he was flogged for it.

Despite having a small but loyal support base on the Board, Elizabeth Surr evidently occupied a minority position within both the Industrial Schools Committee and the Board as a whole. This left her with little alternative but to resort to pressure group activity in order to try and force the Board's hand. Her actions were rewarded by the appointment of a new governor, modifications to the timetable to allow longer periods of recreation, and the purchase of new beds, their predecessors having been a mere 18 inches wide! Eager to castigate both her and her female supporters, opponents appeared ready to turn a blind eye to male supporters like Benjamin Lucraft, while singling out Elizabeth and Helen for especial criticism. For instance, there was a heated exchange in the course of a debate over Elizabeth's motion to appoint a small number of ladies and gentlemen as visitors to each of the board's industrial schools. Without mincing his words, Lyulph Stanley voiced his objections to the proposal on the grounds that she and Miss Taylor were quite capable of concocting a committee which would overturn the discipline of the establishment. When Mrs Surr countered his objections by retorting that such a proposition was only right and proper considering the scandal that had occurred at Upton House, he immediately questioned her judgement, undermining her position still further by his response to her comment regarding the 'ungentlemanly' quality of his remarks:

> Mrs Surr was rather squeamish considering the epithets she often launched right and left whenever the Board discussed this subject. Mrs Surr and her supporters wanted a sort of holiday house instead of Upton House. She wished to give the boys sweets and toys. Such over kindliness of feeling totally unfitted persons from being the managers of a semi-penal establishment. The discipline of institutions of the kind must be reformatory.
>
> (*School Board Chronicle*, 1 November 1879: 424–6)

Significantly, Lyulph Stanley was the leader of the Progressive majority on the Board and the rhetoric clearly suggests the hegemony of a macho culture that places a premium on toughness and force. As a consequence, political practices involving demagoguery and aggression posed real problems for female representatives working within the doctrine of the separation of spheres. These qualities were culturally accepted in men but not in women and were therefore alien to the majority of female members who were anxious to remain 'womanly' in the eyes of women as well as men. Hence the appeal to male chivalry is particularly telling. What was perhaps more surprising was that previous to this, Lyulph Stanley and Elizabeth Surr had been united in their opposition to what they and other members of the Board considered to be the excessive levels of expenditure upon the *Shaftesbury* training ship – which also opened in 1878. Here, boys were actively encouraged to develop a taste for life on the ocean wave on board a specially converted vessel in the hope that they would eventually join the navy. School work was conducted on the half-time system, with the rest of the time devoted to industrial training – principally seamanship – and such extra-curricular activities as gun, rifle and cutlass drill (LCC Report with regard to Industrial Schools, 1870–1904: 53).

The case of the *Shaftesbury* training ship

Although Benjamin Lucraft was the first to raise the issue of financial misman-agement, by querying members' travelling expenses in July 1878, it was Florence Fenwick Miller, Elizabeth Surr and Helen Taylor who kept the issue in the public eye. Unlike the majority of their colleagues, the women refused to be swayed by arguments used to support the ever-increasing allocations of rate payers' money to be spent on the ship and its tender. In October 1878 the Board authorized the expenditure of a further £6,000, the Industrial Schools Committee having exhausted the £28,000 already voted. Three months later members voted a further £2,000, despite the note of caution sounded by Elizabeth and Helen. Not unreasonably the two women recommended that they wait to see the findings of a special committee appointed to inquire into levels of expenditure on the *Shaftesbury*.

On this occasion it was Lyulph Stanley who urged that the Board appoint a special committee to consider the allegations against the Industrial Schools Committee. The motion was carried and he was then appointed chairman – a much more immediate and substantive reward for his actions than that achieved by Elizabeth in relation to her charges against the mismanagement of Upton House. Measuring power in terms of the ability to move successful resolutions, it is worth remembering that certain external attributes members brought with them may well have been particularly effective when it came to determining positions of power on the Board. Educated at Eton and Balliol, Lyulph Stanley was a peer of the realm and practising barrister who served his apprenticeship in politics as an unsuccessful Liberal candidate at Oldham in 1872. By contrast, Elizabeth Surr was a doctor's daughter married to an eminent City merchant, but with no previous experience of public work. She did not have access to the considerable resources of public networks, political contacts, policy experience, and technical and social skills that helped make Stanley such an authoritative figure.

Elizabeth's difficulties in exerting authority in public are in keeping with the contradictory position she occupied within the conventional Victorian vision of the separate spheres of paid employment for men and private domesticity for women. As Carol Dyhouse (1987: 26–7) has shown, the barriers that boxed middle-class Victorian women into the home were particularly effective in the areas of finance and what she defines as public exposure generally. Hence, while female Board members enjoyed a greatly enhanced social status, they were also involved in the very complex task of negotiating gender constraints and social taboos in order to forge new roles for themselves as publicly accountable figures and recognized authorities. Moreover the issue of overspending would undoubt-edly strike a more resonant chord among Board members than the possible mistreatment of recalcitrant working-class children detained in a reformatory institution.

The debate over the *Shaftesbury* also accentuates the contrasting position occupied by Alice Westlake. Far from sharing the rather isolated position of her female colleagues, she was a trusted member of the Industrial Schools Committee, often presenting their reports to be rubber stamped by the Board. Unlike Elizabeth, Florence and Helen, who proudly asserted their independence from the party machines, Alice had conventional Liberal contacts and held orthodox Liberal views. She adhered strictly to the party line – placing party loyalty above support for female colleagues (*School Board Chronicle*, 19 November 1881: 516). Like Ruth Homan, her housewifery skills appear to have been especially prized by male colleagues. Thus it was Alice who 'shopped around' to furnish the ship, who supervised the cutting out and arranging of needlework materials and who persuaded friends to help in supplying the embroidery. Yet she herself felt that she later came in for special criticism from Lyulph Stanley who lay a great part of the blame for withholding information about expenditure at her door. This was because bills and documents had been kept in the private houses of members of the Industrial Schools Committee and she had been ill when the investigation was in progress. Despite public concern over what was fast developing into a financial scandal, Florence Fenwick Miller's attempt to secure the dissolution of the Industrial Schools' Committee was supported by only four members (including Elizabeth Surr and Benjamin Lucraft). As a result, those responsible retained their positions of authority on the Committee and the Board (*School Board Chronicle*, 22 March 1879: 270–1).

While such experiences may have been behind later allegations concerning the operation of an 'official ring' (see Chapter 5), as using a caucus is fairly standard political behaviour, Florence's concern with the relationship between authoritative position holders and those in their confidence may well be a reflection of her relative inexperience in the body politic. Whether it amounted to a rejection of the accepted rules of male-dominated politics, as inferred by Annmarie Turnbull (1983b: 129) is open to question, although a later edition of the *Women's Penny Paper* would appear to support such an interpretation of the actions of these highly principled and assertive female members. Expressing regret at the attacks upon Julia Augusta Webster by an unnamed member retiring from the Board, the paper has 'no doubt that the public will support Mrs Webster's practical and wide-minded interpretation of party rule. The days have gone by when an unintelligent and unconscientious party vote mechanically given is appreciated' (*Women's Penny Paper*, 17 November 1888: 2).

The case of St Paul's Industrial School

Undeterred by the majority line, Elizabeth remained keen to air her views on the subject of industrial school management whenever she felt there was a need for concern. Hence it was she who, still a member of the Industrial Schools Committee in 1881, was largely responsible for exposing the treatment meted out to boys incarcerated at St Paul's Industrial School. St Paul's was a private church school that received grants of public money and mainly London School Board children,[5] and was owned by Thomas Scrutton, now chairman of the Industrial Schools Committee. This was crucial as it somewhat undermined Lyulph Stanley's claim that it was useless to blame the Board in such cases because the Board inspectors had no right of entry to such establishments (*School Board Chronicle*, 9 April 1881: 343). Again Mrs Surr was treated with derision when she tried to raise the case of two boys held at the institution. Mr Scrutton even said he would 'have the Governor of the School' for failure to inform the Home Secretary that the boys had been declared unfit for industrial training. The allegations revolved around two areas of gross cruelty and mismanagement. The first involved the reallocation of food intended for the boys to the Governor, his family and the rest of the staff. This resulted in the death of one boy from starvation. It seems further that insufficient clothing and footwear had resulted in cases of chilblains so severe that one boy nearly had to have his toes amputated. The punishments meted out included having to stand half naked with bare feet on the cold stones in winter, washing sheets; being imprisoned for several days in the bathroom where it was so cold their cocoa froze; and the use of handcuffs and foot manacles. The likelihood was that the deaths of several weak boys had been hastened by their harsh treatment (*School Board Chronicle*, 8 October 1881: 359; 15 October 1881: 377–9).

After eight inmates had set fire to the school a scandal became unavoidable, but Scrutton doggedly buried his head in the sand, persistently trying to evade the issue. Finding themselves in a majority at one Board meeting, despite Lyulph Stanley's opposition, Elizabeth and her supporters pushed through an amendment (by ten votes to six). This moved that the Board remove the children sent by them to that school, and petition the Home Secretary to withdraw the school's certificate (*School Board Chronicle*, 8 October 1881: 359). Nevertheless, the following week the disconcerted majority succeeded in getting the decision reversed on the grounds that it had not been 'fair play', because the man at the centre of the allegations, Thomas Scrutton, had left the meeting before the issue was raised (*School Board Chronicle*, 15 October 1881: 377–9). Once again it took the intervention of the Home Secretary, now the Liberal Sir William Harcourt, to force the Board into an inquiry, albeit one conducted by a special committee so heavily biased in favour of Thomas Scrutton that Benjamin Lucraft, Henrietta Muller and Edith Simcox refused to serve. These two women were elected for the first time in 1879 (*School Board Chronicle*, 29 October 1881: 426–7). Amidst confusion as to whether Elizabeth would be authorized to question witnesses or not, Helen Taylor dismissed the committee as 'a whitewashing committee', advising Elizabeth that:

> if you can lay the facts before the public in any less laborious and equally effectual way, you may bring pressure to bear on the Board better than through such a sham Committee as it would be if you are precluded from asking in your own words such questions as you deem necessary.
>
> (Helen Taylor to Elizabeth Surr, 20 September 1881)

In the event the Board resolved that the committee should follow the procedures used in a court of law. Elizabeth acted for the prosecution and Thomas Scrutton the defence (*School Board Chronicle*, 5 November 1881: 464–5). While some of their male colleagues lauded the women as 'the champions of the outcasts of the metropolis' (*School Board Chronicle*, 15 October 1881: 378), others followed the lead set by Lyulph Stanley in arguing that, as enemies of the Board, the women were using the case to discredit their opponents (Jones, 1979: 32). In fact, the School Board's organ, the *Chronicle*, consistently aligned Mrs Surr with the so-called 'School Board' party. It seems likely that the controversy legitimized displays of personal animosity, failing to give credence to Elizabeth Surr's very real concern for the issues at stake (*School Board Chronicle*, 21 October 1882: 411). Even though it is difficult to attribute motives with absolute certainty, the stance adopted by Helen Taylor is clearly in line with her Socialist political beliefs. As an evangelical churchwoman, Elizabeth Surr's sympathy with the conditions endured by these boys may have reflected the language of Christian obligation to serve the poor. It also had links with the protecting face of social motherhood.

Amidst a glare of publicity, Thomas Scrutton brought a libel action against Helen Taylor for stating that St Paul's was kept open for the sake of profit and that he himself was morally guilty of manslaughter. Clearly demagoguery was not alien to her communication style and although a settlement was agreed, the plaintiff did not benefit financially since he was ordered to pay the costs of the case (*School Board Chronicle*, 15 July 1882: 40). Unable to escape the censure of public opinion expressed at mass meetings – as at Mile End Waste, Tower Hamlets, when about a thousand mostly working-class people called upon 'the Chairman of this den of torture' to resign his seat upon the Board – he not only resigned his position as chairman of the Industrial Schools Committee but later his seat on the Board (*School Board Chronicle*, 15 November 1881: 515). Ignoring the Director of Public Prosecutions' decision regarding the lack of 'evidence' to support a criminal prosecution, the Home Secretary decided to close the school down and set up a Royal Commission on Reformatory and Industrial Schools, whilst acknowledging Elizabeth's role in a personal letter of thanks.

Despite having her actions vindicated in this way, albeit at tremendous personal cost, Elizabeth decided not to stand for re-election as the Board faced the 1882 triennial elections. That she found it difficult to adapt to the essentially male atmosphere is implied by the following editorial comment:

> Mrs Surr takes an exaggerated view of the seriousness of the difficulties she has encountered. We wish she could find herself able to go on with the battle. This excellent lady, and some of the other lady members of the Board, have shown much lack of appreciation of the true elements and conditions of warfare in public life.
> (*School Board Chronicle*, 21 October 1882: 411)

This gives an indication both of the gendered nature of the public sphere and the gendered dynamics of representational politics. Some women clearly found it difficult to operate in a male-dominated political environment and ran the danger of being marginalized politically. Difficulties were exacerbated on the fourth Board which, as Rosamond Davenport Hill later recalled, was not on the whole favourable to its lady members and showed but scant respect for their opinions (Metcalfe, 1904 : 71–2). Elected to the Industrial Schools Committee in January 1880, Rosamond soon earnt a reputation for being a quiet but exceedingly active and successful member. Consistently supporting the Liberal programme, she avoided the opprobrium associated with involvement in the controversy over St Paul's. However she did help Elizabeth Surr investigate complaints about Brentwood Industrial School, where younger boys were detained (*School Board Chronicle*, 21 April 1883: 387).

Public image and behaviour

What is significant about the contribution made by Rosamond Davenport Hill in rebuilding the shattered reputation of the Industrial Schools Committee, is not so much what she was doing but the way in which it was interpreted. Not only did male Board members make good use of her experience in the field of industrial education, they also freely acknowledged the commitment demonstrated by an unbroken record of attendance at committee meetings. Yet the image presented both during and after her lifetime is characterized by its continual stress upon her 'motherly' qualities and such infamous feminine attributes as reticence and skills like knitting. It effectively demonstrates the conditions on which women were acceptable to men in public life.

While both she and Henry Spicer (Thomas Scrutton's successor as chairman of the Industrial Schools Committee) are credited with having achieved greater advance and improvement in this than any other department of the Board's work, in the eyes of the *School Board Chronicle*: 'The most satisfactory indication of her influence is her remarkable popularity with the Industrial School children' (10 October 1885: 361–3). It is her involvement with the boys at Brentwood Industrial School – sending one boy for a trip to the seaside, paying for trips to the zoo and giving them parties afterwards at her home – rather than her administrative abilities which her biographer and subsequent historical accounts have chosen to stress. Clearly she may have been seen as the 'friend and mother of the boys' who 'inspired the whole staff *with a feeling of rectitude*' (my emphasis) (Metcalfe, 1904: 86). She was also a social reformer who firmly believed in the stringent retraining programmes followed by institutions like Brentwood. These were not designed to elevate the boys. The idea was that they would be prepared for a life of unremitting honesty and strenuous labour in their social station.

The instances chosen illustrate the relative importance of gender in shaping the way in which women Board members operated. They also show the way in which their actions were interpreted by their male colleagues and a wider audience interested in, or affected by, the workings of the London School Board. Clearly members with minority views had little power and were therefore obliged to use alternative means to get their message across. In one sense Board members shared an anomalous position, for while membership conferred an element of control, the Board also secured an element of control over them by incorporating them within its organizational structure.

Nevertheless, as the case studies make clear, it was possible for a small, self-motivated group to take up an issue and successfully pursue it using the only channel available to them, that is, reaching out to a wider audience than the potentially hostile one composed of fellow colleagues on the Board. These controversies were the backdrop to a successful intervention by principled and assertive female representatives. It will be argued that industrial school management and organization was to provide female Board members with an additional area within which to develop their expertise above and beyond that of the domestic curriculum.

In appealing to public sensibilities about the physical abuse of children, Elizabeth Surr showed the ways in which traditional female activities could mark out an independent public role for women. Thus, she was asked to give evidence before the 1882 Committee to Enquire into Reformatory and Industrial Schools, initiated by Sir William Harcourt. Thirteen years later Margaret Eve was appointed as one of the Royal Commissioners to inquire into the management of industrial schools (*School Board Chronicle*, 25 May 1895: 586). Traditional social stereotypes about women and their interests brought another key policy area to the fore. Obviously some women did behave differently to other members, but the language of social motherhood was used by all female representatives. Although the women politicians were divided over the question of the administration of the industrial schools, the evidence suggests that it is possible to trace a consistent line of concern over the issue of child welfare from Elizabeth Surr onwards. Created to reform those children characterized as being 'of the street Arab' type, against this background even a male enthusiast found himself forced to admit:

> The only possible criticism one could make regarding the discipline of a Truant School is that it is a little too good. There is something almost uncanny in the grim stolidity of the boys, the stiffness and precision of their every movement. They have intervals for play – it is true – but for the greater part of the day they are under orders, performing every duty by word of command. Watch them, for example, coming to take their places in the dining-room for the afternoon meal. They march in single file and sidle along to their places with the short, rhythmic steps of soldiers 'closing up' on parade.
>
> (Philpott, 1904: 193)

Even more important, such descriptions help one understand Helen Taylor's wish to bring the boys on board the *Shaftesbury* under the 'civilising influence of female teachers, instead of leaving them under the brutalising influence of old soldiers' (*School Board Chronicle*, 17 December 1881: 607). Ruth Homan later sought to challenge the prevailing definition of reformatory treatment by supporting moves towards the use of day industrial schools. In response, a vociferous though decreasing minority of Board members opposed these proposals for two reasons. First, they did not entail the child's total removal from their existing 'haunts and associates'. Second, they made it harder to replace 'defective' parents and neighbourhood influences with surrogate parents in those institutions designated as suitable by the local education authorities. As was pointed out, the moralizing and corrective training was part of a deliberately adopted system aiming at a definite end:

> the weakness of these boys has been their indolent, irregular ways and unwilling-
> ness to submit to authority; therefore every possible means must be taken to incul-
> cate habits of industry, regularity and obedience [...] The Truant School is not a
> home, but a sanatorium for the morally infirm.
>
> (Philpott, 1904: 194)

A sanatorium for the morally infirm?

Some female board members did challenge prevailing notions of reformatory treatment and while they could not effect policy changes, sought to mitigate some of the more punitive aspects by focusing upon the subject of corporal punishment. Consequently, an echo of Elizabeth Surr's concern was heard in 1898, when an attempt was made to obtain Home Office approval for a change of policy to enable the Board to birch boys re-admitted to truant schools. It was argued that the abolition of birching in 1894 had led to a large increase in such re-admissions. Once again a woman – Ruth Homan – led the opposition with an amendment to give the 'recidivists' an extra dose of school work, as well as with-drawing them from manual labour, while her colleague Honnor Morten was highly contemptuous of the 'birch-thirsty men'. Although Ruth's amendment was defeated by sixteen votes to twenty, it received the support of all the women members except Emma Maitland. She ensured that the motion was returned to the Industrial Schools Committee for consideration and report (*The Board Teacher*, 1 April 1898: 84). Later that same year Honnor Morten and Ruth Homan formed an alliance in an attempt to ban the use of corporal punishment in all the Board's truant and industrial schools. According to Ruth: 'these chil-dren were so used to being knocked about in their homes that an entirely dif-ferent treatment was needed for their salvation' (*School Board Chronicle*, 17 December 1898: 683). Not only does this engender developing notions con-cerning children 'in need of care and protection' it is also reminiscent of argu-ments advanced by Helen Taylor, one of the most outspoken critics of the use of corporal punishment in Board schools among the early female Board members (see Chapter 7).

Yet Ruth Homan's motion was watered down by an amendment put by two clerics. The Reverend Russell Wakefield and the Reverend Scott Lidgett suc-cessfully slanted the issue to the question of whether to abolish the practice of public floggings. The following year their amendment was carried and put into effect – despite the outspoken opposition of Honnor Morten and Mary Bridges Adams. Mary even resorted to the use of props on this occasion, bringing in an example of what she claimed was the commonly used instrument of birching, a small besom broom. Here again she proceeded to describe the Board as 'blood-thirsty' rather than 'birch-thirsty' (*The Board Teacher*, 1 March 1899: 68). Such sentiments may well have struck a chord with the working-class recipients of such punitive treatment:

'If you did anything wrong like stealing or anything like that you got birched. That birch was like a besom broom ... real birch. At the apex it'd be twelve to fourteen inches wide and tapered down. And this is what they birched you with. Drew blood – oh, it cut you ... I myself was birched because I played truant from there. When I first went there I was very unhappy and I played truant. Anyway they got me and they took me and I was sentenced to five strokes of the birch. And the caretaker was a vicious old man called Paggin. .... He did the birching and he took a delight in everything.'

(Thompson, 1975: 170)

Conclusion

As the struggles over penal practices in the industrial schools clearly demonstrate, School Board women experienced considerable difficulties in exerting authority in public. There were various reasons for this, ranging from the general contemporary tide of public opinion to the male bias in the positional and organizational balance of the London School Board. Obviously the most publicly acceptable style of authority women could adopt held strong overtones of motherliness and it is hardly surprising that the notion of social mothering was an important element for successful entry to local government. Without wishing to reinforce the stereotype that women are more caring and compassionate than men, it is important to acknowledge that there may be a gender difference on social issues. Moreover the evidence suggests that gender influences policy priorities. On the whole, women members tended to express greater concern over social policies concerned with the moral regulation of children, but there were tensions between those who gave high priority to working in committees and developing and defending party policy and those who challenged the dominant policy agenda. Supporting Elizabeth Surr in her successful opposition to the attack on married women teachers in 1881, for instance, Florence Fenwick Miller launched the following invective against the childless Alice Westlake who had instigated the proposal to remove married women teachers with children under two from the Board's employ:

> She [Mrs Miller] was thankful that this Board was not composed entirely of married ladies without children. It was the motherly eye of Mrs Surr that had discovered the deficiencies of Upton House and St Paul's School. The true womanly instinct and feeling and sympathy for children did not arise in a woman until she had had children of her own in her arms.
>
> (*School Board Chronicle*, 26 November 1881: 531)

But of course however useful the maternalist discourse, it was fraught with contradiction and such exchanges clearly expose the anomalies of women's political role in late Victorian and Edwardian England. On the one hand, the concept of social mothering was severely limiting for women politicians since a language of justification built around the need for a feminine contribution also implied an acceptance of the prevailing sexual division of labour. On the other, it was a discourse with which they were most familiar and one that reflected the social and cultural values shaping the gender order of which they were a part.

This had class implications, of course. The parents most likely to come into conflict with the school authorities were poor and working class; the women politicians were not. In broad terms, female Board members could utilize the resources of financial security and social status in their dealings with the urban poor. This was not true of relations with the majority of their male colleagues. Significantly, cultural attributes may have been a factor shaping alliances with working men like Benjamin Lucraft and George Potter, who were also in a distinct minority. Such relationships are complex but crucial to any consideration both of women's political role and of their impact on the politics of education. Indeed the decision to appeal beyond the Board to an implied popular constituency in the capital at large was a direct result of the very substantial prejudice against policy initiatives pressed by women members. At the same time, a shared experience as women entering a male space did not always transcend political divisions. But whatever their different goals, by holding positions of responsibility and public accountability they were all 'taking one step beyond the old idea of what is womanly work' (*Shafts*, November and December 1894: 349). Indeed the very fact that women in local government could gain official recognition for their actions prompted Henrietta Muller's self-confident assertion that:

> Women like Mrs Elizabeth Surr ... leave their mark on our day. They create a type
> – the hard-headed and large-hearted woman who has a keen scent for 'a job', who
> routs out dirty corners, is beloved by the people and detested by the official.
> (*Women's Penny Paper*, 10 November 1888: 4)

Concerned about penal practices in the industrial schools, Elizabeth Surr kept a watchful eye on these new institutions. Independent of party discipline, she must have infuriated the majority of her colleagues who consistently prevaricated on the issues raised. As a result, when speaking in debate the masculine ethos of formalized politics was reflected in a tendency to trivialize her calls for action which were frequently represented as emotive and irrational. In short, Elizabeth Surr was willing to act on the evidence of the male truants. The great majority of her colleagues were not. Yet according to David Finkelhor, what has made the difference to the treatment of victims of child sexual abuse in contemporary America 'is that there are huge numbers of women working at all levels of the criminal justice system. In a male system, people don't listen to children' (*Guardian*, 22 March 1997: 30).

Notes

1. The last bye-law incorporates the statutory provision for a penalty of five shillings, including costs, for any neglect or violation of the bye-laws.

2. Under London's scheme of education, absence from school for one whole day or two half-days in a week, or frequent irregularity, was deemed a breach of the bye-laws (Spalding, 1900: 124).

3. Appointed on 15 March 1876, the Special Committee on Incorrigible Truants was composed of Mr Buxton, Prebendary Irons, Mr Lovell, Mr MacGregor, Mr Peek, Mr Picton, Dr Rigg, the Reverend J. Rodgers, Mr Scrutton and the Reverend Benjamin Waugh (Minutes, 15 March 1876: 537).

4. 'Universal testimony is borne to the wonderful healthiness of Hackney as a whole, and Hackney Wick and Clapton Park are the only parts of which there is general complaint. The health is due partly to the soil, which is largely gravel, partly no doubt to the large area of open spaces [and] broad streets with gardens at the rear of the houses' (Report on Hackney Health, Booth Collection A35, by George Duckworth: p. 80) with acknowledgements to Dr Judith Ford for this reference.

5. Under the Youthful Offenders Act of 1854, voluntary societies were authorized to establish reformatory schools with the necessary powers of compulsory detention, industrial schools being added three years later. Schools were governed by the 'Managers', the body of subscribers who framed their school's rules, but they had to be certified satisfactory by the Home Secretary who could veto any rules he thought undesirable and withdraw certification if the managers, after due notice, failed to meet any request with regard to the modification of their rules. Wherever possible, parents were required to make some financial contribution to the upkeep of their children whilst in the school, those who had committed a crime having to serve a fourteen-day period of imprisonment as an expiation for their crime, before being remitted to the custody of a reformatory (Pinchbeck and Hewitt, 1973: 477).

Introduction

As the debate over reformatory institutions for persistent truants made clear, in pragmatic terms, simply meeting the needs of accommodation and provision was not enough. Faced with stark economic realities embodied by underfed and impoverished school children, successive School Boards for London found themselves having to re-define their educational remit in the light of broader social welfare concerns.

Relating the ideas of the women involved to the wider political, economic, social and cultural contexts, this chapter examines the use of education as social policy by focusing on what appears to be at the very heart of school organization: discipline. It will be argued that the distinctive character of elementary education as a form of rigid social control was established through disciplinary procedures underpinning Board policy on compulsory attendance, the payment of school fees, school meals, corporal punishment and the propagation of specific social values such as self-discipline, temperance and thrift. In particular, the analysis of issues which often seem peripheral to the provision of schooling provides a framework within which to explore both gendered notions of duty and citizenship and broad arguments about the limits of philanthropy and the scope of state intervention, the nature of charity, and the most efficient way of relieving poverty in the first place.

Serving the poor?

Despite Henrietta Muller's self-confident assertion quoted at the end of the previous chapter, women members were keenly aware of the difficulties faced by women in authority. Indeed, the sentiments expressed by Florence Fenwick Miller show the social and cultural pressures against what may be defined as public exposure generally:

> To be looked on as an oddity, and an unpleasant one, too; to be expected, as a fore-gone conclusion, to be repellant in looks, manners and voice; to be regarded as hat-ing, and, therefore to be shunned by the entire opposite sex, instead of only hating the evils that had naturally gathered around their absolute rule, as about every other despotism since history began; to be presumed to have no taste in feminine matters, no capacity for dressing well, no ability for housekeeping, no childward tenderness, no inclination for the ordinary pleasures of life; to be told perpetually

that one was 'unsexed', 'a shrieking sister', 'revelling in the discussion of matters that even men whisper about', and much more of the same sort, was as painful to bear, and even seemed as dangerous to one's future and one's personal position and safety as the bullets of Inkerman can have been to our brave soldiers.

(*Woman's Signal*, 4 January 1894)

Written exactly 40 years on, the reference to the battle of Inkerman is striking here. This was the bloodiest, most fiercely contested, and decisive battle of the Crimean War and it is significant that Miller should use this particular military metaphor to magnify the deeply ingrained misogyny of the society in which she lived.

Yet if Jane Chessar's obituary is interpreted at face value, it would seem that women could and did transcend these difficulties. At the time of her death Jane enjoyed a greatly enhanced social status. One of the first female professionals, personal qualities like 'zeal and intelligence' were crucial to the ways in which she negotiated the constraints of gender. Apparently she disarmed 'the opposition of those critics who considered the office too "public" a one for women to hold with propriety' (*The Athenaeum*, 18 September 1880: 370). As the previous chapters make clear, the suffragist movement considered it essential that women should step forward to prove their capacity for responsible and effective public service. Claiming that it was the duty of women to take an interest in the well-being of their parish, feminist periodicals accentuated the links between successful and orderly management of such local issues as the nurture and education of children, and the internal prosperity of the country. Obviously it was expedient that candidates should be 'conscientious and religious' women, motivated by the 'simple straightforward wish to do good in the most effectual manner' (*Englishwoman's Review*, 15 May 1879: 211). At the same time, pioneering status lent added responsibility:

If a man fails, the blame is attributed to himself alone, if a woman has shortcomings, the general voice somehow attaches the responsibility to her whole sex. It is, however, with reason that we set up a higher standard of moral qualifications for women candidates, as we believe that their influence is specifically wanted to refine and elevate, to bring something of the tenderness and the purity of feeling found in our home into social politics.

(*Englishwoman's Review*, 15 May 1879: 211–12)

From the feminist point of view, the force of women's political presence would be a softening and humanizing one. Essentialist notions of woman's 'nature' and mission were used to justify the presence of a female figure on the political platform and the strategy delineated here both accepted and propagated the idea of women as the 'natural' guardians of a society's moral order. This framework placed activist women in a double bind. On the one hand, they sought to enter the public realm on the same terms as men. On the other, they grounded this analysis firmly in a culturally determined theory of sexual difference. Activists worked within clear structures of prescription and existing social activity so the slippage between the question of rights and the question of duties is understandable. Honnor Morten may have referred to the 'spirit of service' women devoted to the poor but it was obviously advantageous to undermine the 'shrieking sister' tag by reference to women's particular interests in the social welfare needs of working-class mothers and children.

Nevertheless, the association between the moral qualifications of women and their capacity to 'refine and elevate' is deeply suggestive of the complexities of class and gender power. Of course the target audience here is middle-class women, free from domestic drudgery and with the educational and financial resources to supervise state schooling procedures. Women joined notions about their sense of mission to different political agendas, but the reliance on exhortation to social improvement through moral regeneration, as well as aid, typified the new approaches to voluntary initiative in child welfare, workhouse living conditions and model housing. These approaches were pioneered by such outstanding individual women as Mary Carpenter, Louisa Twining and Octavia Hill.

A founder member of COS (see Chapter 4) whose object was to rationalize and professionalize philanthropy by working within the framework of the Poor Law Amendment Act of 1834, Octavia Hill was inspired to social action by a strong Christian impulse. Like the society to which she belonged, Hill was impressed by the need to rescue the deserving poor from vice and crime. Sound housing and strictly supervised living habits were to provide the means by which to inscribe good housekeeping on the working-class home. The work of housing management was to provide the route by which Hill made the transition from theory to practice. Tenements were bought and reformed through the use of middle-class, largely female, rent collectors who were set the task of improving the carefully vetted inhabitants and their surroundings. By collecting the rent at regular times it was envisaged that tenants would clean their homes to receive their lady visitors, while informal pressure was exerted through a system of spot checks designed to place standards of cleanliness on a more permanent footing. Finally, a tidy profit was envisaged for those who, like John Ruskin, provided both moral support and financial backing.

As Jane Lewis (1992) has shown, practical social work of this kind stressed the importance of developing character. It also facilitated the development of new techniques of investigation, based primarily on the collection of statistical information about the urban population, and new administrative apparatuses designed to impose norms of conduct on that population. As one volunteer rent collector, Beatrice Potter (later Webb), recalled, on 4 June 1885 she was:

> Working hard. Buildings unsatisfactory. Caretaker hopelessly inadequate. Tenants, rough lot – the aborigines of the East End. Pressure to exclude these and take in only the respectable – follow Peabody's example. Interview with superintendent of Peabody's. 'We had a rough lot to begin with, had to weed them of the old inhabitants – now only take in men with regular employment.' The practical problem of management: are the tenants to be picked, all doubtful or inconvenient persons excluded or are the former inhabitants to be housed so long as they are decently respectable?
>
> (*Diary of Beatrice Webb, Volume One 1873–1892*, 1986: 134)

For educated middle-class women, private sector voluntary associations provided a variety of experience which was a very useful introduction to government, administration and the law. Their object was to serve, to be useful. Philanthropy was a reflection of virtue and they infused their construction of domesticity with a strong dose of civic maternalism.

This association between women and welfare clearly held implications for the role of women as social reformers, political activists, educators, and nurturers of working-class childhood. It also shows how ideologies of femininity impacted on educational theory and practice. Giving evidence before the Cross Commission on Elementary Education in 1886–88 Mrs Burgwin, headteacher of the Orange Street School, was asked to consider whether she had 'set up a centre of humanising influence in one of the worst areas of London'. She told the Commissioners that in her opinion:

> You could hardly in years gone by bring a person down that street without a blush of shame; the people did not think of putting window blinds up; they pitched everything out of the windows into the street regardless of passers-by. ... Some Christmases ago I sent a new short curtain to every house to give it a bright appearance for Christmas Day, and now the people feel a sense of shame in various ways. If they attempt to come near you dirty they would even apologise. I know that in many instances a woman will borrow a neighbour's apron to come up and speak to me so that she may come up looking clean. I felt it my duty to tell her that she should have enough self-respect to wash her face before she came to see me.
>   (Cross Commission 1886-8, Evidence of Mrs Burgwin: 121)

The fact that the idea of reform by example was valued both by women teachers and their elective representatives is indicative of the broader social expectations underpinning mass schooling. Like other interventions into the lives of the working classes, education offered its recipients the possibility of self-improvement through individual effort. Those who failed to rise into respectability, as conceived by the middle-class reformers, were felt to be incapable of moral regeneration. Hence the teachers were involved in a process of first constructing and then appealing to the reasonable parent. As Jenny Shaw (1981) has argued, by claiming to stand *in loco parentis*, schools were able to take over some of the powers that accompany parenthood. Essentially an ideological formula deriving from ideas about parental rights, the concept permitted a substantial encroachment on parental freedom and ultimately facilitated the process by which educational professionals sought to impose middle-class standards of child-rearing on working-class parents. Education did provide genuine opportunities for advancement for some working-class children, but of far greater significance for the majority were the effects of social policy in constituting new and different forms of social relations.

Never simply establishments for the transmission of official knowledge, board schools were also the sites of 'welfare' and 'moral' interventions. As Sir Charles Reed (chairman of the London School Board 1873-81) admitted in 1874:

> Of the school work and its results I do not say one word. It is too soon altogether to speak upon the question. Tens of thousands of children are in our schools who

are, I regret to say, grossly ignorant and utterly uninstructed, and the only thing we can do is to look to their cleanliness and give them habits of order, and promote their regular attendance, and then leave the question of results.

(Gautrey, n.d.: 91)

Corroborating Reed's statement, Thomas Gautrey (connected with the Board throughout its 34 year life as teacher, union leader and member) recalled that inspections for cleanliness and tidiness took precedence over other activities at his school. Boys who did not reach a 'fair standard' in the playground inspection were either sent to the school washbasins before entering the classroom or, in the worst cases, sent home. Since this was their working environment, teachers obviously had a vested interest in establishing standards of cleanliness. When 'Board school laryngitis' caused concern during the 1880s, its virulence was attributed to 'air reeking with the stench of pupils' dirty skin and clothes' (Gautrey, n.d.: 91–2) and the search for 'nits' or head lice provided a frequent source of conflict between the home and the school. Not surprisingly, there is clear evidence that working-class parents resented the judgemental labelling associated with what was seen as an unwarranted interference on the part of certain school staff. As one indignant mother demanded in a letter to her daughter's headmistress:

I should like to know how much more spite you intend to put upon my child for it is nothing else. First, you send the Sanitary Inspector and I have my home taken away, then my husband has to get rid of his few rabbits and chickens, and now you cut the few hairs my girl was just beginning to get so nice. I think you had better hang her and be done with it. I know she had no need to have her hair off as it was washed with soft soap last night. The child is thoroughly heartbroken.

(Gautrey, n.d.: 91)

In such circumstances the ideological construction *in loco parentis* effectively legitimized a whole range of interventionist measures above and beyond that of simply removing children from parental control for a certain portion of the day.

School Board women trod an uncertain path that had to be negotiated with care. To assert that their object was to serve the children of women who were less fortunate than themselves provided a socially acceptable means of breaking down the prejudice in the world of local government, hitherto dominated by men. As the example of women who supported the expansion of the domestic curriculum for girls revealed, women on the London School Board could and did develop areas of expertise upon which to build a power base, albeit in areas synonymous with conventional sex role stereotyping. Here the pragmatic and theoretical impact of their work will be considered in relation to the wider social, economic and political contexts, by exploring the ways in which the women's conception of education as social welfare was influenced and shaped by the aspirations of politics and philanthropy.

Most Board members saw mass compulsory schooling as a way of instilling literacy, obedience, industry and manners. It also opened up the working-class family to new forms of surveillance and control. I shall concern myself here with two themes: the notion of compulsion and the disciplinary procedures underpinning Board policy on free education, school meals and corporal punishment.

All were crucial to the ascendancy of the school's claim to be in authority over and to control elementary schooling without interference from the competing claims of the family economy and culture.

School fees

Theoretically, the principle of compulsion ignored social divisions among the working classes. Those who interpreted it did not. In practice, a growing residential segregation among the urban population effectively generated a hierarchical grading of schooling based on an officially graduated fee structure ranging from 1d to 9d a week. Here tensions over the payment of fees will be used to illustrate the ways in which women members responded to the social and economic realities shaping the lives of the very poor.

Although difficult to generalize between representatives of the Tory Anglican 'economical' and 'Church Party', (which became known as the Liberal Nonconformist 'Progressive Party') and Socialist Board members, the first group adopted the most rigid position on the issue of school fees. Putting the case that church education would encourage working-class docility and reduce the School Board rate, these members opposed moves to remit fees on the grounds that they would pauperize the masses and undermine the position of church schools which did not have the necessary financial resources to subsidize such schemes. By contrast, Progressives were increasingly ready to support more humanitarian impulses. However many remained firmly wedded to a conventional Liberal philosophy of self-help and the market economy, espousing a moralistic attitude that virtually denied poverty as a cause of absenteeism.

Inevitably the question of the school pence raised problems of definition and classification. One familiar argument against the remission of fees incorporated versions of the conviction that non-payment reflected an inability on the part of rough working-class parents to appreciate the importance of regular attendance. Whatever the poor's initial disadvantages might be, these were either held to be the result of individual propensities like idleness and dissipation, or the uncaring ways of their parents. From its establishment in 1871, the Local Government Board campaigned to eliminate the provision of outdoor relief for the poor and while workhouses in London were subsidized from 1867 through the Metropolitan Common Poor Fund, out relief was financed through local rates and was much more at the discretion of the poor law guardians. Hence Elizabeth Garrett vigorously opposed a proposal that, for a renewable period not exceeding six months, the Board pay all or part of the school fees of children whose parents were unable to do so from poverty. According to her, such a scheme:

> might lead to a stimulation of pauperism [...] it would be subsidising improvidence [. . .] the money wasted in the public-house would pay for the children's pence several times over [. . .] the most truly humane policy would be to direct the

managers of the schools to remit no fees, except in the case of widows who had several children to educate, and children whose fathers were permanently disabled, and possibly in the case of paupers.

(School Board Chronicle, 22 April 1871: 298)

Both the 1834 Poor Law and the tenets of the COS incorporated versions of the conviction that charity, if it were not to be positively disempowering, was to be used judiciously. Accentuating the parallels, Jane Lewis maintains that 'regular payment of fees was part and parcel of the discipline of school life but was imposed on the parent rather than the child, much as Octavia Hill's insistence on the regular payment of rent in her tenement was designed to inculcate regular habits' (1982 : 299). Clearly the formally structured aspects of the school day were part and parcel of a wide-reaching attempt to promote changes in the values and codes of behaviour that operated within working-class families.

While Garrett Anderson upheld the principles of the 1834 law by seconding motions to limit the remission of fees of school children with able-bodied fathers, Emily Davies did not. Less pessimistic than her friend about the intractability of human nature, she wanted to keep help with the payment of fees personal and individual. In a social philosophy which is heavily reminiscent of Hill's conception of ideal social work practice, Emily pointed out the relationship between persons underpinning the 'gift' of charity (Stedman Jones, 1984). Social contact formed a crucial component of the alms-giving solution that she proposed, rather than the use of public funds. Moreover the fact that she rejected the idea of inspection suggests her appreciation of the ways of living of the poor was genuine, and may well have stemmed from her charity work in Gateshead and Greenwich. She was not alone. The educational press also warned against a policy that would effectively consign families to the workhouse: 'the course marked out for the Board is very simple. They have to consider whether a parent is unable from poverty to pay fees. In going beyond that they exceed their province' (*School Board Chronicle*, 10 May 1873: 304). In the event, the humanitarian impulse gained ground and members defeated proposals to exclude children with able-bodied parents from provisions for the payment or remission of fees.

Quite apart from the question of remission, the legal requirement on the Board to charge fees provided an unofficial means of excluding children on the basis of the scale of fees charged. According to Charles Booth's description and classification of London poverty, by the late 1880s it was possible to grade the elementary schools in accordance with the poverty–comfort spectrum identified within the population of London as a whole. Far from stereotyping the working classes as an undifferentiated mass, Booth exposed the distinction between the residuum: those in want (category B), in distress (category A) and the remainder (30.7 per cent) he found in poverty. Of the 69.3 per cent in comfort, categories, E/F were defined as those in working-class comfort, category G as the lower-middle-class, and category H the servant-keeping class. As William Marsden makes clear: 'This servant-keeping criterion formed one of the most clear-cut discontinuities in the whole social spectrum. It was reflected by the fact that category G families often used the higher-status elementary schools while category H did not' (1985: 128).

Stoutly defending the operation of a differentiated fees mechanism in his own division of Tower Hamlets, Thomas Scrutton admitted he would rather pay the fees of ragged school children himself than have them pass through the portals of London's Board schools. Asserting that 'he hardly ever saw a parent who did not show, absolutely by her dress, that she was able to pay the fees of her children', Scrutton considered it 'a great mistake to suppose that the East-end was poor' (*School Board Chronicle*, 28 June 1879: 608). While the conflation of parent with the female gender is hardly surprising, his vociferous assertion that both he and the other divisional members opposed the remission of fees acquires added significance in the light of subsequent abuses at St Paul's Industrial School. Helen Taylor perceptively undermined the circularity of Scrutton's argument. Accepting that no doubt there were rich people in the East End of London, she rhetorically begged the question of what exactly that proved. She summed it up for herself: 'the schools built by the ratepayers were used by himself and his fellow members for the well-to-do class of society' (*School Board Chronicle*, 28 June 1879: 609).

In stark contrast to the avowedly class differentiated attitude espoused by Thomas Scrutton and his supporters, socialist representatives urged dispensing with fees altogether: Helen Taylor's principal concern was to alleviate material hardship. Moving that the Bye-Laws Committee be instructed to take rent into account, she sought to establish a scale of income below which remission of fees was always granted.

> She apologised for occupying the time of the Board with a question so unimportant as the needs of 20 or 30 thousand poor families in London, but she should never scruple to express her opinion of the cruelty of the Board in this matter ... the heavy oppression which the Board were practising on these starving members of the population was a question which she would bring again and again ... she brought the question forward in the hope of alleviating some portion of the suffering of her fellow creatures.
>
> (*School Board Chronicle*, 2 April 1881: 320)

The emphasis on the cost of housing is crucial as rent absorbed far more income in London than in most other parts of the country. In 1885 the Royal Commission on the Housing of the Working Classes found over 85 per cent of London workers paid more than a fifth of their income for rent and nearly half were paying over a quarter. Refusing to support the Board in its policy of sanctions so long as school fees remained, Taylor appealed for a rights-based claim to universal social entitlements as opposed to the more general emphasis on needs met by self-help and the discriminating intervention of philanthropic organizations. Despite the logic of her argument that the Board lost as much in the way of arrears that they had to cancel as would be lost by a more liberal policy of remission, most of her colleagues held firm to the ideas of classical political economy. Unsurprisingly, pleas that educational endowments be used for the remission or abolition of fees were also blatantly ignored.

This point had already been made by George Potter, who had succeeded in getting a committee appointed (with Benjamin Lucraft as chairman) to inquire into the charitable endowments which might (or should) be applied to education. Evidence produced in this and subsequent reports made it clear that here were substantial funds diverted from their proper use. Helen Taylor and Henrietta Muller were among the few to make explicit the underlying hypocrisy of arguments that to abolish or remit fees would pauperize the working classes, in view of the not infrequent diversion of these resources to subsidize middle-class schooling at Eton, Harrow and elsewhere. At one point Helen proposed the use of funds from the City parochial charities to subsidize free schooling yet her pleas for the remission of fees when the family income fell below 6d a day per member went unheeded until October 1884, when the Board finally agreed with her that rent should be taken into account (*School Board Chronicle*, 2 April 1881: 357). Stressing the day-to-day problem of keeping up the school attendance rate, Henrietta predicted 'free education would reduce the numbers sent to industrial schools, gain a large increase in the Government grant, enhance greater regularity of attendance and increase the numbers in average attendance' (*School Board Chronicle*, 22 April 1882: 375).

Moving beyond a pathological interpretation of life in the metropolitan slums, for these two middle-class women sympathy and empathy coalesced within a philosophy that saw education as a means of redress in the face of gross disparities in social opportunity. Deeply critical of Victorian distinctions between the deserving and undeserving poor, Henrietta did not see how they could distinguish between those who were poor through their own fault and those who were not. The remedy was 'to educate the children as much as possible, and to remove every obstacle that stood in the way of their education' (*School Board Chronicle*, 22 July 1882: 54). Both women advocated free schools on an experimental basis, although Benjamin Lucraft feared that limited numbers 'would herd all the worst children together, and the children of the honest poor would be obliged to mix with them' (*School Board Chronicle*, 15 July 1882: 29–31). Yet even though fees stood in the way of attendance, the Board refused to put into effect Section 26 of the 1870 Act allowing the establishment of free schools in special cases. Dismayed at the extent to which girls' domestic work kept them out of school more often than it did their brothers, Henrietta tried to introduce a system of rewards that might remedy this situation but, until the election of Annie Besant in 1888, she and Helen were the only women to challenge the Board's position on the question of fees.

Their decision to prioritize the issue of free schooling may well have reflected the fact that as members for Lambeth and Southwark, Henrietta and Helen represented divisions containing up to 75 per cent of families living in poverty (Booth, 1891: Volume 1, 36). This was in stark contrast to Marylebone, the only division to have a record of continuous female representation during this period, which averaged 26 per cent of families in poverty – with divisions ranging from 13. 5 to 30.4 per cent of the local population. During the 1880s, Alice Westlake (member for Marylebone) and Rosamond Davenport Hill (member for the City), supported and moved motions to tinker with the system of fee collection. They were concerned to minimize the impact of fees on the poorest class of children, whom they felt to be in most need of education (*School Board Chronicle*, 30 June 1888: 669–760). Reminiscent of middle-class fears of the residuum, their arguments reflect a general movement towards an acknowledgement of poverty as an indisputable cause of irregular attendance, irrespective of distinctions on the basis of aid worthiness. As Mrs Burgwin of Orange Street School assured the Cross Commissioners in 1887: 'I have about 75 per cent of attendances and I go very carefully morning and afternoon into the reasons of the absences ... and I really do find scarcely an unreasonable excuse given.'

The fact that Annie Besant and Stewart Headlam (Socialist member for Tower Hamlets 1888–1904) managed to influence the direction of policy in 1890 indicates the changed social and economic contexts. First, internal divisions among working people reflected the co-existence of rising living standards for some, and unemployment and misery for others. Second, a period in which political attention was increasingly focused on social questions, saw the rise of socialism and the 'new unionism' movement into which masses of unskilled London workers were organized. The decision to recommend free education was a pragmatic response to sharp political conflict. In this situation Board members found themselves drawn towards a broader definition of education as social policy. It received parliamentary approval when the then Conservative government bowed to pressure from the Trades Union Congress and the Liberal opposition, and in 1891 passed an act authorizing free schools.

School meals

Unlike free education, the issue of meals for near-starving school children did not enter School Board politics until the founding platform of the Social Democratic Federation, (then simply the Democratic Federation), advocated state-funded school dinners in 1883. Once again, it was an issue adopted by all socialist candidates, following in the footsteps of Helen Taylor; but it also engaged the interest of other women, motivated by rather different reforming impulses.

As with free education, attitudes towards the issue of school meals reached a turning point in the 1880s, previous to which the part played by public administration was a small one. An Act of 1868 empowered guardians to prosecute parents who neglected to provide adequate food for their children but, according to Benjamin Waugh (Board member and founder-director of the National Society for the Prevention of Cruelty to Children), the Act was almost a dead letter. Giving evidence before the House of Lords Select Committee on Poor Relief in 1888, he stated that such abuses were largely disregarded by the police, the public and the guardians alike, though, in his opinion, the cases in which the Boards did habitually take action were mainly those where female guardians were able to influence policy (House of Lords Select Committee on Poor Relief, 1888, Questions 5857, 5858). Similarly, the 1876 Education Act provided for the establishment of day industrial schools which, among other things, set up school feeding on the basis of parental contributions; but despite vigorous

The conflict among the three women encapsulates the debate between statist and voluntarist visions of the aims and appropriate limits of both economic assistance and state intervention. Deep rooted hostility towards this kind of welfare provision played an important part in the debate and a feeling that school feeding was an unwelcome intrusion into family life continued to dog the campaign on behalf of needy school children. The self-supporting meal, with its degree of moral selectivity and denial of the principle of universalism, remained the most desirable form of provision. For most members, the delicate balance between individual and community, private and public, was best served by an advocacy of *laissez-faire* practices. Board policy continued to favour the individualist approach. As with the debate over free education, the over-riding policy objective became the need to avoid pauperizing further sections of the working classes and so enlarge the residuum. Far from meeting the demands of Socialist representatives that the Board petition Parliament to initiate the provision of free school meals, members voted to appoint a sub-committee to investigate the scale and nature of the problem.

Their inquiries revealed a picture of widespread malnutrition, although the problem was most acute in Finsbury, Hackney, Tower Hamlets (Besant's division) and Southwark. Overall, the inquiry found an average daily attendance of some 43,000 (13 per cent) underfed children in London board schools, a quarter of whom were in Tower Hamlets. This report was followed in November by a conference that resulted in the formation of the London Schools' Dinner Association. Seven Board members were placed on the executive committee of the new central association. Its remit was to co-ordinate local provision and so secure more efficient and economical administration of the funds to be distributed among denominational as well as board schools. Most of the large voluntary agencies were merged into this body, of which the then chairman of the London School Board, the Reverend Joseph Diggle, was president. It also enjoyed the support of a distinguished selection of the educational establishment including A. J. Mundella, the veteran radical educationist and former Vice-President for Education.

In 1895 a still Tory board was forced to acknowledge the failure of the self-supporting penny dinners movement, 90 per cent of the meals having been given free; yet it continued to rely on voluntary and charitable contributions through a special charitable fund. A majority attached great importance to the enforcement of parental duty, while a certain complacency about the effectiveness of feeding by the voluntary organizations meant that the over-riding concern remained the need to avoid indiscriminate charity by means of case records kept by women like Lucy Fowler. Nominated by the Committee of Representative Managers to give evidence to Margaret Eve and her colleagues on the Special Committee on Underfed Children in 1895, Lucy stressed the 'need to know the circumstances of every child to help in each case' (Underfed Children Attending School, 1895: 42). In the Committee's view, practical social work of this kind would facilitate the qualitative analysis of the London poor and so provide 'an invaluable guide for local action' (*School Board Chronicle*, 16 November 1895: 556).

In 1897 control of the Board swung back to the Progressives but policy prescriptions continued to promote individualist solutions. In a powerful maiden speech, Mary Bridges Adams backed proposals to supplement voluntary provision, though the Reverand Copeland Bowie moved the previous question. This was a procedural move designed to put an end to debate. It was carried by 28 votes to 15. Impelled by a relentless hatred of injustice, Mary made her feelings on the issue clear:

> The London School Board, composed of people, who for the most part were able to gratify every wish, could not realise what was meant by underfeeding, and she had been pained to hear this debate. It would be a simple thing to have a weighing machine in the schools and the children weighed to see how much they were below the standard weight, and that would be better than all their reports and statistics. The wives of working men, with what were considered comfortable incomes of 30s to 40s a week would tell them it was difficult to provide for 3 children, then what was the case of those with a £1 a week and less to live upon. Poverty was an ambiguous term and they must remember that there was the poverty of the poor as well as of the rich – the poor relatives members pitied who had to manage on £400 a year. As to lowering parental responsibility, they did not hear of that in the case of the rich who used educational endowments and foundations for their children. While the ground landlords existed as they did there was no need for London's children to starve.
>
> (*School Board Chronicle*, 18 December 1897: 677–8)

Addressing a largely hostile audience who still assumed that the function of the Board was to supplement individual initiative, not to replace it, she combines a classic Marxist statement with a caustic reminder that poverty is a relative concept. Significantly, the only other woman to support the proposed change to Board policy was Honnor Morten. Both lived in women's settlement houses where the aim was to promote the welfare of the district through the emphasis upon a non-professional, shared women's world. Indeed, Morten actually lived alone for a year in Hoxton before persuading two friends from Bedford College to join her. Furthermore, Morten's claim that her settlement was run on 'unsectarian and socialistic lines', was a reference to the fact that, unlike other settlements, it was housed in 'workmen's tenements' where the workers did their own cleaning and 'live in friendly intercourse with the neighbours' (Morten, 1899a: 92–3)

In 1898 the question was referred to the General Purposes Committee, now including Mary Bridges Adams among its members, for consideration and report. Progressives exploited the opportunity afforded them and perhaps the most significant development was the legitimation given to an alternate politics and discourse. As one might expect the evidence given before the committee shows the prevalence of a state of affairs very similar to that of earlier years. On the other hand, the majority report and recommendations suggest a greater willingness to embrace the collectivist project. Honnor Morten, for instance, queried the nutritional value of the food frequently supplied to malnourished children which, she argued, was calculated to cause diarrhoea. 'I should expect', the professional nurse continued, 'many children would die from that complaint if fed daily on such a diet, which is almost devoid of nourishment' (Underfed Children Attending School, 1898: 12–14). Despite the example set by the work of Margaret McMillan and the Independent Labour Party in Bradford (Simon, 1980: 278), in London the standard of voluntary provision had deteriorated by the late 1890s. Quite apart from the concern to safeguard against the pauperization of the masses, financial stringency ensured that the most common form of provision was soup. Indeed the London Vegetarian Society, the Bread and Food Reform Society, and the Women's Total Abstinence Union had joined forces to provide strictly vegetarian soups, supplemented by wholemeal bread. In many schools, the addition of cheap and fatty cuts of meat was equally unedifying since the smell of the soup cooking could be nauseating. Mrs Burgwin, who started giving free milk drinks to the most needy children attending her school in 1874, found the preparation of the soup so offensive that 'it is wonderful' she said 'how the teachers endure it' (Hurt, 1979: 119).

Despite the fact that many other witnesses stressed the inadequacies of private and voluntary aid, differences over the mechanism for provision effectively split the committee. The majority were now prepared to countenance measures designed to alleviate the situation of children without the use of exceptions often deriving from moral criteria. Summing up, it seemed to them:

> The first duty of the community to the child . . . is to see that it has a proper chance as regards its equipment for life. If they come to school underfed . . . it would seem to be the duty of those who have a care of the children to deal with it, and to see that the underfeeding ceases.
>
> (Bulkley, 1914: 23)

Nevertheless, a more cautious minority clung to the status quo. In the event members rejected a proposal that the Board be empowered to supplement voluntary provision and acted on the recommendations of the minority.

Two years later Board enquiries revealed the number of children coming into the underfed category was around 55,000. At no time did all these children receive meals and Mary Bridges Adams continued to press the case for state-funded school meals and medical examinations to ascertain the weight, height and chest measurements of every child. But the majority remained reluctant to encourage state collectivism. Like Kate Hart (Church and Board School manager, Sunday School superintendent and COS representative), most held firmly to the view that free meals were not only detrimental to a child's moral fibre, but 'that those families who seem the poorest are generally the most wasteful and extravagant' (Underfed Children Attending School, 1898: 20). Consequently, Mary's argument that meal services could be paid for in one of three ways – the taxation of ground values, a graduated income tax on all incomes above £300 a year, or graduated death duties – fell on deaf ears. Consistent to the end, in 1900 the Board set up a permanent co-ordinating committee to supplement voluntary efforts.

Discipline

The London School Board developed an elaborate system of reward cards, prizes, medals and certificates, as well as punishments, as part of the struggle to secure compliance in the arena of the elementary schools themselves. Adopting a wider definition of discipline than that encapsulated by the notion of corporal punishment, it will be argued that broader issues were at stake. In addition to the use of corporal punishment, this concluding section explores the ways in which the board schools provided a means of encouraging specific social values. This was part of a broader attempt to engender self-discipline amongst the working classes through the development of new moral codes.

To develop an earlier point about the chimera of parental consensus, the gradual re-definition of the parental role also provided the means of establishing that schools had the right to punish their pupils. The institutionalization of schooling was the result of competing definitions, of negotiation and struggle, extending beyond the school gate. Hence the exercise of power in a specifically educational setting reflects the changing social relations between families and the state. Recalling his first day at his first school at Settles Street on the borders of Whitechapel in 1886, teacher Phillip Ballard observed:

> the softening influence of popular education had been at work on the London poor for only a decade and a half and the bulk of the parents were still unschooled and unlettered. In cases of conflict between teacher and child they nearly always sided with the child.
>
> (1937: 63-4)

Faced with a large class of unruly boys of mixed ages who had not passed Standard I, his autobiographical account is littered with military metaphors. In this context a 'little of the fighting spirit' became a crucial component of classroom discipline. For instance, he once came to blows with a boy of his own height but heavier, who had appeared before the magistrates for cruelty to animals and sticking pins into the leg of a smaller boy who sat beside him. The boy refused to leave his seat when requested to do so and put up his fists and, Ballard continues, 'I had to fight him then and there, and I had either to win or throw up my job. It was my Waterloo' (1937: 64).

Just as women members were divided over the use of corporal punishment in the industrial schools, so they adopted various positions over its use as a mechanism for social control in the elementary schools. The fundamental divide, however, was between those who remained outside the Progressive party caucus and those who sought to work within it. Thus the most vociferous opponents of this form of physical punishment among the early women members were the trio of Florence Fenwick Miller, Elizabeth Surr and Helen Taylor, while Honnor Morten earned the hostility of the teachers' press at a later date. In 1901 the *Board Teacher* launched the following invective against Morten for asserting that corporal punishment was on the increase in schools: 'we have scant respect for Miss Morten ... because she cannot tell the truth – she is so blinded by prejudice that she cannot see things as they are' (1 February 1901: 273). In contrast to the attitude of the educational press, the oral history of childhood painfully recalls the sadistic punishments inflicted by some teachers. It also shows the spirited defence of their children advanced by some parental opponents (see Humphries, 1981; Thompson, 1975).

The woman who took most risks was Helen Taylor who also spoke on domestic violence during her term in office. An outspoken member of the Vigilance Association for the defence of personal rights, she argued that boys who were flogged by their teachers were more likely to grow up in the belief that they had the right to beat their wives. Speaking on a public platform, she used a constituency meeting to draw parallels with the use of corporal punishment on adult males confined to the workhouse. She calculated that the breadwinner who had been punished in a brutal manner would be more likely to come back a brutalized tyrant to his family than to keep them out of the workhouse by his exertions. Extending the argument to the elementary schools, she felt that more than any other single act, corporal punishment was the cause of keeping children away from school. Much more controversially, she went on to enunciate a thinly veiled attack on her male colleagues whom she saw as the main obstacle to reform:

> She did not think there lay much difficulty in the matter; the main difficulty was, in fact, with the members of the Board, who had had punishment in their own youth, and intend now to give it to the young, declaring that they had it themselves and it did them much good. It said little for the refinement and civilisation of the age if teaching could not be carried on by reason and sympathy.
> (Mill-Taylor Special Collection, Newscuttings, 28 November 1877)

The significance of her stand should not be underestimated. At this time, violence against wives by husbands was condoned as legitimate chastisement, although Frances Cobbe's exposé of marital violence amongst the working classes led to working women getting the right to legal separation in 1878. Divorce reform slowly followed.

By contrast, Alice Westlake adopted a rather more orthodox response to Elizabeth Surr's attempt to ban the use of corporal punishment on girls. Speaking during the debate on the proposed change to Board policy in February 1878, Alice demurred on the grounds that some of the girls 'were of a very rough class and were insubordinate, and the teachers could not expel them' (*School Board Chronicle*, 2 November 1878: 416). Later that year, Elizabeth succeeded in getting the question referred back to the School Management Committee for consideration and report. The incident is also important for women's claims to humanize the state in that it provides an indication of how women's organizations might interpret her actions. This point was clearly taken by the *Englishwomen's Review* when the periodical defended the right of women to take a distinctive stand over cases affecting their own sex, but admitted that humanitarianism affects both girls and boys and they should be glad to see her include both sexes alike (15 November 1878: 506).

Originally defined by the Huxley sub-committee in 1871, Board policy was to permit the occasional and exceptional use of the cane. Every incident had to be formally recorded in a book kept for the purpose and the head teacher was directly responsible for every punishment of the kind. Blows to the head were forbidden and pupil teachers were not allowed to use physical punishment at any time. In 1874 a resolution extended this ban to all other assistant teachers. Many teachers resented what Ballard called 'these ridiculous restrictions' and sympathetic head teachers in the poorer districts often turned a blind eye to infringements of the regulations in the interests of school discipline. Consequently the question of corporal punishment was a long standing bone of contention between the teachers, who fought hard for the right to engage in this ritual, and the Board, who were all along more inclined to restrict corporal punishment (see Copelman, 1996: 88-92). Matters came to a head in June 1888 when Mark Wilks and Rosamond Davenport Hill tried to get the headmaster of Mansford Street School, Bethnal Green, sacked for allowing his assistants to administer punishment. Though the extent of the infringement was a matter of some dispute among Board members (with the stated number of boys caned for being late for school ranging from one to nine), the motion was defeated and a fine and a reprimand imposed instead (*Board Teacher*, 1 June 1888: 68). A few months later, after a teacher at Dulwich Hamlet School had been the victim of blackmail by a parent for striking a child, the rule was relaxed.

Working-class opposition to the proposed extension of the rights of school personnel to punish children also found expression in the debate during the 1880s – Benjamin Lucraft was a vehement opponent. He and Florence Fenwick Miller introduced a working-men's deputation to the Board and, despite the fact that she had not sought re-election in 1885, Fenwick Miller continued to speak at specially called public meetings on the same issue. Indeed the Finsbury Clubs Radical Association and the Hackney Radical Club were among the most prominent supporters of her argument that the relaxation of the rules would lead to the frequent, hasty, and indiscriminate use of corporal punishment and hence to greater truancy (*School Board Chronicle*, 27 November 1886: 569–70; 4 December 1886: 612–13). The evidence of a mature pupil teacher, in the years 1889–93, would seem to bear her out:

> Every assistant master had a cane and so had the pupil teachers, but we were not allowed to have a crook so that if any questions arose they were only pointers. There were no backs to the desks and backs of boys were straightened by means of a stroke of the cane.
>
> (quoted in Lowndes, 1937: 16–17)

Phillip Ballard, in defence, offers a different interpretation. In his opinion, the lifting of the restrictions on the use of the cane served to facilitate a gradual reduction in physical punishment.

The stance adopted by women like Helen Taylor and Honnor Morten may have earned them the vigorous dislike of the teachers, but Helen was unfailingly popular with her working-class constituents. Her vehemence on the issue lay behind a leafleting campaign (probably financed by teachers) urging residents not to vote for her in the 1879 election but to plump for the Liberals Joshua Hawkins and Mary Richardson. She still finished top of the poll, despite the opposition of the teachers and the manipulation of the electoral register by

E. H. Bayley and other Liberals. They used the Southwark Parliamentary Revision Courts to illegally exclude about 10,000 qualified (but poor) householders from the parliamentary and school board voting lists. Significantly, the exclusions did not include better off women. Presumably these were considered the basis of Mary Richardson's support – the woman the Liberals chose to run against Taylor.

Irrespective of the punishment of the body (embodying both repressive and ideological methods of control), the selection of school knowledge and the provision of after school leisure activities also lent support to the deliberate attempts to inculcate habits of self-discipline among the working classes. Lessons in elementary social economy were a case in point. One of eight essential subjects in the curriculum proposals adopted by the Board in 1871, this was not a subject for which the education department offered a grant. As a result it was only taught in a few schools and by 1883 was almost non-existent. Concerned at this omission Florence Fenwick Miller raised the issue of recommended texts in an attempt to rejuvenate the teaching of a subject which she considered to be of immense value. With an eye to the civic responsibilities of those who would benefit from such instruction, Florence articulates a moral philosophy in which the work ethic emerges as central to her citizenship ideal:

> It was necessary that men should work. It was utterly impossible to live without working; and the more people who worked the better it would be for everyone in the community. ... By social economy they would teach the first principles of these matters – the absolute necessity of certain things being done, certain courses being adopted, and certain classes of action being followed.
> *(School Board Chronicle,* 13 January 1883: 29)

Significantly, Helen Taylor challenged the political element of this definition by emphasizing that the teaching should only cover 'those laws which actually and indisputably governed society' (*School Board Chronicle,* 13 January 1883: 29). Essentially she wanted to deepen the children's understanding of the world in which they lived was an important shift in emphasis from the implicitly shared understanding of the subject advanced by other members of the Board. To summarize with the representative words of William Bousfield (twice chairman of the COS), he:

> hoped the Board would deal with this matter in some way, as a little instruction in it would make the rising generation really good citizens, and nothing was more wanted at the present time than to teach widely the laws which govern thrift and temperance in other matters.
> *(School Board Chronicle,* 13 January 1883: 29)

Thrift and temperance were further encouraged by the establishment of penny savings banks and instruction in the dangers of intoxicating liquor. This later innovation was the suggestion of Florence Fenwick Miller and Helen Taylor in 1877. Objecting to the use of diagrams to highlight the diseases caused by heavy drinking, Alice Westlake had other ideas as to how the Board might control the social behaviour of children outside school. She suggested that the Board 'place children in the way of other occupations and . . . pleasures' (*School Board Chronicle*, 21 April 1877: 406). Hence the introduction of after school play programmes, like the Happy Evenings organized by the Children's Happy Evenings Association started in Marylebone in 1888.

Elected representatives were simply the tip of the iceberg in the predominantly women's world of school-based social work. The idea of reform by example was crucial to an alternative set of values corresponding to the ethic of public service aspired to by women unable or unwilling to be assimilated to the older, leisured, gentle tradition. In the words of an early student and later senior staff lecturer in maths at Royal Holloway College:

> A new world was being created and I remember the zest with which we all carried on our daily affairs. Our way of life was intended to be a training in virtue, we all looked forward to 'Doing good' somehow, somewhere.
>
> (cited in Bingham, 1987: 109)

Founded by Ada Heather-Bigg (with the Princess of Wales as its benefactor), the aim of the Children's Happy Evenings Association was to provide a range of after-school activities, usually in a single-sex setting. By 1904 the movement had 113 branches, meeting in 83 schools and providing amusement periodically for more than 16,000 children. Among the 800 voluntary helpers were Mary Ward and her daughters Janet and Dorothy, operating under the auspices of the Women's Work Committee of University Hall, the first of Ward's settlement projects. From these beginnings emerged the Evening Play Centres run from a new settlement, Passmore Edwards, which opened in 1897 (Brehony, 1987: 554–60; Koven, 1993: 109–16). Under the guidance of Mary Ward, the women ran recreation schools after official school hours and summer vacation schools during holidays. The focus of all these programmes was play: storytelling and crafts, colouring and board games in the classrooms, with dancing and children's singing games in the school hall on the girls' evening, boxing and tug-of-war on the boys'. Tickets were usually allocated to children as a reward for being regular and punctual. Inevitably many of the poorest were excluded but the teachers supported the movement if only, Hugh Philpott mischievously observed, 'because it tends to improve the school attendance' (1904: 305).

The Children's Country Holiday Fund was another example of child-saving intervention. It existed to supply poor London children with assisted country holidays (part of the cost was almost always met by the parents) in the homes of respectable cottagers who were paid 5s a week for each child they received. Its establishment coincided with the opening of the first settlement house, Toynbee Hall, in Whitechapel. Both organizations owed their inception to the Reverend Samuel and Henrietta Barnett who had been experimenting with the idea of sending East End children for country breaks since 1877. Their work was formalized with the amalgamation of the Fresh Air Mission, the Country Holidays Committee, the Summer Outing Committee and the Marylebone Children's Country Holiday Committee under the auspices of the Children's Country Holiday Fund in 1884 (Minutes of an Executive Committee of the Country Holiday Fund, 27 March 1884). During the 1890s both Emma

Maitland and Maude Lawrence served on its Council, while Constance Elder, Margaret Eve and Honnor Morten joined local committees in their constituencies. Margaret Gladstone, daughter of John Hall Gladstone, Board member and future wife of the Labour leader James Ramsay Macdonald, was just one of the female school managers who joined Morten in Shoreditch. Further, Ruth Homan's daughter assisted her mother's work in Tower Hamlets by serving on the local committee for Poplar East. Whatever the motivations behind such work, it was clearly only ameliorative in character and not designed to effect radical social change. As the self-supporting principles underlying the Poplar Board School Children's Boot and Clothing Help Society (established by Ruth Homan) accentuate, for some of these women at least, it was difficult to break with the fear of pauperism. As she told the *East End News* 'the children pay small weekly subscriptions, and, when two thirds of the cost has been paid the boots are supplied, the society finding the remaining third in very necessitous cases' (Fawcett Library, Schools Boards, 'Newscuttings', *East End News*, 1897).

Conclusion

The sharing of a common culture was an important source of identity for women seeking a pathway into the public sphere. Yet serving the poor was not a unitary practice and women members did not all act together. Ideas about the particular nature of women provided a common discourse within which to articulate their policy recommendations but this did not mean a lack of divergence in their response to social problems. Using the typology of social motherhood proposed by Eileen Yeo (1992) it becomes possible to identify patterns among the women members, without losing sight of the dissonances and contradictions mentioned above.

The three recurring archetypes of social mothering are an empowering mother, a protecting mother and a disciplining (or punishing) mother, though it is not suggested either here or by Yeo that real women expressed only one of these tendencies. Here Annie Besant, Mary Bridges Adams, Florence Fenwick Miller, Honnor Morten, Henrietta Muller and Helen Taylor are used to illustrate the nurturing and empowering side of mother love. All were committed to helping the poor develop the skills for self-organization and to giving them the chance to speak with their own voice. By contrast, the protective face of mothering became sharply visible, first in relation to Emily Davies' position on re-mission of fees, second in relation to Elizabeth Surr's stance on the issue of corporal punishment, and third via the stance adopted by Margaret Ashton Dilke on the question of school feeding. The language of protection and advocacy also linked Alice Westlake's emphasis on school-based leisure provision after official school hours and Ruth Homan's role as policy-maker and care-provider. The third face of motherhood was a punitive face that, as Yeo makes clear, 'often appeared more disciplining and harsh when turned to the poor' (1992: 78). Rosamond Davenport Hill may have seen the family (and women as mothers within it) as central to her conception of herself and her work, but education for all was explicitly justified as 'gentling the masses'. So she chose to emphasize the rehabilitation of working-class boys and girls in institutions promoting gender-specific behaviours, values and skills. Elizabeth Garrett, like Davenport Hill after her, opposed state-initiated welfare schemes. Not without reason, they both were cautious about giving offence. Not only was Elizabeth roundly attacked for her lack of compassion in upholding the principles of the 1834 law, but Rosamond Davenport Hill clearly felt it necessary to temper her opposition to school feeding with an expression of warm-hearted concern.

Despite the claims that women politicians would humanize political economy and the state, the issues chosen accentuate the way in which their attitudes to working-class children in school were shaped by the predominant social theory of the 1860s, epitomized by the fear of that undifferentiated residuum. As the political landscape changed, a rhetoric linking school welfare services to the language of national efficiency became the dominant idiom of early twentieth-century discussions about the health of the nation. The movement for school feeding and child welfare received a tremendous impetus from the appointment in 1903 of an interdepartmental committee to enquire into 'physical deterioration', but the provision of school meals remained controversial precisely because it challenged the absolute responsibility of the father to maintain his family. In the event, the 1906 Education (Provision of Meals) Act secured a measure of school feeding. More importantly, although the legislation was permissive in character, it effectively bypassed the presumption of male maintenance to approach deserving non-earners directly.

Thus, as with the issue of industrial school governance, the evidence suggests that women members tended to give stronger priority to welfare issues, although party divisions and attitudes towards institutional norms and procedures overrode the gender gap in terms of proposed solutions to particular social problems. Hence the tendency for more radical women politicians to be marginalized politically, while those who shared the dominant discourses on social policy were more likely to experience career promotion. As a social group these latter women shared that personal approach towards social problems advocated by Octavia Hill and her disciples in the COS. As she succinctly states: 'My only notion of reform is that of living side by side with people, till all that I believe becomes livingly clear to them' (Maurice, 1928: 211). In effect, considerable faith was placed in the power of education to act as a form of social control, aided and abetted by a simple notion of 'reform from above' – in this case by the example set through increased social contact between the classes in order to instil specific social values and moral codes. As one such 'beneficiary' recalled:

> The lady who judged the work was quite elderly and wore a straw bonnet the shade of Parma Violet, tied with 2 velvet ribbons of the same shade. The straw of the bonnet was peaked over the face and each peak had a shaded Parma Violet on it. Our teacher said to us afterwards 'Class take note of the lady we have just met and her perfect speech'. The lady had called us 'gels', not the so often heard 'girrls'.
>
> (Bark, n.d.: 1)

Making or Unmaking the Difference?

Introduction

As elected representatives, the women members of the London School Board shared a novel political and administrative experience. Nonetheless, only a feminist with a leaning to essentialism would conclude that therefore these women may be said to form a simple, homogeneous social category. My picture is more nuanced. Irrespective of the high degree of social homogeneity and the confident reformers' zeal for social action, no two biographies were (or could be), the same. Unsurprisingly, the strategies and tactics they proposed and used in relation to the constraints and problems they faced were much more heterogeneous.

Political auto/biography

Helen Taylor was perhaps the most spirited elected representative of them all. The women who preceded her had been firm in establishing their ground and holding it. They had learned to walk on to public platforms where ladies were not expected or welcome, they had learned to persuade where persuasion was the best tactic and to speak out in support of their position. Intelligent, energetic and hard-working, Elizabeth Garrett in particular had made a striking impression on the public imagination before Helen Taylor added her own emphases. Like her predecessors on the first Board, Helen was a national figure, albeit with less conventional contacts among the politically organized radicals and Socialists. Additionally, Taylor created a stir by adopting a more open and generalized popular appeal to the working-class electorate which centred on questions of active participation and control. Elected three times in one of the Board's four poorest divisions, Southwark, she was able to command considerable support among trades unions, local radical clubs and the Irish community, thereby ensuring working-class perspectives were not absent from the Board. Moreover she frequently held open constituency meetings to canvass public opinion on such issues as the use of corporal punishment. She also used her power as a divisional member to appoint local people (in particular working men), as school managers.

Yet Helen's real love was the theatre, although her brief career as a professional actress finished on her mother's death in November 1858 (see Kamm, 1977: 115–31). Perhaps partly because of that she was not frightened by appearing in front of an audience, which surely helped her develop the graceful, easy style of oratory remembered by those who heard her speak. Many years later, an editorial in the *Lancashire Evening Post* was fulsome in its praise for the way in which she 'carefully enforced her points step by step, interspersing her observations at times with flashes of humour, at others with touching pictures of life among the London poor' (21 October 1886). Further, in his memoir of a life in education, Thomas Gautrey conceded her voice was pleasant and she never raised it. Nonetheless, as her obituarist claimed: 'when she felt it right to be angry her anger was a white heat. Her passionate hatred of cruelty or oppression could scorch like a furnace seven times heated' (*Women and Progress*, 8 February 1907: 229).

Opinions towards her were mixed. Fellow suffragists such as Lydia Becker, Barbara Bodichon and Emily Davies found her tactless and overbearing, male opponents nicknamed her the acid maiden. Lyulph Stanley, for one, said that she and Elizabeth Surr reminded him of the old fairy tale of two girls, one with jewels and pearls in her mouth, one with toads and vipers. 'He would leave the Board to decide as to which Miss Taylor resembled. (Laughter)' (*School Board Chronicle*, 15 October 1881). In contrast the radical, William Rendle, was convinced the women teachers and female pupils needed a representative like Helen, since she would 'be able to take the necessary stand and by force of pure reason and the public opinion which is behind you get the girls lifted up a step or two at least' (William Taylor to Helen Rendle, 3 December 1876). As described earlier, there was popular support for her policies among the electors of Southwark, but Helen's inability to ally herself with powerful forces inside the Board weakened her effectiveness in advancing the cause of the working class.

As this suggests, the hostility and resentment she experienced brought out what Josephine Kamm (1977) describes best as her positive, dramatic personality. Although William Rendle argued that Helen should lead the 'women element' owing to the tendency for the 'man power' to adopt a condescending attitude towards their female colleagues, her force of character and socialistic views antagonized the Liberal party machine. Consequently, she could record few successes in the causes she adopted. Thomas Gautrey, for example, reports an exchange that took place between Helen Taylor and the Reverend John Rodgers (vicar of St Thomas, Charterhouse, member of the School Board for London, 1870–80), at the end of which she exclaimed: 'So, Mr Rodgers, you would not allow us poor women any sphere!' He retorted: 'Oh yes, I would; get a house full of children, then stay at home and mind them' (n.d.: 79). The incident is important because John Rodgers, Lyulph Stanley and the Congregationalist minister, the Reverend Mark Wilks, dominated Liberal politics on the Board for its first years. By the time Helen was elected, for instance, Rodgers and Wilks were affectionately known as Mark and John the education evangelists. Thus despite constant critical pressure, Helen's clear vision for extending the scope of elementary education was not realized during her period in office. On the whole, she irritated colleagues to such an extent that crucial support was withheld by the official Liberals (she herself stood as a Radical Democrat from 1879), as well as the Anglican clergy. As a consequence, Helen's persistent agitation about the proper use of educational endowments failed to secure even modest schemes of fee remission; the ability to mobilize an independent power base and the intervention of a sympathetic Home Secretary were crucial to her victory over the question of corporal punishment within industrial schools. Her other aims, especially democratic control of the schools, remained more elusive.

At the same time, other women experienced difficulties in the gendered dynamics of political representation. For example, after the defeat of the woman standing as her successor (Emily Guest), Emily Davies confessed to Barbara Bodichon that many voters felt unhappy about the fact that 'I did not fight hard enough for needlework but left it to an old bachelor' (quoted in Stephen, 1927: 285). Twenty-five years later, tensions between a traditional female role and women's activism resurfaced amid reports that Honnor Morten had been seen walking down Fleet Street smoking a cigarette. Indeed her action provoked such a hostile reaction from the church faction that she was forced to resign her seat in Hackney and transfer to Southwark instead (Gautrey, n.d.: 79).

Despite these anomalies, the significance of having had women participate in municipal life and legislation should not be denied. Pat Thane (1993: 350–1) has noted the unique quality of the British situation by highlighting the fact that no other major state in Europe or America offered women a comparable role at such an early date. For the German feminist, Helene Lange (1848–1930) writing in 1895, the example of English women who could vote and hold office at the local level was sufficient to encourage the advocacy of a gradualist approach to reform, rather than risk antagonizing the establishment (see Meyer, 1985: 34). Interviewed by the editor of the feminist *Woman's Signal* in 1894, Graham Wallas acknowledged the value of School Board women and admitted he 'had never found sex made any difference in the quality of the work accomplished' (22 February: 125).

Yet the most fundamental comment that can be made about the progress of women members is that some of them did challenge the status quo, whereas the men hardly ever did. The trio of Florence Fenwick Miller, Elizabeth Surr and Helen Taylor sought to challenge the dominant policy agenda in the late 1870s and early 1880s, as did their political successors Annie Besant, Mary Bridges Adams and Honnor Morten. However, whereas Miller, Surr and Taylor (along with Henrietta Muller) were marginalized politically, Besant was able to respond strategically to the changed opportunities around her after the 1888 School Board election. Nonetheless, it would seem that these women politicians did behave differently to their male counterparts and had a distinctive set of priorities reflecting their involvement in feminist and radical politics. Perhaps partly because of that, Lyulph Stanley was said to have appreciated the quintet of Liberal women who served eleven years or more (Margaret Eve, Rosamond Davenport Hill, Ruth Homan, Emma Maitland and Alice Westlake) and seem to have been loyal, if not inconspicuous, party supporters (Gautrey, n.d.: 96). Allied to Mark Wilks, Alice Westlake led the Liberal opposition to the dominant church–Tory group after Lyulph Stanley lost his seat in the 1885 election, while Margaret Eve and Rosamond Davenport Hill had a lasting impact on programmes for the rehabilitation of recalcitrant boys and girls. But whereas Margaret Eve, Rosamond Davenport Hill and Ruth Homan focused attention on girls' subjects, Emma Maitland made a conscious effort to spread her energies. Unlike her colleagues, she wanted to offer a female perspective on all aspects of the Board's work, confidently acting in the belief that the administration of local services was a crucial testing-ground of women's political abilities.

Examined as a whole, power within the Board did not automatically reflect status, intellect or even administrative experience. As Florence Fenwick Miller recorded, between 1876 and 1885 it depended before all else upon membership of the Progressive group, at which time the Liberal chairman, Edward North Buxton, was deposed by one vote in favour of the leader of the Moderate party, the controversial Reverend Joseph Diggle, who remained chairman until 1894. In general, women contributed to those aspects of Board work that were considered especially appropriate, such as the general concerns of women teachers and female pupils. For independent, radical women like Mary Bridges Adams, Florence Fenwick Miller, Honnor Morten, Henrietta Muller, Elizabeth Surr and Helen Taylor, the experience was both trying and exciting. Elizabeth Surr later described it as 'a wearing, wearing life', although she went on to reminisce to Helen Taylor about the 'amusement' they got out of 'the many disagreements we went through together' (Elizabeth Surr to Helen Taylor, 17 November 1888).

A notable exception to this rule was the service of Annie Besant, fresh from her triumphs as an organizer of the Match Girls' strike. The only daughter of an Irish mother and half-Irish father, at 20 she married the Reverend Frank Besant and went on to have two children, although the marriage broke up in 1873. Between 1874 and 1888 she was one of the leaders of Freethought, while her advocacy of notorious birth control doctrines cost her the custody of her 8-year-old daughter, Mabel, in 1878. By this time her name was anathema to the general public who did not appreciate this militant non-Christian, while her espousal of radical causes did not endear her to the more conservative leaders of the women's suffrage movement. Yet her work on the Board was an unqualified success: largely contributing to the abolition of school fees, better and more organized school feeding, and fair labour conditions in all of the Board's dealings.

In a period when the practised woman orator was a rarity, Annie's reputation as a speaker carried great weight. The traditional mass rally was crucial in the triennial elections to the Board and during the autumn of 1888 she appealed to the populace nearly every night at open meetings which attracted enthusiastic audiences of as many as a thousand people. Physically attractive and barely into her forties, the memories of Malcolm Quin (writing of the mid-1870s), provide a clear indication of the charismatic influence she wielded over like-minded contemporaries:

> She was young and attractive, with dark eyes, a face alive with emotion and expression, and a voice full and sonorous, but musical and not unfeminine. [...] She was facing a hostile world on behalf of liberty and truth; and we young men, who had the passion of these things in our souls, responded readily to the passion with which she pleaded for them. We were carried away.
>
> (Quin, 1924: 53)

By contrast, from the perspective of Beatrice Webb, Annie Besant was 'a woman unsexed by the loss of her child, embittered by the fact that the law robbed her of her child but ... lifted by work and trouble out of all pettiness of nature and smallness of aim' (*The Diary of Beatrice Webb, Volume One 1873–1892*, 27 November 1887: 223). Further, Beatrice Webb was under no illusions about the precarious position Annie then occupied within the male-dominated labour movement. Writing in 1887, Webb considered her position uncertain for two reasons. First, Socialists are not characterized by devotion to leaders. Second, men are jealous of women who assume leadership. But while her scandalous reputation preceded her on to the Board, shortly after her election the Christian Socialist and Anglican parson, Stewart Headlam, was writing in the *Church Reformer* that it was Mrs Besant, not the nominal leader Lyulph Stanley, who was the 'real leader of the advanced party' (quoted in Rubinstein, 1970: 24). Indeed evaluations like these led Annie to remark in her autobiography that 'I largely conquered public prejudice against me by my work on the London School Board' (1908 edition: 342). Unlike Helen Taylor, whose close ties with John Stuart Mill meant the Liberal leadership was initially receptive to her, Annie Besant had the gift of public persuasion and knew how to build alliances to secure her political objectives. She also had the advantage of a new diffusion of Socialist ideas through a growing list of reform magazines, newspapers and periodicals, including her very own *Our Corner*. Her eloquence was undeniable and as Annie herself frankly declared when recalling her first speech in Sibsey church:

> I shall never forget the feeling of power and delight – but especially of power – that came upon me as I sent my voice ringing down the aisles [...] and as the sentences flowed unbidden from my lips and my own tones echoed back to me from the pillars of the ancient church, I knew of a verity that the gift of speech was mine, and that if ever [...] the chance came to me of public work this power of melodious utterance should at least win a hearing for any message I had to bring.
> (Besant, 1893: 115–16)

Unlike the personally controversial Annie Besant, however, it was the cultivation of character that Ethel Metcalfe chose to stress in her biography of Rosamond Davenport Hill. This is important because it serves to illustrate the moral sensibilities and cultural assumptions embedded in wider social attitudes in this period. In practice, as Stefan Collini (1993: 91–118) suggests in his discussion of the idea of character, descriptive and evaluative elements were embedded in a language which accentuated the value of personal qualities developed and displayed by hard labour; although 'it was also true that character was an ascribed quality, possessed and enjoyed in public view' (Collini, 1993: 106). In Rosamond's case, the animating effect of public work ensured that: 'Whatever she imagined to have been her outward shortcomings in youth, by the time middle age was reached the beauty and strength of her character shone out clearly upon the surface, where all could see and appreciate it' (Metcalfe, 1904: 17–18).

In general terms, the notion of character played an important part in the politically contested struggle to transform national and social identities through mass education. All along the way School Board politics opened up debates about the nature of working-class education, with the outcomes epitomized by an increasingly complex and differentiated curriculum in which class and gender structures were dynamically interrelated. For women political candidates, the emphasis on the need to both help and socialize the working class served them well. Drawn from a higher social class than the children who attended the Board schools, they clearly possessed the necessary cultural capital to reach and transform the urban poor. In many ways the actions of women like Margaret Eve, Rosamond Davenport Hill, Ruth Homan and Alice Westlake resemble those of organic intellectuals (see Chapter 1), who emerge with the formation of new economic classes. From this perspective the role of organic intellectuals rested upon the need to organize a whole range of structures and activities as well as the values, attitudes, beliefs and morality embedded in the consciousness of a particular social group (Gramsci, 1971: 5–16). Within capitalism, organic intellectuals like the Victorian state- and bureaucracy-builders who served on the Board played a key role in the process by which particular social attitudes found expression in the London school system. For, as this account underscores, the theme of rescue and reclamation was to become increasingly potent in late Victorian London. Indeed it was promoted by a language of social imperialism and eugenics shared by many social and political movements.

By the 1890s, the tide was running in favour of those hostile to the school board system. On the one hand, Anglican dissatisfaction with the compromise of 1870 became more vociferous. On the other, the Bryce Commissioners (investigating the structure of secondary education in England in 1894–95), focused public attention on the developing crisis over secondary education. From the 1880s more advanced school boards, with popular support, had sought to extend the scope of elementary education by fostering the development of higher grade schools and evening classes, as well as pupil teacher centres in Birmingham, Bradford, Liverpool and London. All of these were spheres regarded by the orthodox and certainly by the voluntarists (church and Tory interests) as the proper province of secondary education. As a consequence, in 1895 the Bryce Commission suggested that they be recognized as secondary schools under the control of the county and county borough councils, operating through education committees (see Simon, 1980: 176–86). The new authorities were not slow to invade the field of education and the prevention of unnecessary overlapping made a struggle for control over secondary education inevitable. In the event, a Conservative election victory in the Khaki election of 1900 brought the possibility of education reform that much nearer.

Women not wanted?

Eager to protect women's role as voters and elected representatives, the last nine women members of the London Board joined the old radical alliance, now fortified by the newer socialist ones, in favour of the school boards. For instance, seven of the nine female representatives (Mary Bridges Adams, Margaret Eve, Ruth Homan, Susan Lawrence, Emma Maitland, Ellen McKee, Hilda Miall-Smith and Honnor Morten), belonged to the Women's Local Government

Society (WLGS). This was a non-party, London-based feminist organization founded to promote the eligibility of women to elect to and serve on all local governing bodies (see Chapter 4). At the same time, we can see evidence of divided loyalties. This was because both working people and women had much to lose from the educational reorganization that followed the Education Act of 1902: working people because the division between elementary and secondary schooling was more firmly defined; women because they were disqualified by sex for election to the new local education authorities.

Although Mary Bridges Adams and Honnor Morten had been elected for their radical views, this was not true of the five other women who fought long and hard in favour of the school boards. Accordingly, while the Liberals Margaret Eve, Ruth Homan, Susan Lawrence, Emma Maitland, Ellen McKee and Hilda Miall-Smith focused attention on the position of women, the Socialist Mary Bridges Adams expressed concern at the emerging class-based system of state education. She believed in equality of opportunity for all and her educational philosophy is clearly reminiscent of the ideas articulated by Annie Besant during the late 1880s. Further, it was as a member of the Gasworkers' and General Labourers' Union that Mary launched the National Labour Education League (NLEL) in November 1901. Described by W. P. McCann as 'the most interesting attempt to develop a positive labour educational policy' (1960: 423–4), the NLEL had five main aims: First, to publicize trade union views. Second, to develop a constructive programme which would not only 'give a lead' to educational reforms, but set a standard by which educational legislation might be judged. Third, to strengthen and develop the educational side of the Labour movement. Fourth, to free popular education from the control of sectarians and the lobbying pressures of political wirepullers. Finally, to secure by legislation a three-tier education system, re-classified as successive, age-defined stages through which every child should proceed. Organized around the demand for educational expansion in egalitarian forms, the League's campaign slogan was 'Education Frst, Machinery Second'.

As a prominent London radical, it was inevitable that Mary should draw on the complex world of working-class politics for her power base. Indeed the League's original Appeal was signed by three Lib-Lab MPs (Richard Bell, Thomas Burt and Charles Fenwick), eight members of the parliamentary committee of the Trades Union Congress, seven Labour members of the LCC, as well as Ben Jones, Alexander McLeod, Thomas Arnold and H. J. May from the cooperative movement. By the end of the month 45 unions had joined the League and the organization continued to give expression to the educational demands of the Labour movement as the legislation progressed through Parliament. As Mary told an enthusiastic audience at Exeter in May 1902, the bill 'did nothing to promote education or efficiency, and aimed a blow at the fundamental principle of democratic government, that where there was taxation there should be representation' (*Comradeship*, June 1902: 8).

Meanwhile the WLGS struggled to win support in a society that was far from favourably disposed towards feminism. Both Rosamond Davenport Hill and Alice Westlake came out of retirement to argue the case for direct female involvement, while Hilda Miall-Smith sought to mobilize support among local branches of the Women's Liberal Federation. Although the women's movement was split on the issue (with some putting the case for education reform irrespective of the problems of women), the WLGS continued to petition and pamphlet both influential politicians and potential supporters. In April 1902 Emma Maitland joined her close friend Annie Leigh Browne (1851–1936) on a sub-committee intended to focus attention on the disabling character of the proposed legislation. From then on the WLGS circulated thousands of leaflets promoting the work of School Board women like Margaret Eve, Rosamond Davenport Hill, Ruth Homan and Emma Maitland. Prominent members also distributed petition forms to provincial Liberal associations and organized meetings without end. Besides the individual signatories on the petition presented to Lord Salisbury, for example, 233 women's organizations rallied to support the WLGS line that the claims of women transcended party considerations. Significantly, these included the Association of Assistant Mistresses, the National Union of Women Workers, the Women's Co-operative Guild, the Women Guardians Society, the Women's Industrial Council and the Women's Liberal Federation (WLGS Report, 1902). At the same time the women used men as figureheads to support their campaign and to gain access for them to Parliamentary debates. Hence the leading parliamentary educationalist James Bryce (Assistant Commissioner to the Schools Inquiry Commission in the 1860s, Chairman of the Secondary Education Commission of 1894–95), Sir Joshua Firth (LCC) and Dr T. J. Macnamara (London School Board 1894–1904, MP for North Camberwell and editor of *The Schoolmaster*), were among their most prominent male supporters. The suffragists, meanwhile, did what they could to highlight the strength of feeling on the issue of female exclusion.

At all events, the offer to allow women to be co-opted as specialists onto the new local education authorities came as a direct result of this agitation. Yet Ellen McKee still signed a letter to *The Times* arguing that it would be wrong for women to acquiesce, while Ruth Homan addressed a non-party women's protest meeting to demand a voice as an elected representative. Furthermore, Elizabeth Garrett Anderson, Emily Davies and Alice Westlake came out of retirement to meet Walter Long, president of the Local Government Board, to press the case for female enfranchisement. Outraged at the injustice of the 1902 Act, which did not cover London, the WLGS concentrated on winning parliamentary allies in the months preceding the special act for the metropolis that was passed in 1903. Hilda Miall-Smith, for example, persuaded the members for St Pancras to support the School Board women and later met Sir William Anson, parliamentary secretary to the Board of Education in the Balfour administration. She was part of a WLGS deputation to the Commons that included Mary Bridges Adams and Ellen McKee, as well as Mrs Heberden of the committee of representative managers of London's board schools (see Chapters 4 and 7). Doggedly determined to publicize their cause, the WLGS distributed thousands of leaflets attesting to the value of the female contribution, including the text of speeches by Sir William Collins (LCC) and Lord Reay (Chairman of the London School Board) reaffirming the accomplishments of women as public officials. Ruth Homan and Florence Fenwick Miller were both moved to write to the press, while the energetic Hilda Miall-Smith addressed various local groups of the Women's Liberal Federation, as well as meetings convened by women activists in the London Board Mistresses Union.

Opponents of the LCC takeover raised three main objections. First, that control would be relegated to persons who were not directly chosen for their views on education. Second, that women were not eligible to stand for county council seats. Finally, that local democracy would suffer because the decision-making process would take place behind closed doors. Still active, the National Labour Education League (NLEL) also continued to argue the case for preservation of the School Board as the local education authority, 'urging all London workers strenuously to oppose any Bill which did not provide for the election of such an authority' (*School Board Chronicle*, 21 March 1903: 238–9). At the same time, the London Progressive Education Council issued a manifesto calling for resistance, while the London Trades Council, Woolwich Trades Council, the Metropolitan Radical Federation, the National Democratic League and the Metropolitan Free Church Federation joined forces to organize a mass demonstration in Hyde Park in May. Despite initial attempts to restrict the size of the meeting, twelve platforms were arranged round the Reformers' Tree. It was estimated that a quarter of a million protesters carried the following resolution put by prominent School Board supporters:

> That this mass meeting of citizens of London emphatically condemns the Education Bill now before Parliament because it destroys the London School Board, excludes women from the election to the education authority, imposes religious tests upon the teachers, and does not provide for the free teaching of elementary, technical and higher grade education in suitable day and evening schools entirely controlled and administered by a body directly elected for that purpose.
>
> (*School Board Chronicle*, 23 May 1903: 471)

Perhaps the last major example of the old radical alliance at work, *The Times* described it as the 'largest, most earnest, and the most intelligent demonstration that has been seen in Hyde Park for a score of years' (*School Board Chronicle*, 23 May 1903: 471). Accordingly, the list of 100 speakers included educationalists and teachers, administrators and experts of the region, feminists (including Margaret Eve, Ruth Homan and Hilda Miall-Smith), and nonconformists, as well as the leaders of the organized Labour movement. Despite two more demonstrations at the Passmore Edwards Settlement and Whitfield's Mount, the London question was settled at the end of July. The final meeting of the Board took place on 28 April 1904. Interestingly, one conspicuous difference between this and the Board's first meeting at London's Guildhall, was that ladies predominated among the audience of past members and supporters of the dying institution. Final votes of thanks went to Lords Reay and Sheffield (the former Lyulph Stanley), now excluded from his educational responsibilities since the new Progressive majority on the LCC failed to choose him as an Alderman. Thomas Gautrey thought they may have feared his powers and knowledge, while Graham Wallas recalled:

His boundless personal force and driving power were combined with a nervous irritability that often daunted those who came in contact with him for the first time, and made him a constant source of terror to anyone, either among his friends or his opponents, who pretended to knowledge which he did not possess.

(Wallas, 1940: 84)

But Lyulph Stanley was not the only past member of the School Board to be snubbed in this way. Accordingly, neither Stewart Headlam, nor Mary Bridges Adams found a place on the new body. Again, they each led the fight against the legislation outside Parliament. Denouncing the 'treachery' of London Progressives who backed the Education Act of 1903, in the words of Headlam's biographer he: 'fought to the end for the doomed institution he so much loved' (Bettany, 1926: 156). Hence 38 men served on the LCC Education Committee (LCCEC), alongside five women. The women were: Dr Sophie Bryant (the first Englishwoman to be awarded a doctorate, headmistress of the North London Collegiate School and member of the semi-autonomous Technical Education Board of the LCC), Margaret Eve, Ruth Homan, the Honourable Maude Lawrence and Susan Lawrence.

Maude Lawrence, it will be recalled, was the daughter of the first chairman of the London School Board and had been co-opted as representative for Westminster following the resignation of Constance Patey (née Elder) in 1900. In 1905, as part of the re-organization of the Board of Education, she was invited by Sir Robert Morant to take up the newly created post of chief woman inspector and her place on the LCCEC was filled by Henrietta Adler, the Liberal daughter of the chief Rabbi. Significantly, Maude Lawrence provides us with a clear example of a woman who achieved successful entry and career promotion without challenging the fundamental rules of mainstream politics. The LCCEC held its first meeting on 20 April 1904 and within a week she became one of the two women acting as vice-chairman (the other was Dr Bryant), when she was appointed to serve under Mr A. A. Allen on the Special Schools Sub-Committee, an area of work she had made her own when on the School Board. Important social connections were fundamental to her promotion to the inspectorate since Robert Morant argued Maude Lawrence would confer prestige and be able to subdue the warring factions within the women's inspectorate. Cultural capital, rather than professional qualifications or teaching experience (and she had neither), was crucial here. Moreover her feminist credentials are unclear. Giving evidence to the Royal Commission on the Civil Service in 1930, for instance, she advocated retention of the marriage bar and unequal pay. This was in direct opposition to the wishes of organized women civil servants.

In these various ways, the example of Maude Lawrence did not expose the contradictions or tensions inherent in being a public woman. Rather, her actions served to bolster the dominant male nature of mainstream political institutions and traditional notions of the female role. The same was true of those School Board women who developed a gender-specific power base via active participation in the expansion of the domestic curriculum. Officially sanctioned by the Education Department and an accepted part of Progressive party policy, the language of domesticity enabled them to play a part in the development of an

English school system that was class divided. Moreover their actions clearly support Anna Davin's thesis (1979, 1996) that state schooling was designed to impose a middle-class family form consisting of a male breadwinner and an economically dependent, full-time housekeeping wife and mother, and dependent children. At the same time, it was ironic that these pioneer female politicians should so rigidly reinforce the domestic ideal, not least because they themselves had sought to break down the boundary between the public and the private. Like their male colleagues, however, the great majority of the women found it hard not to exhibit class prejudice. Hence the expansion of the domestic curriculum was viewed with favour by the social and political élites of the period, because it was seen as a corrective to the inadequate child care and household management, and the overwhelming degeneration of the urban population.

By the mid-1880s all the women candidates stood on a party ticket and it is noticeable that all save Eugenie Dibdin, Frances Hastings and Susan Lawrence were returned as Progressives. Nonetheless, School Board women embraced a multitude of organizations, at the centre of which lay the equal rights feminist groups, like the WLGS, which maintained the fight for elected status at local government level. As Mary Hughes (1992: 263–4) explains, 'co-options are supposed to enhance the experience and expertise of committees, but co-optees do not have the authority or public support of elected members; in this instance they could not fight for resources at finance committees nor steer their proposals through the full Council'. Less than two years after her abolition as an elected member, Susan Lawrence complained about the exclusion of previously powerful women from Council deliberations on the best method of teaching cookery. Thus, harking back to Mrs Homan's position on the Board, she:

> could not help feeling that if Mrs Homan had been able to put her own points herself she would have put these much better, because she would have been able to put them with the force and weight that only long personal experience can give.
> (WLGS *Report*, 1906)

The climax to the struggle for the local government vote came in 1907 with the passing of the Qualification of Women (County and Borough Councils) Act, but it was not until the LCC election of 1910 that women were once more returned as full members. Two women candidates were successful at the polls, Susan Lawrence and Henrietta Adler, who was elected for Hackney. In addition, the Women's Labour League ran Margaret Bondfield in Woolwich and Ethel Bentham in Kensington (see Hollis, 1989: 414-16). Moreover in March 1913 Hilda Miall-Smith also contested the LCC elections, as an unsuccessful Progressive candidate for East Marylebone (WLGS Report 1912–13, Elections in 1913: 17).

Yet, just as the non-party WLGS created an important bridge between Conservative, Liberal and Socialist women politicians at this time, so did the social and ideological frameworks which shaped women's lives. In particular, the service ethic of work provided some coherence to the women's actions, as did the topics of the girls' curriculum, the issue of child welfare and the subject of women staff. But while nuanced, the separate spheres model of a political world divided into male and female activities posited by Patricia Hollis (1989) may be a little misleading here. On the one hand, female politicians chose to speak on certain questions frequently regarded as being of concern to women. On the other, as the case studies in Chapters 5, 6 and 7 made clear, women local government members did not argue from a shared feminist perspective above that of party. As important were the way diagonal relations between classes featured in the feminist challenge to the status quo on the curriculum and the creation of the industrial schools in the 1870s and early 1880s. In this study the emphasis on the School Board for London allows for a more detailed consideration of the different kinds of alliances and networks invoked at different periods of time and in response to a variety of issues. Moreover the biographical approach assists our understanding of the contexts in which political action was taken, while the material on female networks clearly highlights the links between public lives and private commitments. In particular, the concepts of class, gender and power relations, as well as notions of democracy, participation, accountability and citizenship, are insightful in pointing out how biases work and how resistances might be possible.

Against this background it becomes evident that the cultural politics of difference were crucial to the women's suffrage movement and its demand for political representation. Because the private and the public worlds were clearly distinguished through gender, the case for female participation stressed women's distinctive contribution to public office, as well as principles of equity and justice. Nonetheless, the social patterning of gender had ambiguous results for democracy, participation and the implementation of social citizenship. For the sample of female representatives in this study, there is much to suggest that internal male resistance exacerbated the difficulties experienced by more radical women. By contrast, those who internalized institutional norms were rewarded with promotion to decision-making positions of power and responsibility where they took supervisory charge of girls and women as their primary political constituency. Posed in these terms and against this background, the concept of social mothering might foster inequality, as in the expansion of the domestic curriculum or the close personal supervision of the poor. At other times, it was undercut by the moral sensibilities embedded in the culture of altruism and the language of character (Collini, 1993). Indeed, for women like Honnor Morten feminism was just part of the equation. Driven by the spirit of service to suffering humanity, her personal integrity depended upon the doctrine of work to alleviate social injustice. Reiterating the links between middle-class women educators and the much larger world of social reform politics, she emitted the heartfelt plea:

> I have asked for a holiday and am off home for a week [...] home to the fields and flowers the place was joyless, the days were empty, nature had become nothing to me. [...] How could I be happy there when I knew there was all this misery here? Father, I choose; I will not take a heaven haunted by shrieks of far-off misery [...] Oh Eden, Eden! I have eaten the apple, and the gates are closed behind me!
>
> (Morten, 1899b: 28-9)

Conclusion

As the foregoing chapters have shown, this study supports the view that women were able to play an active public role in late Victorian and Edwardian England and made a positive contribution to the formation of a state education system. Quite apart from the more prominent Liberal women, some of whom (like Rosamond Davenport Hill) retained a foothold in the subsequent history of educational and penal reform, it is possible to argue that their Socialist colleagues also had a lasting impact on the creation of policy and the practice of social welfare. In particular, Mary Bridges Adams achieved renown as a rank and file propagandist for the educational demands of the organized labour movement, whereas Honnor Morten largely fought for the cause of children with special needs. Although largely forgotten today, both women were prolific writers and speakers. They challenged the educational establishment in their support for recreational and educational evening classes, as well as the provision of services to promote the welfare of students. For instance, Honnor Morten founded the School Nurses' Society in 1898, in order to organize a supply of women nurses to visit Board Schools in the poorer parts of London. Four years later she retired from the Board to open a home for 'helpless and defective' children at Rotherfield, Sussex, where she lived until her death in 1913 (*The Times*, 15 July: 11). During the same period Mary Bridges Adams continued to argue for state responsibility for social services. She focused the attention of prominent male trade unionists like Will Thorne (General Secretary of the Gas Workers' Union 1889–1934) on the demand for school welfare services. Her actions were a qualified success since the informal welfare networks begun in the 1880s were expanded after the Education Acts of 1906 and 1907 and provided the machinery for publicly-funded school feeding and medical inspection. Finally, as these case studies show, it was possible for people of middle-class origins or life styles to understand the lives of the poor.

Above all, for a 34-year period School Board women sought to 'field a voice', just as the feminist Henrietta Muller would have wanted. By the turn of the century this new spirit was making itself felt in the numbers of women involved in the various aspects of the Board's work and the ways the different suffrage organizations confidently assumed responsibility for promoting women's public work. For instance, writing a handbook for women seeking elected office in 1911, Jane Brownlow (herself an unsuccessful candidate in the 1894 election for the London School Board), offered the following words of advice to women with the necessary leisure and desire to work for the general welfare:

> The woman who takes up any form of public service literally gives herself, her time, her powers and sympathies to help to uplift the nation. She must be guarded in word and deed, for she is subject to public criticism; humble, for she is human and there is more to be learnt than one lifetime can compass; dignified, because she represents womanhood; judicial, because there are two sides to every question and those who ask for fairness must be ready to give it; kind, for it is woman's task to help the desolate and oppressed. Above all, she should never forget that she stands not for mere material welfare alone, but also for the highest interests of the

human race, spiritual forces which make for the righteousness which alone can truly exalt a nation.

(Brownlow, 1911: 6)

Like Honnor Morten, Jane Brownlow looked forward to a new social world in which women would play their full part as citizens and workers in the community. Younger than Henrietta Muller, both women were optimistic about the future. Despite setbacks, the metropolitan woman's movement had achieved a number of significant goals. The development of social policy was now but one way in which female reformers might help others and gain public respect for their work.

Bibliography

Primary sources

Archive collections
Bedford College papers, Royal Holloway, University of London, London.
Children's Country Holidays Fund papers, London.
Emily Davies papers, Girton College, Cambridge.
Garrett Letters, Fawcett Library, London.
Girton College papers, Girton College, Cambridge.
Karl Pearson Papers, University College, London.
Royal Arsenal Co-operative Society papers, Royal Arsenal Co-operative Society, Woolwich.
Edith Simcox, *Autobiography of a Shirtmaker*, Bodleian Library, Oxford.
Helen Taylor papers, London School of Economics, London.
Gertrude Tuckwell Collection, Trades Union Congress Library Collection, University of North London.
Women's Local Government Society papers, London Metropolitan Archives, London.

Parliamentary papers
British Parliamentary Papers Population: Census of Great Britain, 1851, Education (England and Wales) (1852–3) XC.
British Parliamentary Papers Education: Report of the Commissioner on the State of Popular Education in England with an Index (Newcastle) 1861.
British Parliamentary Papers Education: Report from the Commissions on Reformatory and Industrial Schools with Minutes of Evidence, Appendices and Index 1884.
British Parliamentary Papers: Royal Commission on the Housing of the Working Classes, Minutes of Evidence 1884–5.
British Parliamentary Papers Education: Royal Commission on Elementary Education (Cross) 1886–8.
British Parliamentary Papers Education: Royal Commission on Secondary Education (Bryce) 1894–5.
House of Lords Select Committee on Poor Law Relief 1888.

Voluntary societies, papers and printed reports

Annual Reports of the Kensington Committee for Organising Charitable Relief and Repressing Mendacity.

Children's Country Holidays Fund, Minutes and Annual Reports 1884–1902.

Journal of the Women's Educational Union.

Women's Local Government Society, Annual Reports, 1888–1925, Minute books, correspondence and accounts, 1888–1914. Reports of the annual general meetings, 1905–14.

Public bodies and local authorities, papers and printed reports

London County Council, Report on Industrial Schools, 1870–1904.

School Board for London, Minutes, 1870–1904.

School Board for London, Minutes of Evidence taken before a Special Committee Regarding Upton House Industrial School.

School Board for London, Minutes of sub-committee appointed by School Management Committee in November 1878 to enquire into the necessity of having a more complete system of Physical Education for Girls.

School Board for London, Annual Returns of Managers of Board Schools, 1882–1904.

School Board for London, Meals for School Children, Report of a Special Sub-Committee of the School Management Committee, 1889.

School Board for London, Meals for School Children, Report of a Special Committee on Underfed Children, 1895.

School Board for London, Meals for School Children, Report of a Special Sub-Committee of the General Purposes Committee, 1899.

Autobiographies, memoirs, diaries, letters

Ballard, P.B. (1937) *Things I Cannot Forget*. London, University of London Press.

Bark, J. 'The Thimble Prize in "Memories"'. Undated typescript in Tower Hamlets Local History Library.

Besant, A. (1893) *An Autobiography*. London, Fisher Unwin.

Bosworth Smith, R (1883) *Life of Lord Lawrence*. London, Smith, Elder and Company.

Cobbe, F.P. (1904) *The Life of Frances Power Cobbe*. London, Swan Sonnenschein.

Davenport Hill, R. and Davenport Hill, F. (1878) *The Recorder of Birmingham. A Memoir of Matthew Davenport Hill*. London. Macmillan.

Dolman, F. (January 1896) 'The lady members of the London School Board', *The Young Woman*, London, Horace Marshall and Son, 129–32.

Dyer, G.H. (1882) *Six Men of the People: Biographical Sketches with Portraits*. London, Dyer Brothers.

Fawcett, M. (1924) *What I Remember*. London, T. Fisher Unwin.

Gautrey, T. (n.d.) *'Lux Mihi Laus': School Board Memories*. London, Link House.

Grant, C.E. (1929) *Farthing Bundles*. London, Fern Street Settlement.

Macdonald, R. (1912) *Margaret Ethel Macdonald*. London, Allen and Unwin.

Metcalfe, E. (1904) *Memoir of Rosamond Davenport Hill*. London, Longmans, Green and Co.

Morrison, M. (1897) 'Ladies on the London School Board', *Newscuttings*, 'School Boards', Fawcett Library.

Quin, M. (1924) *Memoirs of a Positivist*. London, George Allen & Unwin.

Rackham, C.D. (Spring 1948) 'Susan Lawrence', *Fabian Quarterly*, 20–23.

Reed, A. and C. (1863) (eds) *Memoirs of the life and philanthropic labours of Andrew Reed D.D.* London.

Reeves, J. (c. 1915) *Recollections of a School Attendance Officer*.

Russell, B. (1967) *The Autobiography of Bertrand Russell*. London, George Allen and Unwin.

Smalley, G. (1909) *The Life of Sir Sydney H. Waterlow Bart*. London, Edward Arnold.

Stephen, B. (1927) *Emily Davies and Girton College*. London, Constable.

Stevenson, G.J. (1884) 'Sir Charles Reed: A life Sketch'. London, Dyer and Sons.

Strachey, R. (1988) *The Cause*. London, Virago Press.

Tweedie, A. (ed.) (1898) *The First College for Women Queen's College London Memories and Records of Work Done 1848–98*. London, Queen's College.

Twining, L. (Dec 1890) 'Women as public servants', *The Nineteenth Century*.

Webb, Beatrice (1986) *The Diary of Beatrice Webb, Volume One 1873–1892*. J, MacKenzie and N. MacKenzie, eds. London, Virago.

Williams, G. (n.d.) *The Passionate Pilgrim: A Life of Annie Besant*. London, John Hamilton.

Other contemporary books and pamphlets

Bartley, G.C.T. *Journal of the Society of Arts*, Vol. XVII, 1868–9, 1888–94, 224.

Bartley, G.C.T. (1871) 'The education of girls', *The School Board Chronicle*, 20 May, 53.

Bartley, G. (1875) 'Elementary education', *Journal of the Women's Education Union*, 15 July, 97–8.

Bateson, M. (ed.) (1895) *Professional Woman Upon Their Professions*, London, Horace Cox.

Besant, A. (1886) *Modern Socialism*. London, Annie Besant and Charles Bradlaugh.

Bodichon, B.L.S. (1857) *Women and Work*. London, Bosworth and Harrison.

Booth, C. (ed.) (1891) *Life and Labour of the People in London. Vol. 1*. London, Williams and Norgate.

Bosanquet, H. (1914) *Social Work in London 1869–1912. A History of the Charity Organisation Society*. London, John Murray.

Brownlow, J.M.E. (1911) *Women's Work in Local Government (England and Wales)*. London: David Nutt.

Bulkley, M.E. (1914) *The Feeding of School Children*. London, G. Bell.

Fenwick Miller, F. (1892) *In Ladies' Company. Six Interesting Women*. London, Ward and Downey.

Greg, W.R. (1862) 'Why are women redundant?', *National Review*, 15.

Grey, M. (1871) 'Meeting of Working Men and Women at the Cadogan Rooms' address delivered 28 November 1870, *The School Board for London: three addresses of Mrs William Grey in the Borough of Chelsea with a speech by William Groves, Esq. QC, FRC*. London, W. Ridgeway.

Huxley, T.H. (May 1865) 'Emancipation – black and white', *Reader*, 5.

Huxley, T.H. (February 1888) 'The struggle for existence', *The Nineteenth Century*.

Jameson, A. (1859) 'Sisters of Charity and the communion of labour'. London, Longmans.

Lonsdale, M. (March 1884) 'Platform women', *The Nineteenth Century*.

Mearns, A. (1883) *The Bitter Cry of Outcast London. An Enquiry into the Condition of the*

Abject Poor. London, Congregational Union.

Morley, C. (1897) *Studies in Board Schools*. London, Smith and Elder .

Morten, H. (1899a) *Questions for Women (and Men)*. London, Charles and Black.

Morten, H. (1899b) *From a Nurse's Note-book*. London, The Scientific Press.

Muller, H. (1888) 'Some aspects of the London School Board', *Westminster Review*, January.

Philpott, H.B. (1904) *London at School: the Story of the School Board*. London, T. Fisher Unwin.

Potter, G. 'The 1st point of the New Charter: improved dwellings for the people', *Contemporary Review*, Vol. 18, November 1871.

Spalding, T.A. assisted by T.S.A. Canney (1900) *The Work of the School Board for London*. London, P.S. King.

Webster A. (1879) *A Housewife's Opinions*. London, Macmillan.

Yoxall, A. (1914) *A History of the Teaching of Domestic Economy*. London, Association of Teachers of Domestic Subjects in Great Britain.

Secondary Sources

Theses

Brehony, K. (1987) 'The Froebel Movement and State Schooling 1880–1914: A Study in Educational Ideology', unpublished PhD thesis, The Open University.

Koven, S. (1987) 'Culture and Poverty: The London Settlement House Movement, 1870–1914', unpublished PhD thesis, University of Harvard.

McCann, W.P. (1960) 'Trade unionist, Co-operative and Socialist Organisations in Relation to Popular Education, 1870–1902', unpublished PhD thesis, University of Manchester.

Martin, J. (1987) 'The Origins and Development of Gendered Schooling', unpublished MA dissertation, University of Warwick.

Martin, J. (1991) 'The Role of Women in the Education of the Working Classes, 1870–1904', unpublished PhD thesis, The Open University.

Turnbull, A. (1983b) 'Women, Education and Domesticity: A Study of the Domestic Subjects Movement, 1870–1914', unpublished PhD thesis, Polytechnic of the South Bank.

Worzola, D.M.C. (1982) 'The Langham Place Circle: The Beginnings of the Organised Women's Movement in England, 1854–70', unpublished PhD thesis, University of Wisconsin, Madison.

Modern articles

Annan, N. (1955) 'The intellectual aristocracy', in Plumb, J.H. (ed.) *Studies in Social History: A Tribute to G.M. Trevelyan*. London, Longmans, Green.

Davin, A. (1979) 'Mind that you do as you are told', *Feminist Review*, 3, 80–98.

Dyhouse, C. (1976) 'Social Darwinistic ideas and the development of women's education in England, 1880–1920', *History of Education* 5 (1), 41–58.

Dyhouse, C. (1977) 'Good wives and little mothers: social anxieties and the schoolgirls' curriculum, 1890–1920', *Oxford Review of Education* 3 (1), 21–35.

Gardner, P. (1991) ' "Our schools"; "their schools". The case of Eliza Duckworth and John Stevenson', *History of Education*, 20 (3), 163–86.

Goodman, J. (1995) 'Committee women: women school governors in early nineteenth-century England', *History of Education Society Bulletin*, 56, 48–57.

Hartmann, H. (1976) 'Patriarchy, capitalism and job segregation by sex', *Signs* 1(3), 137–68.

Hughes, M. (1992) '"The Shrieking Sisterhood": women as educational policy-makers', *Gender and Education* 4 (3), 255–72.

Lewis, J. (1982) 'Parents, children, school fees and the London School Board, 1870–1890', *History of Education* 11 (4), 291–312.

Levine, P. (1990) 'Love, friendship, and feminism in later 19th century England', *Women's Studies International Forum*, 13 (1/2), 63–78.

Marsden, W. (1985) 'Residential segregation and the hierarchy of elementary schooling from Charles Booth's London surveys', *London Journal*, 11(2), 127–45.

May, M. (1973) 'Innocence and experience: the evolution of the concept of juvenile delinquency in the mid-nineteenth century', *Victorian Studies*, 17, 7–19.

Rubinstein, D. (1970) 'Annie Besant and Stewart Headlam: the London School Board election of 1888', *East London Papers*, 13, 3–24.

Van Arsdel, R.T. (1979) 'Florence Fenwick Miller: feminism and the *Woman's Signal* 1895–1899', University of Puget Sound, Washington.

Van Arsdel, R.T. (1986) 'Victorian periodicals yield their secrets: Florence Fenwick Miller's three campaigns for the London School Board', *History of Education Society Bulletin*, 38, 26–42.

Vicinus, M. (1982) '"One life to stand beside me": emotional conflicts in first-generation college women in England', *Feminist Studies*, 8 (3), 603–28.

Walkowitz, J. (1986) 'Science, feminism and romance: the men and women's club 1885–1889', *History Workshop*, 37–59.

Yeo, E.J. (1992) 'Social motherhood and the sexual communion of labour in British social science, 1850–1950', *Women's History Review*, 1, (1), 63–87.

Yeo, E.J. (1995) 'Gender and class: women's languages of power', *Labour History Review*, 60(3), 15–22.

Other books and chapters

Aldrich, R. and Gordon P. (1989) *Dictionary of British Educationists*. London, Woburn Press.

Alexander, S. (1994) *Becoming a Woman and Other Essays in 19th and 20th Century Feminist History*. London, Virago.

Ashby, M.K. (1961) *Joseph Ashby of Tysoe*. Cambridge, Cambridge University Press.

Attar, D. (1990) *Wasting Girls' Time. The History and Politics of Home Economics*. London, Virago.

Banks, J.A. and Banks, O. (1965) *Feminism and Family Planning in England*. Liverpool, Liverpool University Press.

Banks, O. (1986) *Becoming a Feminist*. Brighton, Harvester Wheatsheaf.

Bellamy, J.M. and Saville, J. (1978) *The Dictionary of Labour Biography*. London, Macmillan.

Bettany, F. G. (1926) *Stewart Headlam: A Biography*. London, John Murray.

Bingham, C. (1987) *The History of Royal Holloway College 1886–1986*. London, Constable.

Blunden, M. (1967) *The Countess of Warwick*. London, Cassell and Company.

Bourdieu, P. (1976) 'The school as a conservative force' in Dale, R. *et al.* (eds) *Schooling and Capitalism*, London, Routledge and Kegan Paul, pp. 110–17.

Bourdieu, P. (1977) *Reproduction*. London, Sage.

Briggs, A. (1977) *Victorian Cities*. Harmondsworth, Penguin.

Bryant, M. (1979) *The Unexpected Revolution*. Studies in Education, University of London.

Burrow, J. (1988) *Whigs and Liberals: Continuity and Change in English Political Thought*. Oxford, Clarendon Press.

Burstyn, J. (1980) *Victorian Education and the Ideal of Womanhood*. London, Croom Helm.

Caine, B. (1982) 'Feminism, suffrage and the nineteenth-century English women's movement' in Sarah, E. (ed.) *Reassessments of First Wave Feminism*. Oxford, Pergamon Press, pp. 537–50.

Caine, B. (1992) *Victorian Feminists*. Oxford, Oxford University Press.

Clarke, J. (1975) *The Three R's – Rescue, Repression and Rehabilitation*. Birmingham, Centre for Contemporary Cultural Studies, University of Birmingham, Occasional Papers.

Clegg, S.R. (1989) *Frameworks of Power*. London, Sage.

Collini, S. (1993) *Public Moralists: Political Thought and Intellectual Life in Britain 1850–1930*. Oxford, Clarendon Press.

Connell, R.W. (1987) *Gender and Power*. Cambridge, Polity Press.

Copelman, D.M. (1996) *London's Women Teachers: Gender, Class and Feminism 1870–1930*. London, Routledge.

Davidoff, L. and Hall, C. (1987) *Family Fortunes*. London, Hutchinson.

Davin, A. (1996) *Growing Up Poor: Home, School and Street in London 1870–1914*. London, Rivers Oram Press.

Deem, R., Brehony, K. and Heath, S.J. (1995) *Active Citizenship and the Governing of Schools*. Buckingham, Open University Press.

Delamont, S. (1978a) 'The contradictions in ladies' education' in Delamont, S. and Duffin, L. (eds), *The Nineteenth Century Woman: Her Cultural and Physical World*. London, Croom Helm, pp. 134–63.

Delamont, S. (1978b) 'The domestic ideology and women's education' in Delamont, S. and Duffin, L. (eds) *The Nineteenth Century Woman: Her Cultural and Physical World*. London, Croom Helm, pp. 164–87.

Digby, A. and Searby, P. (1981) *Children School and Society in Nineteenth Century England*. London and Basingstoke, Macmillan.

Dinnage, R. (1986) *Annie Besant*. Harmondsworth, Penguin.

Donald, J. (1985) 'Beacons of the future: schooling, subjectivity and Social Relations' in Beechey, V. and Donald, J. (eds) *Subjectivity and Social Relations*. Milton Keynes, Open University Press, pp. 214–49.

Drewry, G. and Butcher, T. (1988) *The Civil Service Today*. Oxford, Basil Blackwell.

Dyhouse, C. (1981) *Girls Growing Up in Late Victorian and Edwardian England*. London, Routledge and Kegan Paul.

Dyhouse, C. (1986) 'Mothers and daughters in the middle-class home *c.*1870–1914' in Lewis, J. (ed.) *Labour and Love: Women's Experience of Home and Family 1850–1940*. Oxford, Basil Blackwell.

Dyhouse, C. (1987) 'Miss Buss and Miss Beale: gender and authority in the history of education' in Hunt, F. (ed.) *Lessons for Life: The Schooling of Girls and Women 1850–1950*. Oxford, Basil Blackwell, pp. 22–39.

Ellsworth, E. (1979) *Liberators of the Female Mind: the Shireff Sisters*. London, Greenwood Press.

Finch, J. (1984) *Education as Social Policy*. Harlow, Longman

Forster, M. (1986) *Significant Sisters: The Grassroots of Active Feminism 1839–1939*. Harmondsworth, Penguin.

Foucault, M. (1980) *Power/Knowledge*. Brighton, Harvester Wheatsheaf.

Gardner, P. (1984) *The Lost Elementary Schools of Victorian England*. Beckenham, Croom Helm.

Gleadle, K. (1995) *The Early Feminists: Radical Unitarians and the Emergence of the Women's Rights Movement, 1831–51*. London, Macmillan Press.

Gorham, D. (1978) 'Victorian reform as a family business: the hill family' in Wohl, A.S. (ed.), *The Victorian Family*. London, Croom Helm, pp. 119–47.

Gramsci, A. (1971) *Selections from Prison Notebooks*. Edited/translated by Hoare, Q. and Nowell-Smith, G. London, Lawrence and Wishart.

Hall, C. (1979) 'The early formation of Victorian domestic ideology' in Burman, S. (ed.) *Fit Work for Women*. London, Croom Helm, pp. 15–32.

Harris, J. (1972) *Unemployment and Politics*. Oxford, Clarendon Press.

Harrison, B. (1978) *Separate Spheres*. London, Croom Helm.

Harrison, B. (1987) *Prudent Revolutionaries*. Oxford, Clarendon Press.

Hayek, F.A. (1959) *John Stuart Mill and Harriet Taylor: Their Friendship and Subsequent Marriage*. London, Routledge and Kegan Paul.

Herstein, S.R. (1985) *A Mid-Victorian Feminist: Barbara Leigh Smith Bodichon*. New Haven and London, Yale University Press.

Hobsbawm, E. (1983) *Industry and Empire*. Harmondsworth, Penguin.

Hobsbawm, E. (1989) *The Age of Empire 1875–1914*. London, Cardinal.

Holcombe, L. (1977) 'Victorian wives and property' in Vicinus, M. (ed.) *The Widening Sphere*. Bloomington and London, Indiana University Press, pp. 3–27.

Hollis, P. (1989) *Ladies Elect*. Oxford, Clarendon Press.

Holton, S.S. (1986) *Feminism and Democracy: Women's Suffrage and Politics in Britain 1900–1918*. Cambridge, Cambridge University Press.

Holton, S.S. (1996) *Suffrage Days*. London and New York, Routledge.

Horn, P. (1978) *Education in Rural England 1800–1914*. Dublin, Gill Macmillan Limited.

Humphries, S. (1981) *Hooligans or Rebels?* Oxford, Basil Blackwell.

Hunt, F. (1987) 'Introduction' in Hunt, F. (ed.) *Lessons for Life: The Schooling of Girls and Women 1850–1950*. Oxford, Basil Blackwell, pp. xi–xxv.

Hunt, F. (1991) *Gender and Policy in Elementary Education 1902–1944*. London, Harvester Wheatsheaf.

Hurt, J. (1977) 'Drill, discipline and the elementary school ethos' in McCann, P. (ed.) *Popular Education and Socialisation in the Nineteenth Century*. London, Methuen and Company, 167–91.

Hurt, J. (1979) *Elementary Schooling and the Working Classes 1860–1918*. London, Routledge and Kegan Paul.

Johnson, R. (1972) 'Administrators in education before 1870: patronage, social position and role' in Sutherland, G. (ed.) *Studies in the Growth of Nineteenth Century Government*. London, Routledge, and Kegan Paul, pp. 110–38.

Jones, A. W. (1979) *Lyulph Stanley: A Study in Educational Politics*. Waterloo, Wilfrid Laurier University Press.

Kamm, J. (1958) *How Different From Us: A Biography of Miss Buss and Miss Beale.* London, Methuen.

Kamm, J. (1965) *Hope Deferred: Girls Education in English History.* London, Methuen.

Kamm, J. (1977) *John Stuart Mill in Love.* London, Gordon and Cremonesi.

Kean, H. (1990) *Challenging the State? The Socialist and Feminist Educational Experience, 1900–1930.* London, Falmer Press.

Koven, S. (1993) 'Borderlands: women, voluntary action, and child welfare in Britain, 1840 to 1914', in Koven, S. and Michel, S. *Mothers of a New World: Maternalist Politics and the Origins of Welfare States.* London, Routledge.

Koven, S. (1994) 'Henrietta Barnett (1851–1936). The (auto)biography of a late Victorian marriage' in Pederson, S. and Mandler, P. *After the Victorians: Private Conscience and Public Duty in Modern Britain.* London, Routledge.

Lawson, D. and Silver, H.(1973) *A Social History of Education in England.* London, Methuen and Company.

Lees, L.H. (1990) 'The survival of the unfit: welfare policies and family maintenance in nineteenth-century London', in Mandler, P. (ed.) *The Uses of Charity: The Poor on Relief in the Metropolis.* Philadelphia, University of Chicago Press, pp. 69–91.

Levine, P. (1987) *Victorian Feminism 1850–1900.* London, Hutchinson.

Levine, P. (1990) *Feminist Lives in Victorian England.* Oxford, Basil Blackwell.

Lewis, J. (ed.) (1986) *Labour and Love: Women's Experience of Home and Family 1850–1940.* Oxford, Basil Blackwell.

Lewis, J. (1992) 'Women and late-nineteenth century social work', in Smart, C. (ed.) *Regulating Womanhood.* London, Routledge.

Liddington, J. and Norris, J. (1985) *One Hand Tied Behind Us.* London, Virago.

Lovenduski, J. (1996) 'Sex, gender and British politics' in Lovenduski, J. and Norris, P. (eds) *Women in Politics.* Oxford, Oxford University Press, pp. 3–18.

Lowndes, G.A.N. (1937) *The Silent Social Revolution: An Account of the Expansion of Public Education in England and Wales. 1895–1937.* London, Oxford University Press.

McKenzie, K.A. (1961) *Edith Simcox and George Eliot.* Oxford, Oxford University Press.

Maclure, S. (1990) *A History of Education in London 1870–1990.* London, Penguin Press.

McWilliams-Tullberg, R. (1975) *Women at Cambridge.* London, Victor Gollancz.

Mandler, P. (ed.) (1990) *The Uses of Charity: The Poor on Relief in the Metropolis.* Philadelphia, University of Chicago Press.

Manton, J. (1965) *Elizabeth Garrett Anderson.* London, Butler and Tanner Ltd.

Martindale, H. (1938) *Women Servants of the State 1870–1938.* London, Allen and Unwin

Maurice, E.S. (1928) *Octavia Hill.* London, George Allen and Unwin Limited.

May, M. (1981) 'Innocence and experience: the evolution of the concept of juvenile delinquency in the mid-nineteenth century' in Dale, R. *et al.* (eds) *Politics, Patriarchy and Practice.* Lewes, Falmer Press, pp. 269–83.

Mendus, S. (1989) 'The marriage of true minds: the ideal of marriage in the philosophy of John Stuart Mill' in Mendus, S. and Rendall, J. (eds) *Sexuality and Subordination: Interdisciplinary Studies of Gender in the Nineteenth Century.* London, Routledge.

Meyer, A.G. (1985) *The Socialism and Feminism of Lily Braum.* Bloomington, Indiana University Press.

Mitchell, H. (1977) *The Hard Way Up.* London, Virago.

Nethercot, A. (1961) *The First Five Lives of Annie Besant.* London, Rupert Hart-Davis.

Nethercot, A. (1963) *The Last Four Lives of Annie Besant.* London, Rupert Hart-Davis.

Norris, P. (1996) 'Women politicians: transforming Westminster?' in Lovenduski, J. and Norris, P. (eds) *Women in Politics*. Oxford: Oxford University Press, pp. 91–104.

Oram, A. (1987) 'Inequalities in the teaching profession: the effect on teachers and pupils, 1910–1939' in Hunt, F. (ed.) *Lessons for Life: The Schooling of Girls and Women 1850–1950*. Oxford, Basil Blackwell, pp. 101–23.

Oram, A. (1996) *Women Teachers and Feminist Politics 1900–39*. Manchester, Manchester University Press.

Owen, D. edited by MacLeod, R. (1982) *The Government of Victorian London 1855–1859*. Cambridge, Mass., Harvard University Press.

Pateman, C. (1989) *The Disorder of Women: Democracy, Feminism and Political Theory*. Cambridge, Polity Press.

Pearson, G. (1975) *The Deviant Imagination*. London, Macmillan Press.

Perkin, J. (1989) *Women and Marriage in Nineteenth Century England*. London, Routledge.

Pinchbeck, I. and Hewitt, M. (1973) *Children in English Society*. London, Routledge and Kegan Paul.

Platt, A. (1969) *The Child-Savers*. Chicago, University of Chicago Press.

Prochaska, F.K. (1980) *Women and Philanthropy in Nineteenth Century England*. Oxford, Clarendon Press.

Pugh, M. (1992) *Women and the Women's Movement in Britain 1914–1959*. London, Macmillan.

Purvis, J. (1985) 'Domestic Subjects Since 1870', in Goodson, I. (ed.) *Social Histories of The Secondary Curriculum*. Lewes, Falmer Press, pp. 145–76.

Purvis, J. (1991) *A History of Women's Education in England*. Buckingham, Open University Press.

Reeder, D. (1982) 'Conclusion perspectives on metropolitan administrative history', in Owen, D. edited by MacLeod, R. *The Government of Victorian London 1855–1859*. Cambridge, MA, Harvard University Press.

Rendall, J. (1985) *The Origins of Modern Feminism: Women in Britain, France and the United States, 1780–1860*. Chicago, Lyceum Books.

Rendall, J. (1989) 'Friendship and politics: Barbara Leigh Smith Bodichon (1827–91) and Bessie Raynor Parkes (1829–1925)' in Mendus, S. and Rendall, J. (eds) *Sexuality and Subordination*. London, Routledge.

Rendall, J. (1994) 'Citizenship, culture and civilisation: the languages of British suffragists, 1866–1874' in Daley, C. and Nolan, M. (eds) *Suffrage and Beyond: International Feminist Perspectives*. Auckland, Auckland University Press.

Riley, D. (1983) *War in the Nursery*. London, Virago.

Riley, D. (1988) *'Am I That Name?' Feminism and the Category of 'Women' in History*. Basingstoke, Macmillan.

Rowbotham, S. (1973) *Hidden From History: Three Hundred Years of Oppression and the Fight Against It*. London, Pluto.

Rubinstein, D. (1969) *School Attendance in London 1870–1904: A Social History*. Hull, University of Hull.

Rubinstein, D. (1977) 'Socialisation and the London School Board 1870–1904: aims, methods and public opinion' in McCann, P. (ed.) *Popular Education and Socialisation in the Nineteenth Century*. London, Methuen and Company, pp. 231–64.

Rubinstein, D. (1986) *Before the Suffragettes: Women's Emancipation in the 1890s*. Brighton, Harvester Wheatsheaf.

Rubinstein, W. (1987) 'The geographical distribution of middle class income in Britain 1800–1914' in Rubinstein, W. (ed.) *Elites and the Wealthy in Modern British History.* Brighton, Harvester Wheatsheaf.

Ryan, M.P. (1983) 'The power of women's networks' in Newton, J.L., Ryan, M.P. and Walkowitz, J.R. (eds) *Sex and Class in Women's History.* London, Routledge and Kegan Paul, pp. 167–86.

Sanderson, K. (1990) 'Meanings of class and social mobility: the public and private lives of women civil servants', in Corr, H. and Jamieson, L. (eds) *The Politics of Everyday Life.* London: Macmillan.

Sarah, E. (ed.) (1982) *Reassessments of First Wave Feminism.* Oxford, Pergamon Press.

Savage, M., Barlow, J., Dickens, P. and Fielding, T. (1992) *Property, Bureaucracy and Culture: Middle-Class Formation in Contemporary Britain.* London and New York, Routledge.

Sayers, J.E. (1973) *The Fountain Unsealed: A History of the Notting Hill and Ealing High School.* Welwyn Garden City, Broadwater Press.

Scott, J. and Griff, C. (1984) *Directors of Industry.* Cambridge, Polity Press.

Shaw, J. (1981) 'In loco parentis: a relationship between parent, state and child' in Dale, R. *et al.* (eds) *Politics, Patriarchy and Practice.* Lewes, Falmer Press, pp. 257–68.

Shanley, M.L. (1989) *Feminism, Marriage and the Law in Victorian England, 1850–1895.* London, I.B. Tauris and Company.

Shonfield, Z. (1987) *The Precariously Privileged.* Oxford, Oxford University Press.

Silver, H. (1965) *The Concept of Popular Education.* London, MacGibbon and Kee.

Simon, B. (1980) *Education and the Labour Movement 1870–1920.* London, Lawrence and Wishart.

Simon, B. (1981) *The Two Nations and the Educational Structure 1780–1870.* London, Lawrence and Wishart.

Smart, R. (1994) *On Others' Shoulders: An Illustrated History of the Polhill and Lansdowne Colleges, now De Montfort University Bedford.* Bedford, Steven-Howard Press.

Sreberny–Mohammadi, A. and Ross, K. (1996) 'Women MPs and the media: representing the body politic' in Lovenduski, J. and Norris, P. (eds) *Women in Politics.* Oxford: Oxford University Press, pp. 105–17.

Stacey, M. and Price, M. (1981) *Women, Power and Politics.* London, Tavistock.

Stedman Jones, G. (1984) *Outcast London: A Study in the Relationship Between Classes in Victorian Society.* London, Penguin Press.

Steedman, C. (1990) *Childhood, Culture and Class in Britain: Margaret McMillan 1860–1931.* London, Virago.

Stephen, B. (1927) *Emily Davies and Girton College.* London, Constable and Co.

Stone, J.S. (1994) *Emily Faithfull: Victorian Champion of Women's Rights.* Toronto, P.D. Meany Publishers.

Sutherland, G. (1972) 'Administrators in education after 1870: patronage, professionalism and expertise' in Sutherland, G. (ed.) *Studies in the Growth of Nineteenth Century Government.* London, Routledge and Kegan Paul, pp. 263–85.

Sutherland, G. (1973) *Policy–Making in Elementary Education 1870–1895.* London, Oxford University Press.

Taylor, B. (1983) *Eve and the New Jerusalem.* London, Virago.

Thane, P. (1993) 'Women in the British Labour party and the construction of state welfare', in Koven, S. and Michel, S. *Mothers of a New World: Maternalist Politics and the Origins of Welfare States.* London, Routledge.

Thompson, D. (1987) 'Women, work and politics in nineteenth century England: the problem of authority' in Rendall, J. (ed.) *Equal Or Different: Women's Politics 1800–1914*. Oxford, Basil Blackwell, pp. 57–81.

Thompson, E.P. (1955) *William Morris: Romantic to Revolutionary*. London, Merlin Press.

Thompson, P. (1975) *The Edwardians*. London, Routledge and Kegan Paul.

Tsuzuki, C. (1961) *Hyndman and British Socialism*. Oxford, Oxford University Press.

Turnbull, A. (1983a) 'So extremely like Parliament': the work of the women members of the London School Board, 1870–1904', in The London Feminist History Group (eds) *The Sexual Dynamics of History*. London, Pluto Press, 120–33.

Turnbull, A. (1987) 'Learning her womanly work: the elementary school curriculum, 1870–1914' in Hunt, F. (ed.) *Lessons for Life: The Schooling of Girls and Women 1850–1950*. Oxford, Basil Blackwell.

Vallence, E. (1979) *Women in the House*. London, Athlone Press.

Vicinus, M. (1985) *Independent Women*. London, Virago Press.

Walkowitz, J. (1980) *Prostitution and Victorian Society*. Cambridge, Cambridge University Press.

Wallas, G. with a preface by Murray, G. (1940) *Men and Ideas*. London, George Allen and Unwin.

Weiner, G. (1994) *Feminisms in Education*. Buckingham, Open University Press.

Widdowson, F. (1980) *Going Up into the Next Class: Women and Elementary Teacher Training 1840–1914*. London, Women's Research and Resources Centre Publications.

Williams, R. (1965) *The Long Revolution*. Harmondsworth, Penguin.

Winch, D. and Burrow, J.W. (1993) *That Noble Science of Politics: A Study in Nineteenth-Century Intellectual History*. Cambridge: Cambridge University Press.

Zimmeck, M. (1988) 'The new woman in the machinery of government: a spanner in the works?' in McLeod, R. (ed.) *Government and Expertise: Specialists, Administrators and Professionals 1860–1919*. Cambridge: Cambridge University Press.

Index